The
Making of England

55 B.C.—1399

A History of England

GENERAL EDITOR: *Lacey Baldwin Smith*

I

The Making of England 55 B.C.–1399
C. WARREN HOLLISTER
UNIVERSITY OF CALIFORNIA, SANTA BARBARA

II

This Realm of England 1399–1688
LACEY BALDWIN SMITH
NORTHWESTERN UNIVERSITY

III

The Age of Aristocracy 1688–1830
WILLIAM B. WILLCOX
UNIVERSITY OF MICHIGAN

IV

Britain Yesterday and Today: 1830 TO THE PRESENT
WALTER L. ARNSTEIN
ROOSEVELT UNIVERSITY

The
Making of England

55 B.C.—1399

C. WARREN HOLLISTER

University of California
Santa Barbara

D. C. HEATH *and Company:* BOSTON

66-39 26

Library of Congress Catalog Card Number 66–11289

COPYRIGHT © 1966 BY D. C. HEATH AND COMPANY

BOSTON ENGLEWOOD CHICAGO SAN FRANCISCO

ATLANTA DALLAS LONDON TORONTO

Printed May 1966

Preface

CARL BECKER ONCE COMPLAINED that everybody knows the job of the historian is "to discover and set forth the 'facts' of history." The facts, it is often said, speak for themselves. The businessman talks about hard facts, the statistician refers to cold facts, the lawyer is eloquent about the facts of the case, and the historian, who deals with the incontrovertible facts of life and death, is called a very lucky fellow. Those who speak so confidently about the historian's craft are generally not historians themselves; they are readers of textbooks which more often than not are mere recordings of vital information and listings of dull generalizations. It is not surprising that the historian's reputation has suffered; he has become a peddler of facts and a chronicler who says "this is what happened." The shorter the historical survey, the more likely it is for the textbook writer to assume godlike detachment, spurning the minor tragedies and daily comedies of men, and immortalizing the rise and fall of civilizations, the clash of economic and social forces, and the deeds of titans. Nimbly he moves from the indisputable fact that Henry VIII divorced Catherine of Aragon and married Anne Boleyn to the confident assertion that this helped to produce the Reformation in England. The result is sublime but emasculated history. Men wept when Good Queen Bess died, but historians merely comment that she had lived her allotted three score years and ten. Anglo-Saxon warriors were sick with fear when Viking "swift sea-kings" swept down on England to plunder, rape and kill, but historians dispassionately note that the Norse invasions were a good thing; they allowed the kingdom of Wessex to unite and "liberate" the island in the name of Saxon and Christian defense against heathen marauders. British soldiers rotted by the thousands in the trenches of the First World War, but the terror and agony of that holocaust are lost in the dehumanized statistic that 750,000 British troops died in the four years of war.

In a brief history of even one "tight little island," the chronology of events must of necessity predominate, but if these four volumes are in any way fresh and new, it is because their authors have tried by artistry to step beyond the usual confines of a textbook and to conjure up something of the drama of politics, of the wealth of personalities, and even of the pettiness, as well as the greatness, of human motivation. The price paid will be obvious to anyone seeking total coverage. There is little in these pages on literature, the fine arts or philosophy, except as they throw light upon the uniqueness of English history. On the other hand, the complexities, the uncertainties, the endless variations, and above all the accidents that bedevil the design of human events—these are the very stuff of which history is made, and these are the "truths" which this series seeks to elucidate and preserve. Moreover, the flavor of each volume varies according to the tastes of its author. Sometimes the emphasis is political, sometimes economic or social; but always the presentation is impressionistic—shading, underscoring or highlighting to achieve an image which will be more than a bare outline and will recapture something of the smell and temper of the past.

Each book was conceived and executed as an entity capable of standing by itself, but at the same time the four volumes were designed as a unit. They tell the story of how a small and insignificant outpost of the Roman Empire hesitantly and not always very heroically evolved into the nation which has probably produced and disseminated more ideas and institutions, both good and bad, than any state since Athens. The hope is that these volumes will appeal both to those interested in a balanced portrait of the more discernible segments of English history— *The Making of England* (55 B.C.–1399), *This Realm of England* (1399–1688), *The Age of Aristocracy* (1688–1830) and *Britain Yesterday and Today* (1830 to the present)—and to those who seek the majestic sweep of history in the story of a people whose activities have been wonderfully rich, exciting and varied. Erasmus once wrote, "The important thing for you is not how much you know, but the quality of what you know." In this spirit these volumes have been written.

Lacey Baldwin Smith

Contents

ILLUSTRATIONS

MAPS

GENEALOGICAL TABLES

Acknowledgment for the use of illustrations is made to British Information Services (pp. iii, 59); the British Museum (pp. 1, 26, 41, 121, 154, 189, 215); the Henry E. Huntington Library (p. 221); and the National Monuments Record (pp. 157, 194). Maps by Aldren A. Watson.

Chapter 1

𝕽𝕺𝕸𝕬𝕹 Britain and the Anglo-Saxon Settlements

Background of the Roman Invasions

History, as the recorded annals of civilized man, began in England in the year 55 B.C. when Julius Caesar's troops waded ashore on the beaches north of Dover.[1] Caesar was a man of remarkable military ability and boundless confidence. He was an astute opportunist who rose to power amidst the violent political turmoil of the late Roman Republic — a great creative statesman who laid the groundwork for Rome's transformation from republic to empire. It was this man, this military adventurer and

---

[1] Several good general accounts of Roman Britain are available. R. G. Collingwood and J. N. L. Myres, *Roman Britain and the English Settlements* (2nd ed., 1937) is the first volume in the Oxford History of England, a monumental and generally up-to-date series covering the whole of English history. The volumes in the Pelican History of England are shorter and place more emphasis on social history. The appropriate volume in the Pelican series is J. A. Richmond, *Roman Britain* (1955). A still more recent series is the History of England edited by Christopher Brooke and Denis Mack Smith and published by Thomas Nelson and Sons. In general, the volumes in the Nelson series are relatively short, accurate, and written in an attractive style. Volume I of the series is Peter Hunter Blair, *Roman Britain and Early England*, 55 B.C.–A.D. 871 (1963). A. L. F. Rivet, *Town and Country in Roman Britain* is a good introductory account. For studies on specific towns see G. Home, *Roman London* (2nd ed., 1948), and G. C. Boon, *Roman Silchester* (1957).

political genius, who first brought England into the orbit of civilization.

Caesar's invasion of Britain was almost an afterthought to his campaigns against the Gauls. Between 58 and 50 B.C., prior to the time of his rise to supreme power in Rome, Caesar undertook the conquest of an extensive territory known as Gaul which corresponds very roughly to modern France and was then inhabited by semicivilized Celts. Although Caesar could not realize it, the conquest of Gaul was to have an incalculable influence on the development of Western Civilization in later centuries. For Gaul extended far to the north of the Mediterranean Basin, and Caesar's victories brought Roman government and Roman culture into the Western European heartland. The Romanization of Gaul proved to be a crucial factor in providing medieval and modern Europe with its enduring classical heritage.

In the course of his campaigns, Caesar discovered that the Celts in Gaul were receiving support from their fellow Celts in the remote island of Britain. Desiring to teach the British Celts to respect the might of Rome, he undertook two military forays into Britain, the first in 55 B.C., the second a year later. Caesar's first raid was inconclusive, but in 54 B.C. he marched across Kent, forded the Thames River, and won a notable victory over a Celtic coalition. He demanded hostages from the defeated Britains, secured a promise of regular tribute payments, and then withdrew across the Channel. The promised tribute was not forthcoming, however, and Caesar was too preoccupied with the consolidation of his Gallic conquest and the advancement of his political fortunes in Rome to return to Britain in force. The first encounter between classical Mediterranean civilization and the distant Celtic island was not followed up for nearly a century.

Still, Caesar's raids had succeeded in bringing Britain to Rome's attention, and with the organization of Celtic Gaul into Roman provinces, the Britons themselves began to feel the impact of Roman civilization. The close relations between Gaul and Britain continued much as before; the two lands remained tightly linked by bonds of commerce and kinship. A group of Celtic inhabitants in Yorkshire called the *Parisi*, for example, was related to a group in Gaul who gave its name to the future capital of France. The Romans, having subdued the Celts of Gaul, were almost bound to undertake one day the conquest of their British kinsmen.

In A.D. 43 the conquest began; the emperor Claudius sent four Roman legions across the Channel into Kent with the intention of bringing Britain under the authority of Rome. The Claudian invasion marks the real beginning of the history of

Roman Britain. Before discussing its outcome, let us examine the two very different cultures that came face to face when Claudius' legions reached Britain's shores.

By the time of Claudius' invasion, Rome had weathered the stormy decades of the late Republic and had submitted to the rule of an emperor. In doing so the Romans abandoned their political tradition of self-determination for a new, authoritarian order that promised stability and political coherence. With the coming of imperial government, the interior districts of the Empire entered a prolonged, unprecedented epoch of security and peace. The empire that Claudius ruled was a prosperous, intelligently governed state embracing the ancient lands along the Mediterranean and extending northward across Gaul to the English Channel. Within its vast frontiers, guarded by well-trained legions, the cultures of Greece, Italy, and the ancient Near East were drawn together into one immense political and economic unit, unencumbered by national boundaries or tariff barriers and spanned by a superb road system and by the protected seaways of the Mediterranean. The relatively beneficent rule of the emperors brought to the ancient world a degree of prosperity hitherto unknown, even though great masses of peasants and urban dwellers remained, as they always had, in a state of hopeless impoverishment.

The Roman economy, like virtually all economies prior to the industrial revolution, was fundamentally agrarian, but the city was the nexus of Roman politics and Roman civilization. The city, with an extensive agrarian district surrounding it, was the essential unit of local government, and it was on their cities that the Romans lavished most of their considerable architectural and engineering talents. Administrators, poets, scholars, even great landowners, made their homes in the cities. As half-civilized districts such as Gaul fell under Roman control, old tribal centers were transformed into cities, and new cities were built where none had existed before. And each city sought to adorn itself with impressive temples, baths, and public buildings on the model of Rome itself. Hence the paradox that the Roman Empire was economically rural yet culturally urban.

These cities, scattered across the Empire, were the foci of a notable cultural synthesis and diffusion, as the component traditions of the Mediterranean world spread and intermingled. But it was above all the Latin culture of Rome itself that inspired the architecture and literature of the western European cities and dominated the curricula of their schools. Great Latin authors and poets such as Lucretius and Cicero, Virgil and Horace, set the canons of style for a Latin literary tradition that spread across the West. United politically by the Roman legions, the Roman Empire was united culturally—at least in its western provinces—by the power and magnetism of Roman literature and art.

Finally, the Empire was united legally by Roman jurisprudence. It may well be that Rome made its most creative and enduring contribution in the field of law. As Rome won its empire, the narrow law code of the early Republic gradually evolved into a broad and humane system of legal precedents and principles—a product of centuries of practical experience—designed to deal justly with conflicts among men of diverse cultural origins. Although essentially empirical in its development, Roman law was influenced by the Greek concept of *natural law*—the belief in universal and discoverable norms of human conduct, applicable not merely to certain civilized peoples but to all men. A concept of this sort was naturally attractive to Roman jurists, faced as they were with the task of bringing all the peoples of the Empire under a single overarching body of jurisprudence.

Such, in brief, was the civilization which Rome brought to Britain. The student of English history must never allow his preoccupation with the British Isles to obscure the fact that Claudius' invasion of A.D. 43 constituted an encroachment by a vast and highly civilized Empire on a small, remote, and backward land. In Roman times, Britain could never be anything but an outwork—a distant frontier district of an age-old Mediterranean civilization.

Britain's history before the Roman contact is utterly undocumented, but the careful investigations of archaeologists provide us with at least a general picture of her economic and cultural development in pre-Roman times. It is a picture of repeated incursions and invasions from across the Channel, of incessant tribal rivalries, of gradual technological and economic progress as Britain's inhabitants evolved from the Stone Age to the Bronze Age and finally, beginning in the fifth century B.C., to the Iron Age. The majestic stone trilithons at Stonehenge—a central religious center of the early Bronze Age—testify to the notable engineering skills which the island's inhabitants possessed nearly two millennia before the Roman invasion.

The pattern of invasions and settlements was governed by the island's geography. Clearly visible from the Continent, England's Kentish shore is separated from France by a channel only twenty-one miles wide at its narrowest point. Accordingly, repeated waves of invaders and traders crossed from the Continent to southern Britain in prehistoric times. England itself is divided geographically into two major districts: a lowlands area—with rich, heavy soil broken by occasional ranges of hills—which covers approximately the southeastern half of England; and a highlands zone dominating the northwestern half of the land – a district of mountainous terrain rich in mineral resources but with generally infertile soil. Cornwall and Devonshire at the southwestern tip of England, Wales in the west, and most of northern England and Scotland are hilly or mountainous, and England's chief mountain range, the Pennine Chain, points southward like a great finger from the northern hill country into the heart of the midland plain.

The earlier prehistoric invaders tended to concentrate in the southeast "lowlands" zone, but they settled chiefly in the hilly portions of that zone rather than in the lowlands themselves. For the lowlands were thickly wooded, and their heavy soil defied the primitive plows of these early settlers. On the eve of the Roman invasion, however, Britain's Celtic inhabitants had developed plows that were adequate to the task of tilling the rich soil of the lowlands. At the same time, the Celts were beginning the age-long process of clearing the land of woods and brush. By the standards of the time, the Celtic settlement of lowland Britain was quite heavy, and grain was being produced in such quantities that it became an important export commodity. A Roman author of the early first century A.D. mentions several other British exports that found regular markets in the Empire: cattle, hides, dogs, iron, and slaves. And for centuries, traders of the Mediterranean world had been aware of the rich tin deposits in Cornwall. The considerable prosperity of some of the Celtic tribes of pre-Roman Britain is illustrated by the fact that a few of the island's chieftains, following the example of neighboring Roman provinces, were beginning to coin money.

As the first century progressed, everything pointed to a Roman invasion of Britain. The independence of the British Celts posed difficulties for the Roman administration of Celtic Gaul. British resources and prosperity suggested to the Romans that from the financial standpoint a conquest of the island would be well worth the effort. Finally, endemic intertribal warfare among the Britons – and occasional appeals by defeated British chieftains for Roman support – indicated that a conquest would not be unduly difficult. The invasion of A.D. 43 was a carefully calculated act of imperial policy, undertaken for sound reasons and with every expectation of success.

Roman Britain

The British Celts, divided among themselves and distinctly inferior to the Romans in military organization, could offer only temporary resistance to the Claudian invasion. In the years following A.D. 43 the Roman legions repeatedly breached the Celtic defenses, storming hilltop fortresses and occupying first the southwestern lowland zone and finally, after some difficulty, the highland districts of the north and west. The administration of the able Roman governor Agricola (A.D. 78–84) marks the essential completion of the conquest. By then, Roman authority extended over virtually all of modern England, Wales, and southern Scotland.

The Roman conquest of the lowland zone was relatively easy, although it was threatened momentarily by a widespread rebellion of several British tribes in A.D. 60 under the leadership of a remarkable woman named Boudicca. Historians of previous generations tended to romanticize this uprising and to picture Boudicca, quite wrongly, as the first British patriot – a kind of Celtic Joan of Arc. After some initial victories the rebels were crushed, and the lowland zone was thereafter securely under Roman control. The consolidation of Roman authority in the highland zone was far more difficult, for the savage hill peoples of Wales, the north, and the northeast could be controlled only by constant vigilance and by the continued presence of large Roman garrisons at strategic points.

Hence, Roman Britain was divided administratively into two districts, corresponding to the island's two great geographical zones: a civil district in the southeast, where Roman civilization flourished in an atmosphere of peace, and a military district in the highland areas where Roman legions remained on guard against uprisings and invasions and where Roman civilization made comparatively little impact. Three legions guarded the military district, each of them consisting of some thirty to forty thousand men. One legion was stationed at Chester where it was in a position to dominate Wales. Another was stationed at Carlisle to overawe southern Scotland and guard the northern frontier. A third made its base at York and served as a strategic reserve. These three legions were generally successful in upholding Roman authority in their respective districts, but they were never able to rid the districts of rebellion.

Under the emperor Hadrian (117–138) construction began on a great wall, more than seventy miles long, spanning the narrow neck between Solway Firth and the mouth of the Tyne River in northern England. This ambitious fortified line was intended to secure the northern frontier of Roman Britain from incursions by savage tribes to the north. Later in the second century another fortified line, the Antonine Wall, was erected still farther northward extending across the narrows between the Firth of Clyde and the Firth of Forth. The Antonine Wall was an advance position which the Romans were unable to hold for long, and during the third and fourth centuries they were usually content to draw their northern line at the Wall of Hadrian.   At times Roman punitive expeditions probed far north of Hadrian's wall, and at other times northern tribesmen broke through the fortifications and carried their devastation far to the south.   But during the greater part of the later age of Roman occupation Hadrian's wall marked t .e northern frontier.

The lowland zone, after Boudicca's revolt, enjoyed unbroken peace and a considerable degree of prosperity.   Here, Roman institutions were gradually imposed upon a Celtic and pre-Celtic substructure, and the Britons came to know not only the high taxes but also the settled life, the thriving economy, and the amenities of urban living that were customary in the Roman provinces.   The military camps and commercial centers of Britain were bound together by a splendid network of Roman roads;   Roman law courts brought with them a rational and enlightened system of justice quite unknown to Britain prior to the Roman conquest.   And with the coming of Roman civilization, towns and cities grew and flourished as never before.

In Britain, as elsewhere in the Empire, the cities were of three basic types: (1) the *colonia*, which was usually a newly established urban center occupied by retired legionaries and their families, (2) the *municipium,* normally a previously existing town whose inhabitants received from the imperial government a charter conveying certain important privileges, and (3) the *civitas,* an older tribal center which developed urban institutions in imitation of the *colonia* and *municipium*.   The inhabitants of *coloniae* and *municipia* were Roman citizens; those of the *civitates* were not.   All three, however, enjoyed a degree of local government and exerted political control over fairly extensive surrounding lands.   All three were governed by local senates comprised of wealthy and notable townsmen. All three had annually elected magistrates who supervised finances, public buildings, and the courts.   And all three sought to adorn themselves with impressive public buildings, temples, and baths in the Roman style.   Still, the *civitates* remained fundamentally Celtic tribal centers and were never so thoroughly Romanized as were the *municipia* and the *coloniae*.

Only four British cities are known to have possessed *colonia* status: Colchester, Gloucester, Lincoln, and York, and there is evidence to suggest only one *municipium:* Verulamium (the later St. Albans).   Extant contemporary documents do not state specifically that London was a *colonia* or a *municipium,* but there can be no question that London was the foremost city of Roman Britain.   Indeed, it was the Romans who made London great.   Whereas most of the chief British cities of the Roman era were between 100 and 200 acres in extent, London occupied some 325 acres.   Situated on the Thames at the crucial point where the river was broad enough to accommodate oceangoing ships yet narrow enough to be bridged, London assumed in Roman times the dominant commercial position that it was destined to occupy in medieval and modern times as well. Then, as now, it was the commercial nexus of Britain.

It was only natural, therefore, that London should be the focal point of the Roman road system. Stretching from London far and wide across the land, the Roman roads formed a vast 5,000-mile system of paved thoroughfares running in nearly straight lines over the countryside, enabling men and supplies to move across the island at a speed unequaled until the nineteenth century.

In Roman Britain, as elsewhere in the Empire, farming was the basic economic activity. Historians of former generations used to distinguish between two radically different agricultural communities: the village—pre-Roman in origin and little affected by the Roman occupation, and the villa—a typically Roman institution which consisted of a luxurious home surrounded by extensive fields. Recent research, based on more sophisticated archaeological techniques and on aerial photography, has necessitated severe modifications of this traditional view. We now realize that the buildings unearthed at a particular site often represent successive levels of development rather than the total agrarian complex from a single moment in time. Consequently, scholars today doubt that the agricultural village played a particularly significant role in Roman or pre-Roman Britain. Rather, the rudimentary agrarian unit of the age was the small family farm, a few acres in extent, consisting typically of a couple of houses, a number of pits for the storing of grain, and farmlands laid out in the form of small, squarish fields. Farms of this type abounded in both Celtic and Roman times, and their inhabitants were little influenced by the coming of the Romans.

The older conception of the villa, with its gracious Roman provincial architecture, its mosaics and rich furnishings, and its central heating, also requires modification. Such villas did indeed exist, but they were highly exceptional. The great majority of the Roman villas were far more modest establishments, and some were actually squalid. Altogether, between 600 and 700 villas have been identified in Britain, the bulk of them concentrated in particular areas of the southeastern lowlands. Villa life, whether luxurious or impoverished, was distinctly Roman in style and organization, and it is through the villas that Rome made its impact on the British countryside. The typical villa owner was a Roman or a Romanized Briton who used hired laborers or slaves, sometimes in large numbers, to work his lands. In the later years of the Roman settlement,

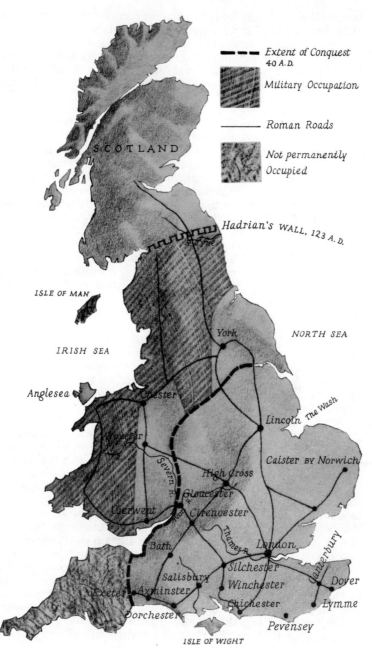

SCOTLAND

Extent of Conquest 40 A.D.

Military Occupation

Roman Roads

Not permanently Occupied

Hadrian's WALL, 123 A.D.

R. Tyne

ISLE OF MAN

IRISH SEA

York

NORTH SEA

Anglesea

Chester

Lincoln   The Wash

Wroxeter

Caister BY Norwich

Severn R.

High Cross

Gloucester

Caerwent

Cirencester

Thames R.

London

Canterbury

Bath

Silchester

Dover

Salisbury

Winchester

Exeter   Axminster

Chichester

Lymme

Dorchester

Pevensey

ISLE OF WIGHT

much villa land was leased to tenant farmers, as was the case elsewhere in the Empire, with the consequence that many of the advantages of large-scale farming were lost.

A sharp distinction still must be made between the Celtic farm and the Roman villa, but it must also be remembered that the laborers on the villa's fields profited no more from Roman civilization than did the Celtic farmers. In Britain, as elsewhere in the Empire, Rome's impact on the agrarian masses was remarkably slight. Rome had always lagged in the field of agrarian technology, and she contributed little to Celtic farming practices because she had little to offer. Some progress was made during the Roman occupation toward the clearing of forests and draining of swamps, but the bulk of that great task was left to the later Anglo-Saxons. And it was the achievements of the pre-Roman Celts that enabled Roman Britain to export agricultural products to the Continent.

The Romans did, however, contribute significantly to the development of the British economy in areas other than agriculture. Britain had been exploiting its mines long before the Claudian invasion, but Rome introduced a mining technology that was far more efficient—and more ruthless—than before. In particular, the Romans developed lead mines in Britain and made lead a major export commodity, along with tin, copper, and bronze.

Perhaps, after all, Rome's greatest gift to Britain was peace. For more than three centuries, lowland Britain was shielded from invaders and freed of intertribal warfare by the Roman legions. It was ruled severely but, on the whole, wisely by a Roman administration. As a frontier province of the Roman Empire, Britain fell under the direct authority of the emperor, but apart from the rare occasions when the emperor actually visited the island, imperial control was exercised by an imperial agent entitled *legatus* who was, in effect, a provincial governor. His responsibilities included both the administration of justice in the civil zone and command of the armies in the military zone. Responsibility for the collection of imperial taxes and the supervision of imperial estates was entrusted to another official, the *procurator,* who was administratively independent of the governor and subject to the emperor alone. It was up to the *procurator* to see that Britain paid its way and that the occupation should be financially worthwhile to Rome.

Such was the administrative structure of Britain in the era following the Claudian invasion. In subsequent centuries, as the Roman Empire evolved steadily toward naked military despotism, its administrative organization underwent several major revisions, and the administration of Britain was altered accordingly. Early in the third century the island was divided into two separate provinces which probably approximated its two zones: military and civil. Toward the end of the same century the emperor Diocletian designated Britain as one of the twelve dioceses into which he divided the Empire. Britain was now ruled by a *vicarius* whose headquarters seems to have been at London. The island was further subdivided by Diocletian into four provinces.

Throughout the epoch of the Roman occupation, the key units of local government were the towns — the *coloniae, municipia,* and *civitates* — which managed their own local affairs through their senates and magistrates and also supervised considerable areas of the surrounding countryside. In the final catastrophic years of Roman Britain it was the cities that took the lead in striving to defend their civilized heritage against the incursions of the barbarians.

Decline and Fall

The Roman age of British history began and ended as a result of causes that far transcended Britain itself. The decline and fall of the Roman Empire in the West is one of history's great problems, and numerous able scholars have devoted many years to it without producing an entirely satisfactory solution.[2]

Many different factors contributed to the transformation from Roman to medieval Europe. For one thing, the educated classes of the Empire underwent a profound change in outlook during the third and fourth centuries, turning from the humanism and rationalism of Greek antiquity and the practical, worldly values of early Rome to the mysticism and quest for eternal salvation which characterized the earlier Middle Ages. This change in mood marked the end of the viewpoint and value system that dominated traditional Greco-Roman civilization. But it may well be asked, did the new transcendental spirit destroy the old humanistic values, or did the failure of these values give rise to the new mysticism?

Much has been written on the political and economic

---

[2] Gibbon's classic account, *The Decline and Fall of the Roman Empire,* is still very much worth reading. For the provocative argument that the fall of Rome was more a blessing than a disaster, see W. C. Bark, *Origins of the Medieval World* (1960). F. Lot, *The End of the Ancient World and the Beginning of the Middle Ages* (new edition, Harper, 1961) is a thorough, solid analysis. Mortimer Chambers (ed.), *The Fall of Rome* (1964) contains thoughtfully chosen excerpts from historical writings that deal with Rome's decline, and provides a most useful summary of the problem.

problems that afflicted the Roman Empire. It has been said that
the Roman political system never solved the problem of imperial
succession—that the Roman economy was inefficient and para-
sitical—that the Roman bureaucracy was bloated and corrupt.
One should be cautious about condemning an empire that
endured for five hundred years in the West and a millennium
thereafter in the East. Nevertheless, some of these criticisms
stand. The economy of the early Empire depended too heavily
on slave labor and on booty from conquered peoples. When,
in the course of the second century, imperial expansion ceased,
the economic system in the West began to falter and finally
broke down almost completely. Rome experienced no industrial
revolution; her cities, particularly those in the West, tended to
be military and administrative centers rather than centers of
industrial production. Many of them harbored large masses of
unemployed paupers and derelicts; others teemed with soldiers
and bureaucrats who consumed the wealth of the Empire instead of expanding it. Soldiers and bureaucrats are essential
to any civilized society, but in the Roman Empire they abounded
to such a degree that eventually the names on the imperial pay-
roll exceeded those on the tax rolls. In the end, the relatively
backward imperial economy proved incapable of supporting
the bureaucracy, the army, and the unproductive cities.

The economic breakdown was marked by widespread
demoralization. Artisans, tenant farmers, even civic leaders
abandoned their jobs, and the emperors of the third century
were obliged to institute laws freezing men to their vocations
and obliging sons to take up their fathers' callings. By the
fourth century a vast hereditary caste system had come into
being. The economy continued to function after a fashion, but
demoralization was growing. To many, an Empire that had
evolved into an immense prison-state seemed hardly worth
preserving. The lightly taxed landed aristocracy remained
prosperous, but the more productive classes of the Empire—
the workers in field and town, and the urban middle classes—
were becoming dangerously alienated.

Economic breakdown was accompanied by political disintegration. The emperors of the second century tended to be
long-lived and dedicated, but as the third century dawned, the
army came to exert increasing power in Roman politics. The
middle decades of the third century were marked by frequent
assassinations, disputed successions, and struggles between
army units for control of the imperial throne. In these years,
barbarians breached the frontiers repeatedly, and large sections
of the Empire repudiated the authority of the emperor in Rome.
At length, the emperor Diocletian (284–305) succeeded in restoring the frontiers and reestablishing imperial control over

the Roman state, but only by resorting to a military despotism of the most thoroughgoing sort and enforcing strict controls over economic activity.

Diocletian's policy of restoration through despotism was carried on by Constantine (306–337) and his successors. Constantine's reign is marked by two epoch-making events: (1) the construction of Constantinople on the Bosphorus – the great city that served as the capital of the Eastern or Byzantine Empire for more than 1100 years thereafter, and (2) the conversion of Constantine to the Christian religion.

Both these events were responses to age-long trends. The center of gravity of the Roman Empire had been shifting eastward for many decades; the older eastern cities were more productive and more prosperous than those of the west, and the eastward movement symbolized the new political order which abandoned the constitutional traditions of the city of Rome for the absolutism of the east. The great autocrat Diocletian had spent nearly all his reign in the eastern half of the Empire, and now Constantine erected his new capital there.

Constantine's conversion may be regarded as a response not only to the growing strength of Christianity within the Empire but also to the gradual drawing together of the Classical and Christian traditions. The growth of a transcendental spirit in Roman culture made the inhabitants of the Empire ever more receptive to the mystical doctrines of the Christian religion; the increasing emptiness and hopelessness of daily life in the Empire created a growing need for the doctrines of human dignity before God and personal salvation which Christianity offered. The Christians, for their part, had incorporated into their theology many fundamental elements from classical philosophy – particularly the philosophy of Plato – and had adopted numerous administrative ideas from Rome itself. The steadily closing chasm between Church and Empire was bridged by the conversion of Constantine.

By the fourth century, Christianity had spread from its Near-Eastern homeland to embrace the entire Empire. In Constantine's time it was still a minority religion, but its adherents were among the most vigorous and dedicated inhabitants of the Roman state. Previous emperors had persecuted Christians intermittently for their refusal to worship the official deities, but persecution seemed to encourage the Church to greater efforts. With Constantine's conversion, the persecutions gave way to a policy of toleration and encouragement, and before the fourth century had ended, Christian emperors were persecuting pagan and heterodox sects. Multitudes of converts now joined the Church, and great Roman intellectuals such as St. Ambrose, St. Jerome, and St. Augustine of Hippo devoted their lives to its service. The new religion harmonized perfectly with the otherworldly mood of the late Empire, and long before the end of imperial rule in the West, Christianity had won the allegiance of the Mediterranean world. By the fifth century, Greco-Roman civilization had virtually fused with the Judeo-Christian religious tradition.

The progress of Christianity in Roman Britain is difficult to trace. Christian archaeological remains from this period are far from abundant, and written references to the Romano-British Church occur only occasionally. Christian evangelism doubtless came late to remote Britain, but by the third century the process of conversion had begun. St. Alban and two fellow Christians were martyred during a persecution of the mid-third century, and three British bishops are recorded as being present at an ecclesiastical council in Gaul during Constantine's reign. Thus, fourth-century Britain possessed an ecclesiastical hierarchy and was active in the affairs of the universal Church. Toward the end of the fourth century, Britain went so far as to produce a heresy all its own: the British priest Pelagius, who emphasized the importance of free will over divine grace, had the distinction of being attacked by the great theologian, St. Augustine of Hippo, and orthodox continental churchmen are recorded as preaching against Pelagianism in Britain in the fifth century. At about the same time, courageous British evangelists such as St. Patrick (*c.* 389–461) were engaged in spreading the Gospel beyond the Roman frontiers, bringing Christianity to the heathen peoples of Ireland and Galloway in southwestern Scotland.

As it turned out, Christianity was Rome's most enduring legacy in Britain. At a time when Roman civilization was losing its hold on the inhabitants of the Empire, Christianity was reaching masses of people and affecting their lives in a way that Greco-Roman culture had failed to do even at its height. In later years, when Roman government was all but forgotten, when heathen Germanic barbarians had occupied the fertile lowlands zone and driven its former British inhabitants into the encircling hills, the British held fast to their Christian faith and built upon it an impressive new culture.

The ebbing of Roman authority in Britain was an inevitable consequence of Roman political and economic disintegration in the West. But because of its isolated location on the periphery of the Empire, Britain was spared much of the agony and chaos of the third century, and her cities remained relatively prosperous throughout the fourth.

The whole history of Roman Britain is punctuated by occasional irruptions of semicivilized peoples from across her frontiers, most notably the Scots and the Picts. The term "Scot" was used by men of this period to refer to members of the various tribes of Ireland (not Scotland). These "Scots" undertook periodic attacks against Britain's western shore, but met with no permanent success. "Pict" was the common term for the tribes across the northern frontier in what we would now call Scotland. With a few disastrous exceptions, the northern wall held firm against their incursions.

As the Roman period of British history drew toward its close, signs of increasing insecurity began to appear. An intensification of sea raids by Germanic barbarians is suggested by the appearance of elaborate fortifications along the southeastern coast. In the fourth century these coastal fortresses were placed under the authority of a single military commander known, significantly, as the count of the Saxon Shore. In 367 the British defenses were shattered by a combined attack of Picts from the north, Scots from the west, and Saxons from the south and east. Hadrian's Wall was breached, the count of the Saxon Shore was killed, and London itself was placed under siege. The situation was saved, however, by the timely appearance of a large Roman army from the Continent led by Theodosius, a talented general and future emperor. By 370 Britain was secure once again, and her earlier prosperity returned.

As the fourth century closed, Roman Britain was still vigorous and her cities continued to flourish. But the Roman Empire as a whole was in a desperate plight. One important Germanic tribe, the Visigoths, had crossed the Empire's Danube frontier in 376, and by the first decade of the fifth century the Visigoths were threatening Rome itself. As Roman troops were ordered southward from Britain and the Rhine frontier to strengthen the defenses of Italy, Gaul and Britain were left exposed to invasion. In the winter of 406 a heterogeneous multitude of Germanic tribesmen poured across the frozen Rhine into defenseless Gaul, virtually cutting Britain loose from the Empire. In the chaos that followed, an ambitious Roman-Briton general, Constantine III, led what was left of the Roman garrison in Britain southward across the Channel in an irresponsible and abortive bid for the imperial title.

The year 410 marks the essential termination of Roman authority in Britain. In that year the Visigoths entered Rome and pillaged the city for three days. About the same time, Emperor Honorius wrote a letter to the *civitates* of Britain commanding them to assume responsibility for their own defense. In effect, Honorius was recognizing the fact that the legions had abandoned the island and that the imperial administration in Britain was defunct. Long protected by the armies of the Empire and softened by more than three centuries of imperial peace, the Britons were now on their own.

The Germanic Invaders

There is evidence to suggest that Roman troops may have returned briefly to Britain once or twice during the earlier fifth century in answer to desperate British appeals for help against the Picts and Scots, but thereafter Britain became, from the standpoint of the civilized districts of the Mediterranean Basin, the "land of legend" — "the Isle of the Dead."

To the modern historian the epoch following the Roman withdrawal from Britain is almost equally obscure. Aside from a few oblique, secondhand references from continental writers, the historian must depend on a handful of unreliable Celtic sources and accounts written by descendants of the Germanic invaders. None of these sources is at all satisfactory, yet none can be ignored. Perhaps the most important of them is a history of the conquest of Britain written by a Briton named Gildas sometime in the 540s. Riddled with errors, Gildas' account was actually a bitter and highly emotional outcry against the shortcomings of contemporary British Christians rather than an objective history. Yet it is the only contemporary narrative of the invasion epoch to which historians can turn. On the Germanic or "English" side, there is a certain amount of suggestive but ambiguous material in early epics such as *Beowulf*. The opening sections of the *Anglo-Saxon Chronicle*, which were first written in their present form in the late ninth century, contain some information that was drawn from sources much closer to the invasion age and which can therefore provide illumination if used with care. The talented and rigorous English historian Bede, writing in the early eighth century, gives an account of the invasions that also seems to rest on earlier evidence, now lost, but there is much that Bede leaves out and much else that can be accepted only with hesitation. For despite Bede's remarkable historical skill he was, after all, centuries removed from the invasions.

There are a few other historical sources to which one can turn, but they are fragmentary and still less trustworthy. Archaeological investigations have been helpful in providing additional insights into fifth- and sixth-century Britain, but the archaeologist is handicapped in investigating a society which built not with stone but with wood and other such perishable materials. Finally, patterns of Celtic and Germanic settlement have been investigated with considerable success through the study of place-names. Scholars are able to identify particular names — and especially name endings — with particular peoples and thereby trace the advance of Germanic settlements and measure their intensity. A number of towns and settlements, for example, end in *ing* or *ingas*, which, in Anglo-Saxon, indicates that the original settlers were dependents or followers of a particular leader. Hastings derives its name from a group of early settlers called Haestingas, that is, the followers of a leader named Haesta, and we can conclude tentatively that a Germanic warrior of that name settled with his following in the vicinity of the present town. But place-name studies, valuable though they are, cannot be related to an exact chronological framework. All in all, scholarly investigations of fifth- and sixth-century Britain have been pushed forward brilliantly and ingeniously, yet much remains uncertain and much entirely unknown. The epoch has become a battleground of conflicting scholarly theories, many of which may never be positively proven or discredited.[3]

Before entering this historical wilderness it will be well to establish, insofar as it is possible, the nature of the Germanic peoples as a whole and the significance of their invasions not only of Britain but of the entire Western Roman Empire. Medieval European civilization was a synthesis of three distinct cultural traditions: the Classical or Greco-Roman, the Judeo-Christian, and the Germanic. We have seen how Classical culture in the closing centuries of the Roman Empire began to move toward a mystical, otherwordly outlook, thereby drawing progressively closer to the Judeo-Christian tradition. At the same time, Christian theologians were addressing themselves to the task of interpreting Christian doctrine in terms of Greek philosophy, and the Christian Church was developing a political and legal organization that drew heavily from Roman administrative and judicial practices. Well before the demise of Roman imperial authority in the West, these tendencies had progressed to the point where Classical and Christian cultures had become fused. The making of medieval civilization was in essence the product of a prolonged tension, interpenetration, and eventual fusion between the Classical-Christian tradition, fostered by the early medieval Church, and the Germanic tradition that dominated the barbarian kingdoms which established themselves on the carcass of the Western Roman Empire.

Since the early Germanic peoples were illiterate, our knowledge of their culture must be drawn chiefly from the often ten-

---

[3] On the early Anglo-Saxon period, see Sir Frank Stenton, *Anglo-Saxon England* (2nd ed., 1947)—the appropriate volume in the Oxford History. H. R. Loyn, *Anglo-Saxon England and the Norman Conquest* (1962) is more recent and places more stress on social and economic history. Volume II of the Pelican History—Dorothy Whitelock, *The Beginnings of English Society* (1952)—is authoritative and highly recommended.

dentious testimony of occasional Roman observers.[4] A critical analysis of these writers provides, in broad outline, a reasonably trustworthy picture of the ancient Germans. They were organized, for the most part, into tribes, each of which had its own cultural peculiarities. Some tribes were nomadic, others were sedentary and agrarian, while many were in a process of transition from the first state to the second. Some tribes were far more deeply influenced by Roman civilization than others. Some were converted to Christianity during the course of the fourth century; others remained heathen for centuries thereafter. Nevertheless certain broad generalizations apply more or less to all of them. Indeed, the Romans themselves, while noting tribal distinctions, often spoke of the Germanic peoples as a group. A fastidious Roman country gentleman of the fifth century, for example, made the remark, "Happy the nose that cannot smell a barbarian."

To the Romans, the Germanic barbarians seemed like blonde giants. They devoted themselves chiefly to tending crops or herds, fighting wars, hunting, loafing, gambling, feuding, and drinking beer. They possessed slaves – war prisoners for the most part – but on occasion a free German might gamble himself into slavery. At the time of the invasions their key political unit was the tribe, ruled by a chieftain or king who from time to time sought the advice of a tribal assembly. Ordinarily, a new king was chosen by the assembly from among the sons and other close kinsmen of the former king. Kingship was hereditary, but not strictly so, and an able younger son who had proved his skill as a warrior was often chosen over an incompetent elder son. The most honored profession was that of the warrior, and the warlike virtues of loyalty, courage, and military prowess were esteemed above all others.

The chief military unit within the tribe was the war band or *comitatus*, a group of warriors or "companions" bound together by their allegiance to the leader of their band. It was in the *comitatus*, above all, that the military virtues were cherished. The chief of the band was bound to set a high example of fearlessness and military skill, and his followers were obliged, should their leader fall in battle, to fight to the death if necessary in order to avenge him. The ethical foundations of the *comitatus* – honor, loyalty, courage – remained the norms of

---

[4] *Germania*, by the Roman historian Tacitus, is an exceedingly important source on early Germanic institutions. Its greatest shortcoming is a tendency to view Germanic society too favorably, in order to suggest, by contrast, the shortcomings of Tacitus' own Roman contemporaries. The work is available in paperback: H. Mattingly (tr.), *Tacitus on Britain and Germany* (Penguin, 1948).

the English and continental warrior aristocracy for many centuries thereafter.

Another, much older subdivision of the tribe was the kindred group or clan. Members of a clan were duty-bound to protect the welfare of their kinsmen. Should any man be killed or injured, his kinsmen would declare a blood feud against the wrongdoer and his clan. Since murders and maimings were only too common in the violent and honor-ridden atmosphere of the Germanic tribe, blood feuds were a characteristic ingredient of Germanic society. In order to keep their tribes from being torn asunder by blood feuds, most of the Germanic peoples instituted a crude form of tribal justice. Early Germanic law was concerned primarily with *wergelds** — sums of money that wrongdoers might pay to their victims or their victims' kinsmen in order to appease their vengeance and forestall the feud. In time, *wergeld* schedules became highly complex. Various sums of money were assigned for various injuries — so much for a severed finger, somewhat more for the loss of a hand, etc. And murder *wergelds* varied, too, depending on the social status of the victim. In Anglo-Saxon England, for example, the *wergeld* of a free peasant was 200 shillings while that of a nobleman was 1,200 shillings.

The *wergeld* system mitigated the blood feud but by no means eliminated it, for there was no assurance that the alleged murderer would pay the required sum or even admit his guilt. Gradually the tribes developed bodies of customary law which were intended to determine guilt or innocence. Early Germanic law was exceedingly limited in its jurisdiction — many crimes of violence fell outside its scope. Its basic principle was the presumption of guilt. It was up to an accused man to prove his innocence, and he normally did so by submitting to the ordeal. Each of the several ordeals in Germanic law was regarded as an appeal to divine judgment. The accused man, for example, might be obliged to grasp a red-hot iron and carry it a prescribed distance, or to lift a stone from the bottom of a boiling cauldron. Several days thereafter the hand was examined carefully. If it was healing properly, the court concluded that the accused enjoyed divine favor and was therefore innocent. But if the hand was infected, the accused was pronounced guilty. Similarly, the accused might be bound and thrown into a pond. If he floated, he was deemed guilty, for it was assumed that pure water would refuse to "accept" a guilty man. If he sank, he was judged innocent and was fetched from the water (presumably

---

* Literally, the term *wergeld* means "man money."

still alive) to enjoy the favorable verdict. It has been suggested that this last ordeal might actually have been effective in determining guilt or innocence. The accused, who believed firmly in the validity of the test, may well have had a subconscious compulsion to float or sink depending on his innocence or guilt, much as a modern defendant might betray himself by increased tension when answering falsely in a lie detector test.

However this may be, Germanic law and Germanic institutions were crude indeed when compared with those of the Romans. Yet it was Germanic culture that dominated the barbarian successor kingdoms which arose on the ruins of the Western Empire. And the Germanic contribution to English history and Western Civilization was by no means entirely negative. The Germanic peoples brought to Western Europe a rough but energetic spirit. Their warlike ideals of loyalty and honor evolved slowly and gradually into the medieval notion of chivalry. Their respect for the sanctity of tribal custom, the advisory function of the tribal assembly, and the rough social equality among members of a war band, all contributed to the later ideas of limited government, the rights of subjects, and the superiority of law over the royal will.

It should not be thought for a moment, however, that early Germanic institutions were remotely democratic or even proto-democratic. The sanctity of folk-law and the prominence of tribal assemblies are to be found among many primitive peoples. Far from being politically precocious, the Germanic peoples were simply too crude and ignorant to create efficient despotisms. More than a millennium would pass before these ancient Germanic notions—of mutual respect and honor within the *comitatus*, the inviolability of customary law, and the political role of the assemblies—would evolve into anything resembling a coherent doctrine of limited representative government. The process of evolution is itself far more significant than the faint and ambiguous precedents in primitive Germanic custom.

On the Continent, as we have seen, the fifth and sixth centuries witnessed the beginnings of a gradual fusion between the Germanic culture of the barbarian kingdoms and the Classical-Christian tradition preserved and fostered by the Church. In Britain, on the other hand, the heathen Germanic invaders remained immune to the Christian faith of the indigenous Britons. As British authority receded before the advance of the Germanic barbarians, Christianity receded with it. The failure of the Britons to Christianize their conquerors may be attributed at least in part to the profound hostility that developed between the two peoples and the consequent unwillingness of British missionaries to evangelize among the hated invaders. A century and a half elapsed between the first conquests and the beginnings of serious missionary work among the heathen Germanic settlers in Britain.

The Anglo-Saxon Conquest

According to the great eighth-century historian, Bede, three distinct Germanic peoples invaded England: the Angles, the Saxons, and the Jutes. Although repeated by historians and memorized by schoolboys ever since, Bede's statement seriously oversimplifies the actual situation. It would probably be more accurate to view the invasions as consisting of landings, attacks, and settlements by innumerable small Germanic war bands coming from various points along the long coastline of the North Sea between southern Denmark and the Netherlands. Among these invaders were many warriors from among the Angle and Saxon tribes that had long been known to be settled in northern Europe, but they also included Frisians, Swabians, and other Germanic peoples. On the Continent the invaders came in large tribal groups bent on conquest and settlement; in Britain they came as small marauding bands hungry for booty and land. The organization of the Germanic invaders into larger political units ruled by kings was a product of the decades following the original invasions.

It would also be incorrect to say, as is sometimes done, that the Germanic invasions of Britain began around 450. Britain had long been subject to Germanic attacks, as the establishment of the Saxon Shore and the disaster of 367 make clear. Moreover, even in the days of Roman rule, Germanic warriors had been invited into Britain to serve as mercenaries in the defense of the island. The transition from Germanic raiders and Germanic mercenaries to Germanic conquerors was exceedingly gradual and could not be identified with a particular year in the fifth century even if our sources for the period were adequate. Finally, long after the Germanic invaders — the Anglo-Saxons as they are conventionally called — had set about in earnest to conquer Britain, the Britons themselves maintained a stout resistance. For well over a century the issue remained in doubt.

The general pattern of conquest — as it emerges in the writings of the British monk Gildas, the later history of Bede, and other less-than-satisfactory sources — is as follows: Following the Roman abandonment of Britain in about 410, the British towns inherited the task of defending their land. At first, the most serious threats to the island's security came from the Picts and Scots, and letters were dispatched to Rome begging for military assistance against these enemies. There is evidence to suggest that some assistance was sent, but obviously not enough. For as the fifth century progressed, the Western Empire itself was approaching total political disintegration.

Our evidence indicates that around 425 a Romano-British aristocrat named Vortigern rose to political leadership in southeastern Britain and took upon himself the responsibility of defense against the sea raids of the Picts and Scots. Finding the Britons incapable of defending themselves adequately, Vortigern is said to have invited Germanic warriors to Britain, offering them lands in Kent in return for their military assistance. Gildas calls these warriors "Saxons" whereas Bede describes them as "Jutes" under the leadership of two chieftains named Hengist and Horsa. Many historians have followed Gildas in proclaiming Vortigern's decision an act of incredible folly, but this is scarcely a fair judgment. Vortigern was simply resorting to a policy that the Romans themselves had frequently used in their declining years.

Nevertheless, Vortigern's invitation had disastrous consequences. The Germanic warriors, once settled, invited numerous kinsmen to join them, then rebelled against Vortigern's authority and spread devastation and terror across southeastern Britain.

This rebellion can perhaps be dated around 450. During the next half century Germanic war bands came to Britain in large numbers, settling along the southern and eastern shores and penetrating deep into the interior, chiefly by means of eastern Britain's three great estuaries: the Thames, the Wash, and the Humber. After about 470, however, the British defense began to stiffen, and around the turn of the century the Britons won a major victory over the invaders at a site called Mount Badon. The inadequacies of our evidence regarding these events is well illustrated by the fact that historians are in complete disagreement as to both the site of this battle and its date. (Estimates range between 486 and 516.) On the authority of a ninth-century Welsh writer named Nennius, the great British victory at Mount Badon is associated with a leader named Arthur who became the inspiration for the richly elaborated Arthurian romances of later centuries. Perhaps the original Arthur was indeed a hero of the British resistance against the Anglo-Saxons, but this tempting conclusion is far from assured: Nennius is a dangerously untrustworthy authority and is writing a good three centuries after the event. At any rate, it should be obvious that Arthur's glittering court at Camelot, with its chivalrous knights who paid pretty compliments to their ladies and went on romantic quests, constitutes an idealization of courtly society in the later Middle Ages and has nothing whatever to do with the primitive and insecure world of early-sixth-century Britain.

For a half century after the British victory at Mount Badon, so Gildas tells us, the island enjoyed a period of relative peace and prosperity. The Anglo-Saxons were evidently forced to abandon some of the territories which they had previously conquered, but they were by no means driven from Britain. The period of peace and British hegemony can be dated tentatively as the half century between 500 and 550. Gildas himself was writing in that period, and provides eyewitness testimony to the relative security of the epoch.

The era between 550 and 600 was far different. Shortly after 550 the Anglo-Saxons won the first in a series of notable victories that ultimately drove the Britons into the mountainous fastness of Wales, Devon, and Cornwall. Some left the island altogether, seeking refuge on the great peninsula at the northwest corner of Gaul which was known in later years, appropriately, as Brittany. (Actually, Britons had been migrating to Brittany ever since late-Roman times.) Those Britons who remained in the rich lowland zone, now almost completely under Germanic control, were obliged to acknowledge the Anglo-Saxons their masters.

The details of the Anglo-Saxon invasions are far from certain. Even the broad pattern that has been outlined here is hypothetical in many respects. But we do know this: that the Britons, long accustomed to the ways of peace, and long guarded by a protective screen of Roman legions, nevertheless put up a stout and prolonged resistance against the Anglo-Saxon invaders. Their efforts were fruitless in the long run, however, and the Anglo-Saxon conquest resulted ultimately in a remarkably thorough eradication of the previous Romano-British culture. Always a remote outpost of Roman civilization, Britain was the least successful of Rome's provinces in preserving vestiges of Roman culture into the Middle Ages. Insofar as any land can lose its past, Britain had lost hers, and the history of Anglo-Saxon England begins with a virtual *tabula rasa*. A new language superseded the old; German heathenism took the place of British Christianity; the square Celtic fields gave way to the long strip fields of the Anglo-Saxons; the Celtic family farm was replaced, for the most part, by the Anglo-Saxon village community; and Romano-British town life vanished altogether. In a word, Britain was transformed into "Angle-Land," or England. And the Anglo-Saxons, who had neither the Roman past to build upon nor the Christian Church to teach them the ways of civilization, were ruder and more barbarous than any other Germanic people in the former Empire.

Still, early Anglo-Saxon England began to move almost immediately toward political coherence, at least in a limited degree. As invasions turned into settlements the warriors who had formerly commanded military bands now assumed the additional responsibility of territorial administration. They became important local aristocrats who, together with their military followers, constituted a warrior nobility, sustained by the labors of subject peasants and slaves. English historians of the Victorian era were fond of describing Anglo-Saxon England as a relatively egalitarian society, pregnant with democracy. Today most scholars regard this view as an illusion. Almost from the beginning, Anglo-Saxon society was dominated by an aristocracy of landed wealth and military prowess. And very early in the history of the settlements, war leaders of singular ability or luck began to assert their hegemony over neighboring war bands, thereby inaugurating a movement toward political consolidation that culminated in the establishment of numerous territorial states ruled by royal dynasties.

England in A.D. 600

By the seventh century Anglo-Saxon England had resolved itself into about seven or eight major kingdoms and a number of less important ones — a political configuration that is usually called the Heptarchy. This term can be misleading, since it implies the existence of precisely seven states, all more or less equal in power. In reality the number of kingdoms fluctuated constantly, and tended gradually to diminish as political consolidation advanced. Moreover, the kingdoms of the Heptarchy varied considerably in prestige and military might. Even by 600, if we may trust Bede, it was customary to accord one king the honor of preeminence among his royal colleagues by designating him "bretwalda." This title was not permanently attached to a particular kingdom, but shifted from one dynasty to another with the varying fortunes of politics and war. The earliest bretwaldas were kings whose military strength enabled them to collect tribute from a few smaller neighboring kingdoms and whose fame had spread over much of England. Other important monarchs held the bretwalda in respect, but the degree to which they submitted to his commands is far from certain. Among the more powerful Anglo-Saxon kings his primacy seems to have been largely honorary. In later years, however, the authority of the bretwaldaship was destined to increase significantly and to play an important role in the ultimate unification of the realm.

The preeminent kingdom in Anglo-Saxon England around the year 600 was Kent, in the southeast corner of the island. Bede accords the Kentish king at this time the title of bretwalda, and it does seem clear that Kent exerted authority over the two neighboring kingdoms of Essex and East Anglia.

Kent is the one Anglo-Saxon kingdom whose conquest Bede attributes to the Jutes. Unfortunately, historians are still debating the questions of who the Jutes were and where they came from. It is quite true that Kent exhibits a number of peculiar features not found elsewhere in Anglo-Saxon England. Instead of the usual strip fields and agrarian villages, Kentish agriculture is characterized by consolidated fields and individual farms or "hamlets." In its pottery, its jewelry, its burial methods, and its legal customs, Kent differed from most of the remainder of England. On the other hand, its culture demonstrates marked similarities to that of the Franks, whose kingdom lay directly across the Channel. It may well be that the "Jutes" of Kent were actually diverse peoples who achieved cultural unity only after their migration to Britain, and that their evolving culture was strongly influenced by their trade and intercourse with the Franks.

To the west and northwest of Kent lay three kingdoms associated by name with the Saxon migrations: the kingdoms of the South Saxons, the West Saxons, and the East Saxons, known respectively as Sussex, Wessex, and Essex. Of these Saxon states, only Wessex had the potentiality for future expansion westward at British expense, and in the centuries following A.D. 600 Wessex rose to become one of the three leading kingdoms of the land. Ultimately, Wessex became the nucleus of a united England, and the Wessex dynasty evolved into the English monarchy.

To the north of Kent lay the kingdom of East Anglia, whose inhabitants were divided into two separate groups—the North Folk and the South Folk—occupying the territories that would later become the shires of Norfolk and Suffolk. Subject to Kent in A.D. 600, the East Anglian monarchy was destined in the following generation to acquire the bretwaldaship. The wealth of the East Anglian kings in this epoch is attested dramatically by the richly laden royal burial ship dating from the mid-seventh century that was discovered at Sutton Hoo in 1939. The ship contains an astonishing quantity of gold and silver jewelry, plate, coins, and weapons, some of Frankish provenience, others from distant Byzantium. The discovery at Sutton Hoo leaves no doubt that the trappings of a great Anglo-Saxon monarch two centuries after the onset of the conquest could be splendid indeed.

The English midlands were dominated by the kingdom of Mercia which first emerges into the light of history with the accession of its great king, Penda, in 632. Like Wessex, Mercia could expand westward toward Wales at the expense of the

26

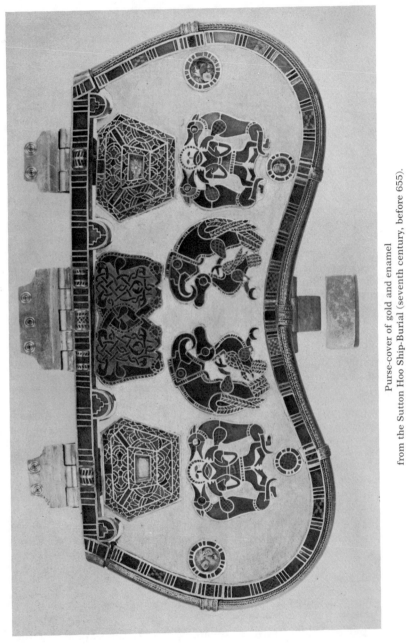

Purse-cover of gold and enamel
from the Sutton Hoo Ship-Burial (seventh century, before 655).

Britons (or, as we should by now call them, the Welsh), and like Wessex also, Mercia was destined to become one of the three dominant kingdoms of England in the centuries to come. Indeed, throughout most of the eighth century the kings of Mercia were the most powerful monarchs in the land.

The third great Anglo-Saxon kingdom of later centuries was Northumbria — the land north of the Humber River. The kingdom of Northumbria arose shortly after A.D. 600 from the unification of two smaller and older kingdoms, Deira and Bernicia, under a single dynasty. In the later seventh and early eighth centuries Northumbria became the setting of a splendid intellectual and artistic revival stimulated by a resurgence of Celtic culture and conversion to Christianity. Perhaps the greatest ornament of this Northumbrian Renaissance was the historian Bede, whose writings have done so much to illuminate the dark epoch when his own savage forebears were ravaging and subduing Britain.

By the early seventh century the chaos of the invasion age had given way to a more stable regime dominated by reasonably coherent Anglo-Saxon kingdoms such as the seven described above: Kent, Sussex, Wessex, Essex, East Anglia, Mercia, and Northumbria. The splendor of Sutton Hoo demonstrates that the early Anglo-Saxons, even though cut off from the Roman past and isolated from the Church, were not without culture or resources. As it turned out, however, the isolation of the Anglo-Saxons was destined to cease. The epoch following A.D. 600 was dominated by the momentous fact of England's conversion to Christianity. The Church returned to Britain at last, gradually winning the allegiance of the Anglo-Saxons and profoundly shaping their historical development. To the Christian conversion of England we must now turn.

Chapter 2

Conversion AND Unification

The Celtic Church

BY THE TIME of the British victory at Mount Badon (*c.* 500) Roman political authority had collapsed in the West. But although the Western Roman Empire was a thing of the past, Roman political institutions survived, in altered but recognizable form, in the organization of the Roman Catholic Church. Indeed, the Church has been regarded as a kind of transfigured Empire, its administration paralleling the old Roman civil administration with dioceses, provinces, parishes, and even a central authority in Rome. Where Roman emperors had once exerted political sway over the inhabitants of Western Europe, Roman popes now claimed responsibility for their immortal souls. And just as the Emperor Constantine had established an imperial capital at Constantinople that rivaled Rome itself, so now an intense spiritual rivalry developed between the Roman pontiff and the patriarch of Constantinople.

Accordingly, the Church has been termed the ghost of the Roman Empire. To be sure, the ghost metaphor belies the very tangible ecclesiastical organization of the early Middle Ages and the significant impact of the Church on the lives of European Christians, yet there is some value in regarding the Church, in the political sense at least, as an institutional legacy of the defunct Empire.

In England, however, Christianity did not survive the Germanic invasions but receded with the Britons themselves into the mountains of Cornwall and Wales.[1] In these rough lands the Britons found sanctuary against the military thrusts of the Anglo-Saxons, and here the British Church endured. Although several generations passed before Celtic Christianity made any headway against the heathen Anglo-Saxons, Celtic missionaries were spreading their faith in other directions. In the fifth century, the fabled British missionary St. Patrick (d. 461) had introduced Christianity to the Scots of Ireland, and other missionaries were undertaking the task of Christian conversion in Galloway (southwestern Scotland). Thus, although Christianity virtually disappeared from England with the completion of the Anglo-Saxon conquest, it continued to flourish in the lands which Englishmen call "the Celtic Fringe": Wales, Cornwall, Galloway, and, above all, Ireland.

In the days of St. Patrick, the Celtic Church had been in contact with continental Christianity, but with the passage of time it became increasingly isolated. Despite its isolation – or perhaps because of it – the Celtic Church flourished remarkably, particularly in Ireland. During the sixth and seventh centuries it far exceeded the Church on the Continent in the rigor of its scholarship, the depth of its sanctity, and the dynamism of its evangelical work. Irish monastic schools were perhaps the best in Western Europe at the time, and a rich Irish artistic tradition culminated in the illuminated manuscripts of the eighth century which were the wonder of their own age and still excite admiration in ours.

Because of its isolation from the papacy and continental Christianity, the Celtic Church developed certain practices and customs that were unique and, from the continental standpoint, peculiar. The tonsure of Celtic monks differed from that of continental monks; the Celtic method of calculating the date of Easter was at variance with the continental method. Matters such as these might well seem trivial to the modern student, but to a continental churchman the Celtic celebration of Easter on the "wrong" day and the markedly peculiar Celtic tonsure (the front half of the head was entirely shaved) set the Celtic Christian apart as a rather exotic and even barbaric individual.

---

[1] For a good recent account of the early English Church see C. J. Godfrey, *The Church in Anglo-Saxon England* (1962). The period of Anglo-Saxon history treated in this chapter is covered in several of the books on Anglo-Saxon England already cited. In addition to these, see R. H. Hodgkin, *A History of the Anglo-Saxons* (3rd ed., 1952). Dorothy Whitelock (ed.), *English Historical Documents*, I (1955), is a splendid and comprehensive selection of original documents in English translation from the period *c.* 500–1042.

Above all, the Celtic Church differed from the continental Church in organization. On the Continent the key unit in ecclesiastical administration was the diocese, ruled by a bishop; in the Celtic Fringe it was the monastery ruled by an abbot. The Celtic Church had bishops, to be sure, but their functions were spiritual and sacramental rather than administrative. Normally they lived in monasteries under the authority of the abbot.

Celtic monastic life was peculiar, too, by continental standards. Celtic monks led simpler, harsher, and less regulated lives than their continental counterparts. The unique combination in Celtic monasticism of profound dedication and relatively loose discipline does much to explain the wide-ranging and highly successful evangelical activities of the Irish monks.

In the sixth and seventh centuries, fervent Irish missionary monks traveled far and wide across Western Europe bringing the Christian Faith into the remaining pockets of paganism, and bringing the intense piety of Celtic Christianity to regions only nominally Christian. For our purposes, the most significant of these Irish evangelists was St. Columba (d. 597) who worked with great success toward the conversion of the Picts. In about 590, St. Columba founded a monastery on the island of Iona, off the west coast of Scotland, which became a fountainhead of missionary activity among the Picts of Scotland and the English of Northumbria.

With the founding of Iona, the Celtic Church took up at last the immense task of converting the Anglo-Saxons. But the Celtic spiritual penetration of Anglo-Saxon England from the north began, as it happened, almost concurrently with an entirely distinct Christian missionary endeavor from the south. In 597, the very year of St. Columba's death, a group of Christian evangelists sent by the Roman pope, St. Gregory the Great, and led by the Benedictine monk, St. Augustine, made contact with King Ethelbert of Kent. So it was that the seventh century saw Anglo-Saxon heathendom under spiritual assault from two independent and historically distinct Christian traditions.

The Roman Church and Benedictine Monasticism

As England was developing from the chaos of the early Anglo-Saxon conquests to the relative stability of the Heptarchy, much larger Germanic kingdoms were evolving on the Continent. A powerful Germanic tribe known as the Franks had established a kingdom in Gaul and the Rhinelands, Catholic in religion but only superficially so, wretchedly governed by Roman standards yet rather more coherent and sophisticated than the contemporary kingdoms of Anglo-Saxon England. The Germanic Visigoths had founded a loosely-organized kingdom in Spain, destined to be overwhelmed in the early eighth century by the advancing Moslems. Italy, after a series of upheavals, was ruled in part by a savage Germanic tribe known as the Long Beards or Lombards, in part by the Byzantine Empire. In Rome itself the papacy maintained a precarious independence. Throughout these lands of Western Europe scholarship was all but extinct, culture had sunk to a primitive level, the cities were moribund, and political and economic organization was rudimentary (except in Byzantine Italy). Germanic culture and Germanic institutions were everywhere in the ascendancy; and among the rough aristocracy of this epoch, fighting skill and loyalty to clan and lord were the appropriate virtues.

The taming of this crude and violent society by the intellectual and cultural values of antiquity and the spiritual message of the Church was yet to be accomplished. The sixth-century Church, throughout much of the barbarian West, was little better than the lay society that surrounded it. Ineffective, ignorant, and frequently corrupt, it stood in desperate need of revitalization and reform. All things considered, isolation was by no means a disadvantage to the Church of Ireland.

Yet the continental Church of the sixth century had within it the strength to recover and to assume its great mission in the world. Its reform centered above all on two institutions: Benedictine monasticism and the papacy.

Christian monasticism arose in Egypt in the third century, but it did not become a significant factor in the life of the Church until the fourth. After the conversion of Constantine and his rise to power in 312, Christianity became a favored religion. Profession of the Christian Faith was no longer the perilous and heroic act that it had been in the days of the martyrs. As converts poured into the now-respectable fold, men of unusual piety began to seek a more rigorous Christian way of life—one that would enable them to withdraw from the iniquitous world and devote all their energies to communion with God. Many of them found what they were seeking in monasticism.

Traditionally, Christian monasticism was of two types: eremitic (hermit monasticism) and cenobitic (communal monasticism). During the fifth and sixth centuries increasing numbers of fervent believers became cenobitic or eremitic monks (not "aromatic monks," as some students would have it). The lives of the hermit monks were bewildering in their variety. Some established themselves atop tall pillars and remained there for many years; others retreated to the desert, living in a state of uncompromising austerity. And the monastic communities of the age tended to be equally diverse. Both hermit monks and cenobitic monks often carried the mortification of the flesh to extreme lengths, indulging in severe fasts, going without sleep for prolonged periods, wearing hairshirts, and even beating themselves.

The great contribution of St. Benedict (*c*. 480–*c*. 544) was to bring sanity and order to the monastic life. A Roman of aristocratic background, his emphasis on the practical Roman virtues of discipline and coherent organization transformed the monasticism of his day and infused it with new vigor. St. Benedict founded many monasteries in his lifetime, the most important of which was Monte Cassino, on a mountaintop between Rome and Naples. But more important than the monasteries that he founded was the rule that he created for their governance.

St. Benedict's rule was characterized by Pope Gregory the Great as "conspicuous for its discretion." Discretion is its most essential quality. The life of the Benedictine monk was austere, but not excessively so. He ate, slept, and dressed simply but adequately. His day was divided into a regular sequence of activities: there was a time for eating, a time for sleeping, a time for prayer, and a time for work. The Benedictine monasteries had no central organization. Each was autonomous (subject to the jurisdiction of the local bishop), and each was under the full and unquestioned authority of an abbot. On important matters the abbot was to consult the whole community of monks, but ultimately his word was final. Still, St. Benedict cautioned his abbots to respect the views of their monks, not to "sadden" or "overdrive" them or give them cause for "just murmuring." Here, as elsewhere, is the element of discretion to which Pope Gregory alludes, and which was doubtless the chief reason for the rule's phenomenal success. St. Benedict tempered his sanctity with a keen knowledge of human nature. His monks must submit to the discipline of their abbot and the authority of the rule, they must practice poverty and chastity, they must work as well as pray. Yet for all that, the life which St. Benedict prescribed was not for spiritual supermen alone, but one that any dedicated Christian might hope to follow.

St. Benedict's rule transformed Western monasticism, revitalized the Church, and inspired many of the most prominent participants in the conversion of England. Benedictine monasteries became islands of peace, security, and learning in a sea of barbarism. They operated the best, often the only, schools of their day. Their extensive estates—the gifts of generations of pious donors—served as models of the most efficient agricultural techniques known in their time. In a word, they were the supreme civilizers of the early Middle Ages.

Benedictine monasticism was one of the two great invigorating institutions in the early medieval Church. The other was the papacy. For centuries the popes, as bishops of Rome and heirs of St. Peter, had claimed spiritual dominion over the Church, but they had seldom been able to exercise it prior to the pontificate of St. Gregory the Great (590–604). A man of humility and deep piety, St. Gregory was the first Benedictine pope. He was also the most powerful pontiff of the early Middle Ages. His pontificate represents in effect a momentous alliance between the papacy and the Benedictine order.

Both parties profited from the alliance: Benedictine monasticism received a powerful impetus from papal support, and wherever the Benedictines went, papal authority followed. When the Benedictines converted a heathen land, they converted it not merely to Christianity, but to Christianity as practiced and interpreted by the Roman Church. Hence, Benedictine evangelism was a potent factor in the spread of papal power and the spiritual unification of Christendom.

The Benedictines in England

Pope Gregory the Great was a man of many talents. Like St. Benedict, he possessed in full the practical genius of his aristocratic Roman forebears and was therefore a brilliant administrator and sensitive pastor. He was a notable scholar by the standards of his day, and is traditionally grouped with the great fourth-century intellectuals, St. Ambrose, St. Jerome, and St. Augustine of Hippo as one of the four "Doctors" of the Latin Church. Much of his theological writing failed to rise far above the level of his day, but his *Pastoral Care* – a practical handbook on the duties of bishops and priests – is a work of originality and keen insight.

Paradoxically, St. Gregory the Great never set foot in England yet is one of the central figures in early English history. Bede relates that prior to his elevation to the papacy, St. Gregory encountered a group of fair-haired young boys from England who were being offered for sale as slaves. Asking the name of their race, he was told that they were Angles. "That is appropriate," he replied, "for they have angelic faces, and it is right that they should become fellow heirs with the angels in heaven." The story seems a bit contrived, and Bede himself is obviously a little suspicious of it, but he includes it to illustrate "Gregory's deep desire for the salvation of our nation."

It was doubtless this "deep desire" that inclined Pope Gregory to send a band of missionaries to begin the conversion of the English. And his devotion to the Benedictine order prompted him to entrust the hazardous task to a group of Benedictine monks led by St. Augustine (not to be confused with the great fourth-century philosopher, St. Augustine of Hippo). The ultimate effect of St. Augustine's mission was not only to win England to the Christian Faith but also to enlarge enormously the scope of the Benedictine order and the authority of the papacy and, indirectly, to reform and expand the continental Church.   For in later years English Benedictines themselves undertook exceedingly fruitful missionary work on the Continent, reorganizing the Church in Frankland and carrying Christianity deep into the forests of heathen Germany.

In 597 St. Augustine's mission arrived in Kent.   This small kingdom was an ideal place to begin the work of conversion. It was the closest Anglo-Saxon kingdom to the Continent; its king, Ethelbert, was momentarily the preeminent monarch of England and was accorded the title of bretwalda; and its queen, Bertha, was a Christian and a member of the Frankish royal family.   At Queen Bertha's request, a Frankish bishop had been established in the Kentish royal household.   Ethelbert received Augustine's mission courteously, permitted the monks to establish themselves in the royal town of Canterbury ("Kent City"), and in time became a convert to the new faith.   Following Ethelbert, a great many Kentishmen were baptized, and significant progress was made in converting the client kingdoms of Essex and East Anglia.   Returning briefly to the Continent, Augustine was consecrated by papal order "archbishop of the English nation," thereby becoming the first in a line of archbishops of Canterbury that extends to this day.

In accordance with the sagacious instructions which he received in letters from Pope Gregory, Augustine permitted his English converts to retain those aspects of their former heathen customs and rites that were not inconsistent with Christianity. Old heathen temples were neither abandoned nor destroyed, but were converted to Christian use.   In general, Gregory and Augustine displayed a respect for the integrity of Anglo-Saxon folk ways that would bring joy to a modern anthropologist.

Almost from the beginning, St. Augustine was aware of the activities and potential rivalry of the Celtic Church.   He attempted to secure its submission to his own archiepiscopal authority, but a series of unsuccessful summit conferences with leading Celtic ecclesiastics made it clear that the Celts would give up neither their unique system of calculating Easter nor their age-long independence.   The tension between Celtic and Roman-Benedictine Christianity was to continue for many decades to come.

It is no coincidence that Ethelbert of Kent, the first Anglo-Saxon monarch to become a Christian, was also the first to issue a series of written laws, or "dooms." The Dooms of Ethelbert are the first in a great series of Anglo-Saxon vernacular law codes running all the way down into the eleventh century. They represent the first literary fruits of the encounter between Christianity and Anglo-Saxon culture. For although Ethelbert's Dooms are concerned largely with Germanic custom, they were undoubtedly committed to writing at the instigation of the Church, which was then the almost exclusive custodian of the written word. Indeed, the first doom in Ethelbert's list provides explicitly for the protection of ecclesiastical property. The following dooms deal with customary fines and wergeld rates: If a man cuts off another's ear he must pay twelve shillings; he must pay fifty shillings for an eye, six shillings for a front tooth; ten shillings for a big toe, etc. In publishing these dooms, Ethelbert was not claiming the right to legislate but was merely specifying and clarifying the immemorial customs of his people. For in Germanic law the authority of the king was strictly limited by the customs of the folk.

The Conversion of Northumbria

Upon the death of Ethelbert in 616, Kent, Essex, and East Anglia underwent a heathen reaction. The bretwaldaship passed momentarily to East Anglia, but the center of evangelical activity shifted to the remote kingdom of Northumbria.

As we have seen, Northumbria came into being shortly after 600 with the unification of two northern kingdoms, Bernicia and Deira, under a single monarch. The real founder of Northumbria was a Bernician warrior-king named Ethelfrith (d. 616) who won a series of notable victories over the British, the Scots, and the Anglo-Saxon inhabitants of Deira, thereby establishing himself as the dominant power in the north and bringing the kingdom of Deira under his sway. The Deiran heir, a talented young warrior-statesman named Edwin, went into exile for a time at the East Anglian court, but in 616 Edwin's forces defeated and killed Ethelfrith and Edwin became king of Northumbria (616–32). Now it was the Bernician royal heirs who were driven into exile. They found refuge in Scotland where they fell under the influence of the Celtic monks of Iona.

Meanwhile, Edwin was proving himself a monarch of rare ability. He maintained a firm peace in Northumbria, led a highly successful military expedition against the Welsh, and even took his army on a triumphant campaign southward across the midlands into Wessex. Edwin was a bretwalda of unprecedented authority, dominating his Anglo-Saxon contemporaries as no king before him had done. Even though his power rested on the ephemeral foundation of his own personal leadership and military skill, his reign represented an important step in England's long evolution toward political unity.

In the pages of Bede, Edwin's warlike prowess and wise statesmanship are given full recognition, but they tend to fade before the momentous fact of his conversion. Like Ethelbert of Kent, Edwin had a Christian wife. Indeed, he was wed to a daughter of Ethelbert himself, Ethelberga, who took with her to Northumbria a vigorous chaplain named Paulinus. King Edwin was subjected to Christian pressure from several quarters: from his devout wife, from Paulinus, and from the pope. In one of his letters to Ethelberga, the pope gave this counsel: "Persist, therefore, illustrious daughter, and to the utmost of your power endeavor to soften the hardness of his [Edwin's] heart by insinuating the divine precepts, etc." To King Edwin, the pope wrote,

> Hear the words of your preachers, and the Gospel of God which they declare to you, to the end that believing . . . [in] the indivisible Trinity, having put to flight the sensualities of devils, and driven from you the suggestions of the venomous and deceitful enemy, and being born again by water and the Holy Ghost, you may, through his assistance and bounty, dwell in eternal glory with Him in whom you shall believe.

After a time Edwin succumbed to this campaign of saturation. In 627 the king held a council at which he and his counselors accepted Christianity in its Roman-Benedictine form. Bede tells of an episode in this council which, whether authentic or not, provides an invaluable insight into the mood of the age. It is one of the most famous anecdotes of early English history — as familiar to English schoolboys as is the story of George Washington and the cherry tree to their American counterparts. According to Bede, one of Edwin's *Witan* (i.e., a member of his council), on considering the question of Christian conversion, advised his monarch as follows:

> The present life of man, O king, in comparison to that time which is unknown to us, seems to me like the swift flight of a sparrow through the hall wherein you sit at dinner in the winter, with your chieftains and ministers, and a good fire in the midst, while the storms of rain and snow rage without. The sparrow flies in

at one door and immediately out at another. While he is within he is safe from the wintry storm, but after a brief interval of fair weather he immediately vanishes from sight into the dark winter from which he came. So this life of man appears for a brief interval, but we are utterly ignorant of what went before or what will follow. So if this new doctrine contains something more certain, it seems justly to deserve to be followed.

As the council concluded, the chief priest of the heathen gods is reported to have embraced the new religion and with him, King Edwin himself. The Roman Church had won a notable triumph in a remote but powerful land.

The chagrin of the Christian party must have been great when, six years after his conversion, King Edwin was killed in battle (632). His adversary, the heathen King Penda of Mercia (c. 632–55), laid waste to Edwin's kingdom, and as a result of the catastrophe Northumbria collapsed briefly into political and religious chaos. But with the fall of Edwin and the Deiran royal house, the two heirs of the Bernician dynasty, long in exile in Scotland, returned to claim their inheritance. These two princes, bearing the engaging names of Oswald and Oswy, brought with them the Celtic Christianity that they had learned at Iona. Oswald, the older of the two, won the Northumbrian throne by defeating the Mercians and Welsh in 633. At this crucial encounter, known appropriately as the battle of Heavenfield, Oswald set up a wooden cross to symbolize his devotion to the new faith. But his victory must have evoked a mixed reaction among the Christians of Edwin's former court whose devotion to the Roman Easter and the Roman tonsure made it difficult for them to accept the alien ways of the Celtic Church.

Under the patronage of King Oswald (633–41) and his successor, King Oswy (641–69) Celtic Christianity established itself firmly in Northumbria. The great Celtic missionary, St. Aidan, founded a monastery on the isle of Lindisfarne off the coast of northern Bernicia which became a great focal point of Celtic Christianity and Celtic culture. And in the middle decades of the seventh century Celtic missionaries carried the Gospel south of the Humber into Mercia and other Anglo-Saxon kingdoms.

But it was Northumbria, above all, that witnessed the collision and cross-fertilization of the Roman and Celtic traditions. The Celtic influence, radiating from Iona and Lindisfarne, was countered by the activities of dedicated Roman-Benedictine missionaries such as the fervent and uncompromising St. Wilfrid of Ripon (634–710). And despite the Celtic leanings of King

Oswald and King Oswy, Roman Christianity, with its disciplined organization, its impressive ceremonial, and its majestic tradition, gradually advanced against the conservative and loosely administered Celtic Church.

The final victory of Roman Christianity in Northumbria was achieved at a momentous synod held at Whitby in 663 * in the presence of King Oswy. Present at this synod were leading churchmen from all over England, representing both the Roman and the Celtic observances. The chief issue in question was the Easter date. Oswy, who had previously celebrated Easter according to the Celtic reckoning, was upset that his wife, who followed the Roman custom, should be keeping the Lenten fast while he was enjoying the Easter feast. The Easter issue may well seem trivial, but it symbolized a far more fundamental question: would England remain in isolation from continental Christendom by cleaving to the customs of the Celtic Christians, or would it place itself in the mainstream of European Christianity by accepting the guidance and authority of the papacy and the customs of European Christianity? St. Wilfrid of Ripon saw the issue clearly when he addressed the Celtic churchmen at Whitby in these words:

> Although your fathers were holy men, do you imagine that they, a few men in a corner of a remote island, are to be preferred before the universal Church of Christ throughout the world? And even if your Columba—or may I say, ours also if he was a servant of Christ—was a saint of potent virtues, can he take precedence before the most blessed prince of the Apostles [i.e., St. Peter, whose vicar and representative the pope claimed to be] . . . ?

The synod of Whitby closed on an almost comic note, as King Oswy, determining that Peter possessed the keys to the kingdom of heaven, agreed to follow Peter's vicar, the pope, in all matters: "Otherwise, when I come to the gates of heaven, he who holds the keys may not be willing to open them." Bede reports this statement in all seriousness, but another source reports that Oswy smiled as he uttered those words. Probably he had decided long before the synod opened to cast his lot with Rome. The question at issue was momentous indeed, but the answer may well have been a foregone conclusion. For by the

---

* Sometimes dated 664. Bede's chronology is disputed.

time of Whitby it must have been growing increasingly clear
that the Roman way was the way of the future.

Celtic Christianity by no means expired with the Synod
of Whitby. On the contrary, it endured long thereafter, contributing much to Christian culture and the Christian life. But
little by little it abandoned its separatist character. In 716 Iona
herself submitted to the Roman observance, and in later years
the churches of Wales and Ireland followed suit.

The Roman Church was quick to consolidate its victory.
The acceptance of Roman authority and customs at Whitby was
followed by a thorough reorganization of the Anglo-Saxon
Church along Roman lines. The architect of this great administrative undertaking was St. Theodore of Tarsus, a distinguished
scholar from Asia Minor who, having traveled to Rome, was
sent to England by the pope to become archbishop of Canterbury. Theodore arrived in England in 669 at the advanced age
of 66. He set about at once to divide the land into a coherent
system of dioceses and selected devout, energetic bishops to
rule them. The rational episcopal structure which Archbishop
Theodore imposed upon the Anglo-Saxon Church was given
unity and direction by a regular series of conciliar assemblies
over which he presided. In the course of his twenty-one year
archiepiscopacy, St. Theodore of Tarsus succeeded in superim-
posing upon the multiplicity of Anglo-Saxon kingdoms a unified
church, with clearly delineated territorial bishoprics, and with
ultimate administrative authority centered at Canterbury. So
it was that the English Church, shaped by the coherent political
principles of the Roman papacy and, indrectly, the Roman Empire, achieved a degree of territorial coherence and administrative centralization that contrasted sharply with the instability
and particularism of the Anglo-Saxon states. As the unity of
the Roman Empire had been perpetuated in the spiritual unity
of the Roman Church, so the unity which St. Theodore imposed
upon the English Church anticipated and prefigured the political
unity of England itself.

Theodore was a notable scholar who had earlier studied
in Athens. He was accompanied on his journey to England
by another scholar of eminence, a North African churchman
named Hadrian. The Latin learning of Hadrian served as a
perfect foil for the Greek scholarship of Theodore. Together,
the two men made Canterbury a distinguished intellectual
center. Theodore established a school there which provided
instruction in Greek and Latin letters and the principles of
Roman law. The Roman legal tradition, which had virtually
disappeared from Western Europe, was well known in Theodore's Byzantine homeland, and he was therefore able to in-
troduce it into England along with his native Greek tongue.

Through their wide experience and broad culture, Theodore and Hadrian brought to seventh-century Canterbury the rich intellectual legacy of the Mediterranean world.

But it was in Northumbria rather than at Canterbury that Anglo-Saxon ecclesiastical culture reached its highest degree of creativity. Here, at the northernmost extremity of Christendom, the stimulating encounter between Celtic and Roman-Benedictine Christianity resulted in an intellectual and cultural achievement of the first order. In Northumbria, during the later seventh and early eighth century, Anglo-Saxon culture — and perhaps the whole of Christian culture in the early Middle Ages — achieved its climax.

One of the great patrons of this Northumbrian Renaissance was a nobleman named Benedict Biscop, a man of vigor and piety and a devoted Benedictine who made a number of journeys to Italy and southern Gaul. There he experienced the ordered life of long-established Benedictine monasteries, and collected large quantities of books and precious works of art which he brought back with him to his native Northumbria. He founded two great Northumbrian monasteries of the strict Benedictine rule — Wearmouth (674) and Jarrow (681) — which he filled with his books and other treasures. These two houses became the foci of Roman-Benedictine culture in Northumbria, while the older establishment at Lindisfarne remained the center of Celtic culture.

Both cultures contributed to the renaissance in Northumbria. The impressive artistic achievements of the age are largely Celtic in inspiration. The magnificently illuminated Lindisfarne Gospels (c. 721) are executed in the complex curvilinear style typical of Celtic art, although scholars have also detected an Anglo-Saxon influence in them. The great Latin literature of the period is, of course, primarily Roman-Benedictine in inspiration, and it has been suggested that the same impulse that gave rise to the Latin writings of the Northumbrian Renaissance also evoked the idea of putting into permanent written form great Germanic epic poems such as *Beowulf* which had been handed down orally for generations.*

The achievements of the Northumbrian Renaissance lay in many fields — in art, architecture, poetry, paleography, and manuscript illumination. But the supreme achievement of the age was the scholarship of the Venerable Bede (c. 673–735). In the writings of Bede, particularly his *History of the English*

---

* Our earliest extant version of *beowulf* is from tenth-century Wessex, but philological evidence demonstrates that the Wessex text is based on an earlier version from central or northern England.

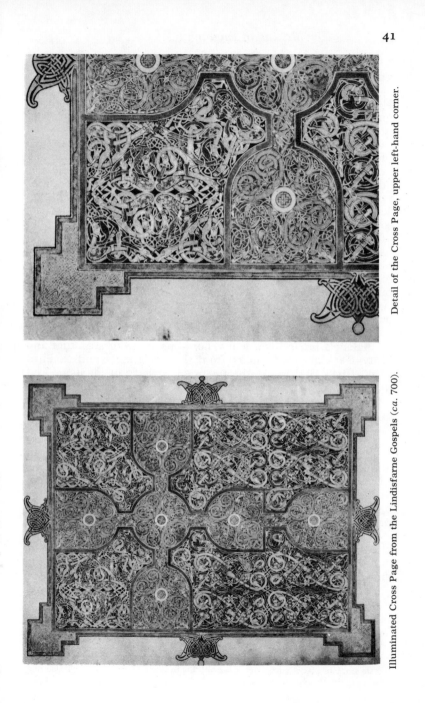

Detail of the Cross Page, upper left-hand corner.

Illuminated Cross Page from the Lindisfarne Gospels (*ca.* 700).

Church and People, the intellectual tradition of Western Europe attained a level unequaled since the fall of Rome.[2]

Bede was a product of the Roman-Benedictine tradition. He spent his life under the Benedictine rule at Jarrow, an exemplary monk and a superb scholar whose investigations were made possible by the fine library which Benedict Biscop had installed in the monastery in 681. Bede seems to have regarded his theological writings as his most important work, but his fame in later centuries rests primarily on his history. It was a pioneer effort, unprecedented in scope, yet at the same time a work of remarkable maturity. Bede possessed a strong historical conscience—an acute critical sense that caused him to use his sources with scrupulous care, evaluating their reliability, and often quoting them in full. Bede was by no means a scientific historian in the modern sense. His history is embroidered with numerous visions and other miraculous events, for he was a man of devoted faith who accepted without question the possibility of miracles. But even in his miracle stories he demonstrates far greater caution—far more respect for the historical evidence—than was customary among his predecessors and contemporaries.

Bede's broad historical vision—his sense of structure and unity—sets his work apart from the dry annals and fanciful saints' lives that typify the historical writing of his day. And his miracle stories fit logically into the basic structure of his work. For it was Bede's purpose to narrate the miraculous rise of Christianity in Britain and its crucial role of imposing coherence and purpose on the chaos of human events. In Bede's hands the history of the Britons and Anglo-Saxons and the rise of Christianity among them take on shape and direction. In effect, Bede is recording the developing synthesis between the Germanic and the Christian cultures—the gradual softening of the savage, martial traditions of the primitive Anglo-Saxons by the peace, love, and humble labor characteristic of the Christian life. And of course to Bede the Christian life *par excellence* is the life of the Benedictine monk. In one of the closing paragraphs of his history, Bede records—doubtless too optimistically—the triumph of monastic peace over Germanic violence:

> As peace and prosperity prevail in these days, many of the Northumbrians, both noble and humble, together with their children, have laid aside their arms, prefer-

---

[2] Bede's masterpiece is most readily available in Leo Sherley-Price (tr.), *Bede: A History of the English Church and People* (Penguin, 1955).

ring to receive the tonsure and take monastic vows rather than study the arts of war. The result of this trend will be seen in the coming generation.

It is characteristic of this man who regarded Christianity as the supreme organizing force in history that he should be the first scholar to use the Christian era as his chronological base – to date events not in terms of kings' reigns or lunar cycles but in terms of Christ's birth. Thus, Bede's sense of chronology and historical development resulted in the division of history into the two eras, B.C. and A.D., that are used to this day.

Finally, Bede gave to his contemporaries the concept of an "English people." At a time when England was divided into numerous individual kingdoms, and loyalties were limited to one's clan or local lord, Bede conceived the notion of "Englishmen" and made it the subject of his history. Thus, Bede accomplished at the intellectual level what Archbishop Theodore had accomplished at the level of ecclesiastical organization. In the face of the savage particularism and petty struggles of Anglo-Saxon kings, both men saw England as one. It is fitting that later ages should honor the administrative genius of Theodore, and celebrate Bede as "the first articulate Englishman."

The Return to the Continent

We have seen how the Benedictine order had its genesis in sixth-century Italy, how it was harnessed by Pope Gregory the Great at the century's end to the mighty task of converting the Anglo-Saxons, and how its encounter with Celtic Christianity in seventh- and eighth-century Northumbria evoked a great cultural flowering. During the eighth century, the dynamic Roman-Benedictine Christianity of England was carried back to the Continent by intrepid Anglo-Saxon missionaries and scholars to reinvigorate the Frankish Church and to spread civilization and the Gospel among the heathen Germans east of the Rhine. The greatest of these Anglo-Saxon missionaries was the Wessex monk, St. Boniface (d. 754). Working under the general direction of the papacy, and supplied with books and assistants by his Wessex countrymen, St. Boniface was the representative of three great dynamic forces of his day: the papacy, the Benedictine order, and the impressive ecclesiastical culture of Anglo-Saxon England. During the 740s, with the cooperation of the Carolingian rulers of Frankland, St. Boniface devoted himself to the reform of the Frankish Church, enforcing the strict observance of the Benedictine rule in

Frankish monasteries, and reconstructing Frankish diocesan organization on the same disciplined pattern that St. Theodore of Tarsus had earlier established in England. It was this reformed Frankish Church that provided the necessary environment for the impressive cultural achievements of Charlemagne's reign a generation later.

St. Boniface also devoted himself to the immense undertaking of Christianizing the heathen peoples of Germany. The task was far too great for a single man or a single generation, but Boniface made a promising beginning. Among the several Benedictine houses which he founded in Germany was the monastery of Fulda, which, like Wearmouth and Jarrow in Northumbria, became a notable intellectual and evangelical center. Boniface devoted himself particularly to the conversion of the Saxons, Hessians, and Frisians, and it was at the hands of the latter that he died a martyr's death in 754.

Northumbria, too, participated in the work of evangelism on the Continent. The fiery Northumbrian Benedictine, Wilfrid of Ripon, had been active in missionary work across the Channel long before Boniface undertook his mission, and much later on, in the reign of Charlemagne (768–814), the Northumbrian scholar Alcuin of York became the leading intellectual at Charlemagne's court. Alcuin was a student of a student of Bede's. A product of the Northumbrian Renaissance, he became the chief figure in the later and better-known Carolingian Renaissance.

In England itself, ecclesiastical culture declined somewhat in the course of the eighth century from the summit which it had attained in Bede's day, and in the ninth century it was virtually annihilated by the Vikings. Norse raiders sacked Lindisfarne in 793, Jarrow in 794, and Iona in 802. But before its demise in the far north, this culture had spread its creative influence among the Franks and Germans. Having transformed the Anglo-Saxon world, the potent civilizing force of Benedictine evangelism now returned to the Continent to provide the intellectual and spiritual foundations for Charlemagne's empire.

The Movement toward Political Consolidation: Mercia

During the 220 years following the death of Bede in 735, the unity of England, foreshadowed in the ecclesiastical organization of Archbishop Theodore and in the historical work of Bede himself, was achieved at the level of secular politics. The great historical theme of these years is the gradual trend toward political consolidation and, at length, the genesis of the English monarchy.

The progressive consolidation of royal power during the seventh and eighth centuries can be illustrated by the evolution of the bretwaldaship. Prior to the reign of King Edwin of Northumbria (616–32), a bretwalda might demand allegiance and collect tribute from one or two small neighboring kingdoms, but elsewhere his preeminence seems to have been chiefly honorary. Indeed, the bretwaldas of southern England appear to have been ignored completely by Bernicia and Deira north of the Humber. Moreover, the bretwaldaship tended to flit rather promiscuously from one small kingdom to another — from Sussex to Wessex to Kent to East Anglia — never remaining in one place more than a single generation. We are dependent on Bede for the names of the early bretwaldas, and it may well be that in attributing the bretwaldaship and its implied hegemony to these early kings Bede was mistakenly injecting into a chaotic past the relative orderliness of his own day.

However this may be, the rise of King Edwin of Northumbria to the bretwaldaship marks a new phase in England's political evolution. The smaller kingdoms of earlier years were gradually absorbed into the larger ones, until, by the later seventh century, three kingdoms — Northumbria, Mercia, and Wessex — had come to overshadow all the others. To speak very generally, Northumbria was the leading Anglo-Saxon kingdom in the seventh century, Mercia in the eighth, and Wessex in the ninth and tenth.

The epoch of Northumbrian hegemony is celebrated in the pages of Bede's history, and the great days of Wessex are recorded in the writings of King Alfred the Great's court and in the *Anglo-Saxon Chronicle*. Mercia, unfortunately for its later fame, left to posterity no impressive scholarly works and no history of its age of greatness. The power of Mercia's eighth-century kings cannot be gainsaid, but local patriotism prevented either the Northumbrian Bede or the later Wessex authors of the *Anglo-Saxon Chronicle* from portraying the rival Mercian state sympathetically. We must therefore use these sources with caution and beware of underestimating the statesmanship of the Mercian kings or the creativity of Mercian culture. Still, it seems unquestionable that the culture of eighth-century Mercia failed to reach the level of either Bede's Northumbria or King Alfred's Wessex.

Mercia's political and military power, however, was impressive indeed. Even in Northumbria's greatest days, she lived under an almost constant Mercian threat. Mercia's powerful heathen monarch, Penda (631–54), had challenged the Northumbrian hegemony more than once in the seventh century, defeating and killing King Edwin in 632 and King Oswald in 641 before being killed himself in battle against King Oswy in

654. During much of his reign, Penda exerted an authority over the kingdoms south of the Humber exceeding that of any of the earlier southern kings whom Bede called bretwaldas. By the end of his reign he had vastly increased the extent of his kingdom by absorbing a number of small neighboring states, and exerted his supremacy over both Wessex and East Anglia. A remarkably effective heathen warrior-king, he is portrayed by contemporary Christian writers as something of a devil.

Penda's Christian son, King Wulfhere (657–74), resumed his father's drive for control of southern England, establishing dominion over Essex and the town of London, cowing Wessex, and winning the allegiance of Kent and Sussex. At his death he was endeavoring to subdue Northumbria itself. Had he succeeded, his authority over England would have been virtually uncontested.

The growth of Mercian power was interrupted for a half century following Wulfhere's death by a resurgence of Wessex, particularly in the reign of its able king, Ine (688–726). Sussex, Essex, and Kent passed for a time from Mercian control to Wessex control. It was obvious by now that these smaller states were far too weak to maintain their independence, and the only question that remained was, which of the two "superpowers" would dominate them—Mercia or Wessex? During the better part of the eighth century Mercia not only successfully reasserted her dominion over these states, but managed by and large to dominate Wessex as well.

Mercian supremacy in the eighth century resulted from the intelligent exploitation of her strategic position and considerable resources by two able and long-lived kings: Ethelbald (716–57) and Offa (757–96). Mercia under the leadership of these monarchs was a powerful state that dominated the midlands and exacted tribute and allegiance from the kingdoms to the south and east. King Offa once described himself in an official document as "king of all England," and the royal boast was not too far from the truth.

The cold reality of Mercian power is well illustrated by a contemporary document known as the Tribal Hidage—a comprehensive assessment schedule which seems to have regulated the tribute payments owed to the Mercian kings by various lesser kingdoms in southern and central England. In the early days of the Anglo-Saxon settlements the term "hide" had denoted a unit of land sufficient in extent to support the household of a single warrior. By the time of the Tribal Hidage the hide had become the key unit of assessment. In the centuries to come, royal governments would exact taxes and military service from their subjects on the basis of the number of hides of land which each subject owned. The fact that the eighth-century Mercian monarchy should produce a document enumerating the hides of most of the Anglo-Saxon peoples south of the Humber testifies unmistakably to a far-flung administrative system and a central organization of unprecedented scale.

The reigns of Ethelbald and Offa witnessed not only an unparalleled degree of political power but also a surprising resurgence of commercial activity. King Offa's minters produced considerable quantities of the silver pennies that would remain the basis of the English currency until the thirteenth century. Indeed, the very term, "penny," was probably derived from the name of Offa's predecessor, King Penda. And the importance of commercial activities between the dominions of Offa and the empire of his illustrious contemporary, Charlemagne, is demonstrated by a most remarkable treaty between these two monarchs. Charlemagne addresses Offa in these words:

> You wrote to us about merchants. We extend to them our personal protection, as is the ancient custom for those engaged in trade. If treated wrongfully, let them appeal to us or our judges, and we will see that they have full justice. Similarly, should any of our subjects suffer injustice in your kingdom, they shall appeal to you for a just remedy, so that no trouble may occur between our subjects.

It is significant that English merchants were sufficiently active on the Continent at this time to require a formal arrangement between two rulers, and perhaps even more significant that Offa should take such a broad view of his royal responsibilities as to intervene in behalf of English traders abroad. In Offa's hands, Anglo-Saxon monarchy was assuming new and larger dimensions.

Many details of Offa's crucial reign are hidden from us by a lack of historical evidence. He has rightly been termed the most obscure great monarch of Anglo-Saxon England. King Alfred spoke respectfully of Offa's laws, but they have since vanished. We have no contemporary account of his reign or celebration of his deeds. But we do know that Offa extended very considerably the limits of the Mercian kingdom and the scope of Mercian royal authority. He advanced his power westward at Welsh expense and delineated his western frontier by constructing a remarkable earthen boundary marker known as Offa's Dike. By his death, the venerable royal dynasties of Sussex, Essex, East Anglia, and Kent had ceased to rule, and the vague suzerainty of the earlier bretwaldaship was in the process of being transformed into a direct control and absorption of subject lands.

Ironically, Offa's program for Mercian hegemony had the effect of temporarily subverting the hierarchical unity which Archbishop Theodore had earlier imposed on the English Church. Under Theodore the archbishopric of Canterbury had stood unchallenged at the apex of the hierarchy, but in 735 a second archbishopric was established at York in Northumbria, inferior in prestige to Canterbury but a potentially dangerous rival nevertheless. King Offa, so it seems, demanded a separate archbishopric for Mercia, and accordingly, in 787 there emerged a new archbishopric at Lichfield. Shortly after Offa's death, however, the Mercian archbishopric of Lichfield disappeared, and thereafter the English Church was dominated by its two remaining archbishoprics of Canterbury and York. Of these two, Canterbury remained preeminent.

The Church was active during Offa's reign. General councils continued to meet, and, at a lower level, country parishes were gradually taking shape. The development of an effective parish system was of immense importance to both Church and society in the early Middle Ages. The Church had emerged from the highly urbanized Roman Empire with a diocesan organization based on the city. With the disintegration of Roman imperial society, the cities declined and the countryside came to the fore, but several centuries elapsed before the Church adjusted its organization to the needs of the rural society in which it worked. Peasants and small freeholders often were obliged to go many months without seeing a priest or attending mass. The answer to this unsatisfactory condition was found in the country parish, administered by a priest who was supported by the enforced tithes of his parishioners. The parish system developed gradually, but in the eighth century, both in the empire of Charlemagne and in the kingdom of Offa, it was making significant progress.

In ecclesiastical and secular affairs alike, Offa's reign marks a crucial stage in the development of the Anglo-Saxons. With the Northumbrian monarchy in the doldrums and Mercian power unchallenged south of the Humber, with a vigorous and statesmanlike monarch who could negotiate with Charlemagne on terms of equality, Offa's England attained a degree of cohesion that Anglo-Saxon England had never before experienced.

The Movement Toward Political Consolidation: Wessex

The eighth-century Mercian kings gave England coherence but fell short of giving it unity. With Offa's death in 796, inspiration departed from the Mercian royal line, and the leadership of southern England gradually passed to Wessex.

In the early Middle Ages sophisticated bureaucratic government was unknown to Western Europe, and whatever the resources of a state might be, its success in the ruthless political competition of the period depended heavily on the military and administrative talents of its ruler. Thus, Mercia prospered mightily under Ethelbald and Offa but declined under their less competent successors. On the Continent, the Carolingian Empire of the Franks declined similarly in the years following the death of its brilliant emperor, Charlemagne, in 814. Accordingly, the rise of Wessex in the early ninth century depended not merely on its wide extent and the relative abundance of its human and material resources but also, and above all, on the impressive ability of its monarchs.

It was the gifted King Egbert of Wessex (802–39) who won for his kingdom the hegemony that Mercia had so long enjoyed. At the battle of Ellendon in 825 he routed the Mercian army, thereby winning control of the lesser states of southern England—Kent, Sussex, and Essex. Shortly afterward he received the submission and allegiance of East Anglia and Northumbria, and for a brief time he ruled even in Mercia itself. Egbert's power was impressive indeed, although it seems to have fallen short of the authority which Offa had earlier exercised. But unlike Offa, Egbert had the good fortune to be succeeded by a series of remarkably able heirs. Egbert's reign was merely the beginning of a long epoch in which the Wessex monarchy, tempered by the fires of a terrifying Viking invasion, endured to become the sole royal power in the land. Egbert's descendants were to become the first kings of England.

The Viking Age and the Birth of the English Monarchy

The era of Mercian ascendancy corresponded approximately to the period in which Charlemagne and his gifted predecessors expanded the power of the Frankish kingdom to such an extent that it became virtually coterminous with continental Christendom. We have already noted the impressive intellectual upsurge at Charlemagne's court, and the crucial role played by the Northumbrian Alcuin in this Carolingian Renaissance. The hegemony of Wessex, on the other hand, was concurrent with the decline of the Carolingian Empire and the coming of the Viking Age. Traveling from their Scandinavian homeland in their famous long ships, the Vikings carried their activities of pillage and conquest far and wide across northern Europe and the Atlantic. They subjected the Franks and Germans to fierce harassment, established a powerful dynasty in Russia, raided in Islamic Spain, settled Iceland, and even touched the coast of North America.

Although the reasons for the Viking outburst are a matter of considerable scholarly dispute, it is at least possible to suggest certain key factors which may have contributed to the advent of the Viking age. For one thing, a steady rise in population and political consolidation in Scandinavia may well have prompted many adventurous spirits to seek their fortunes abroad. For another, improvements in Viking shipbuilding seem to have added significantly to the mobility of these warriors. Charlemagne himself may have contributed unknowingly to the future debacle when he subdued and conquered the Frisians, a powerful maritime people along the northern shore of Europe to the east of the Rhine, who had previously functioned as a buffer between Western Europe and Scandinavia. With the collapse of the Frisian state, the barrier was removed. And with Charlemagne's death in 814, Europe's defensive posture slackened. Three decades thereafter, in 843, Charlemagne's grandsons divided his huge, unwieldy empire into three parts, creating thereby the nuclei of modern France, modern Germany, and the long strip of intermediate lands over which France and Germany have contested ever since. Charlemagne's heirs were by no means weaklings, but they represented a distinct decline in leadership and their internecine struggles created a political-military vacuum that exerted an irresistible attraction on the Viking raiders.

Neither Charlemagne nor Offa had possessed any navies to speak of, and the English Channel had effectively separated the two powers. But to the seafaring Vikings the Channel was less a barrier than a boulevard. They harried the lands on either side without partiality, plundering coastal settlements and sailing up rivers to bring havoc and terror deep into the interior of England and the Continent. Their first raids struck England, for they found it expedient to ignore continental Europe until the passing of Charlemagne. It is said that the great Frankish emperor wept on seeing Viking ships off the north Frankish coasts on their way to England, and Alcuin wrote a letter expressing his profound sympathies when the Danes sacked Lindisfarne in his native Northumbria in 793.

The first Viking raid struck the Dorset coast of Wessex around 787. The *Anglo-Saxon Chronicle* reports that on the arrival of three long ships, the chief royal official of the threatened community — the port reeve — rushed to the shore to inquire their business. They made emphatic reply, killing the reeve and looting and sacking the town. It was a portentous episode, for in subsequent years countless other raiders came from Scandinavia to devastate and plunder the land. When Wessex inherited the political hegemony that Mercia had formerly exercised, it also inherited the ominous and ever increasing Norse threat.

Organized into relatively small groups of ships' crews, the Vikings had the immense advantage of mobility and surprise over their relatively sedentary victims. At first confining themselves to plundering expeditions, they gradually conceived the idea of conquest and settlement. Norwegian Vikings attacked and overran Ireland, founding a state centering on Dublin, and remained in occupation of northern Ireland for generations thereafter. Another Viking band established a permanent settlement in northern Frankland at the mouth of the Seine. Its ruler, a Viking chieftain named Rollo, was converted to Christianity and granted official recognition by a Frankish king in 911. This Seine settlement evolved and expanded in later years into a powerful duchy known as Normandy which gradually assimilated French culture, French institutions, and the French language, but retained the warlike vigor of its Viking past. The establishment of the Norman duchy went unmarked in English annals, but Normandy was destined to play a crucial role in England's later history.

Midway through the ninth century, the Viking attacks on England began to change from plundering expeditions to campaigns of conquest. In 850 a considerable group of Danish Vikings spent the winter on the Isle of Thanet off Kent rather than return to their homeland at the close of the raiding season. In 865 a great Danish host began a series of bloody and highly successful campaigns against the demoralized Anglo-Saxons that shortly won them virtually all of England outside Wessex. The local kingdoms and sub-kingdoms that had survived the eras of Mercian and Wessex hegemony were now destroyed, and of the monarchies of the ancient Heptarchy only Wessex endured.

In the wake of these lightning conquests came Danish settlers in such quantities as to change permanently the social and institutional complexion of large areas of England. These areas of Danish settlement and occupation, known thereafter as the "Danelaw," included (1) Yorkshire (southern Northumbria), where the most intensive settlements occurred, (2) East Anglia, and (3) a large tract of central and eastern Mercia that came to be known as the "Five Boroughs" after its five chief centers of settlement: Lincoln, Stamford, Nottingham, Leicester, and Derby. For centuries these three Danish districts — Yorkshire, East Anglia, and the Five Boroughs – differed sharply from the remainder of England in their traditions and customs.

Alfred the Great

In 870 the Danish attack against Wessex began in earnest. It is almost providential that in the following year there rose to the Wessex throne a man of such remarkable intellect and statesmanship that he has often been described as England's ablest king. This man was King Egbert's grandson, Alfred the Great (871–99), a many-talented monarch who excelled as a warrior, an administrator, a friend of scholarship, and a leader of men. With his reign the history of the English monarchy truly begins.[3]

Alfred's accession occurred at a desperate moment in Anglo-Saxon history. In 872 he was obliged to purchase a truce from the Danes in order to gain the time necessary to put his forces in order. During this brief and expensive intermission he began a thorough military reorganization of his realm which continued throughout his reign. His military reforms rested on three major innovations: (1) His army — or *fyrd* as it is called in the Anglo-Saxon documents — was divided into two halves each serving for six months. Thus, when one half was at home, the other half was under arms, insuring that at no time would Wessex be defenseless. (2) Large fortifications were built at strategic points to defend against Danish invasion and, later on, to serve as forward bases in the reconquest of the Danelaw. These fortifications were known as burghs. An important tenth-century document known as the Burghal Hidage discloses that extensive and precisely delineated territories surrounding each burgh were made responsible for its maintenance and defense, with responsibility being assessed in terms of the hide of land. We have already encountered the hide as the assessment unit of the eighth-century Mercian Tribal Hidage, and we shall encounter it again as the basis for military recruitment and the assessment of the danegeld. In later years many of the burghs of Alfred and his successors evolved into commercial centers, and the meaning of the term gradually changed from "fortress" to "town." (3) Alfred is quite properly regarded as the founder of the English navy. He recognized far more clearly than his

---

[3] On Alfred see Eleanor Duckett, *Alfred the Great and His England* (1957). A biography of Alfred written by one of his own contemporaries is available in English translation: L. C. Jane (tr.), *Asser's Life of King Alfred* (1926). Asser's biography is a crucial historical source for Alfred's reign, and all modern accounts have drawn heavily from it. Quite recently, however, the authenticity of Asser's *Life* has been called into question by V. H. Galbraith, *An Introduction to the Study of History* (1964), pp. 88–128. If Galbraith's doubts come to be shared generally, our picture of Alfred and his reign will have to undergo serious modification.

predecessors or contemporaries, either in England or on the Continent, that the Vikings must be challenged on the seas. His biographer, the Welshman Asser (the authenticity of whose work has recently been questioned) reports that Alfred built numerous ships, both large and swift, "neither after the Frisian design nor after the Danish, but as it seemed to him that they could be most serviceable." This disclosure, if we can trust it, provides a clear illustration of Alfred's creative intellect and imagination as applied to the problems of war.

Alfred's military reforms were far-reaching, but considerable time was required to consummate them. And for Alfred, time was all too short. In 876 a Danish chieftain named Guthrum led a powerful host against Wessex, and early in 878, catching Alfred off guard in the dead of winter, Guthrum led his army across Alfred's kingdom, forcing the king to flee into the marsh country of Somerset where he found refuge at a royal estate on the Isle of Athelney. For a dark moment virtually all England was at the mercy of the Danes.

Athelney was England's Valley Forge. There Alfred held out with a small group of followers through the winter. In the spring of 878 he was able to rally the Wessex fyrd. (The Danish army was far too small to occupy Wessex completely or to prevent the summoning of Alfred's army.) The armies of Alfred and Guthrum met in pitched battle at Edington where Alfred succeeded in winning a total victory. As a consequence of his triumph, he forced Guthrum to come to terms. The Danish leader undertook to accept Christianity and to abandon Wessex forever. One may well doubt the sincerity or depth of Guthrum's conversion, but the fact remains that he was the first important Viking to become a Christian. His baptism in 878 marks a significant foreshadowing of the ultimate Christianization of Viking culture and its incorporation into the mainstream of Western European civilization. It was more than a century after Guthrum's conversion before Christianity was able to make important inroads against Viking heathenism, but with the events of 878 the momentous civilizing process had at least begun.

In an age of bitter warfare when skillful military leadership was essential to a king's very survival, Alfred was blessed with a full measure of military genius. In the years after 878 he was obliged to cope with repeated attacks by Danish raiding parties, and all of these he successfully repelled. Indeed, he was able, little by little, to drive back the Danish power. In 886 he recaptured London, and later in the same year he entered into a new treaty with Guthrum which defined the boundary between English and Danish authority. The frontier ran approximately northwestward, along the old Roman road known as Watling Street, from London to Chester on the Irish Sea. By this new agreement most of Mercia was freed of Danish control, and in that once-proud kingdom Alfred established a sub-king or *ealdorman* named Ethelred. The future allegiance of English Mercia was insured by a marriage between Ethelred and Alfred's daughter, Ethelfleda, who was known thereafter as the "Lady of Mercia."

The struggle with the Danes continued to the close of Alfred's reign and well beyond, but by Alfred's death in 899 the crisis had clearly passed. Southwestern England was secure, London had been recovered, a successful military policy had been established, and the authority of the Wessex monarchy was supreme in non-Danish England.

England's first king was more than a mere warrior, however. The same creative intelligence that we have already encountered in the area of military reorganization was equally evident in law and administration. Several of Alfred's predecessors had issued law codes or "dooms." Ethelbert of Kent had been the first to do so, and he was followed by other monarchs such as Offa of Mercia (whose dooms are now lost), and Alfred's own distant ancestor, Ine of Wessex (688–726). But these earlier kings — Offa, perhaps, excepted — seem to have intended merely to clarify existing law and provide for new conditions. None went so far as to actually repeal old customs or, in the strict sense of the word, make new law. Although no autocrat, Alfred clearly interpreted his lawmaking authority more broadly than his predecessors had done. He was hesitant to create new laws, but he exercised considerable latitude in his selection or rejection of old ones, thereby placing his own distinctive imprint on the legal structure of his day. In the preface to his dooms, Alfred expresses himself in these words:

Then I, King Alfred, collected these [laws] together and ordered that many of them which our forefathers observed should be written down, namely, those that I liked; and, with the advice of my *Witan*,* I rejected many of those that I did not like and ordered that they be observed differently. I have not presumed to set in writing much of my own, because it was unknown to me what might please those who shall come after us. So I have collected here the dooms which seemed to me the most just, whether from the time of Ine, my kinsman, or of Offa, king of the Mercians, or of Ethelbert, the first of the English to receive baptism; I have discarded the rest. Then I, Alfred, king of the West Saxons, showed these to all my *Witan* * who declared that they were all pleased to observe them.

In this significant passage we can glimpse the king at work, surrounded by his council as Germanic monarchs had been since their most primitive days, respectful of past custom as had always been the case, yet injecting into his traditional royal role a novel element of personal volition and creative judgment which marks a new departure in the evolution of Anglo-Saxon kingship.

To Alfred the warrior and Alfred the statesman we must now add Alfred the intellectual. Like Charlemagne a century earlier, Alfred was a notable patron of learning who drew scholars to his court from far and wide – the Welshman Asser, a Frankish scholar from Rheims, several Mercians (including one with the unforgettable name Werwulf) and a number of others. And Alfred himself made a far greater personal contribution to scholarship than the half-illiterate Charlemagne had been able to do.

Specialists in medieval intellectual history have pointed out that the renaissance of Charlemagne's era was less an outburst of creative genius than a great intellectual salvage operation designed to recover and preserve a classical-Christian heritage that was in danger of vanishing on the Continent. Charlemagne's scholars were not original philosophers but gifted schoolmasters who reformed the script, purged the Bible of scribal errors, established schools, copied manuscripts, and struggled to extend literacy and preserve a correct liturgy. These were humble tasks, but they were desperately essential. The Anglo-Saxon renaissance of Alfred's time, generally speaking, was of the same order. By the late ninth century the brilliant intellectual flowering of Bede's Northumbria had long passed. Latin, the linguistic vehicle of classical culture, was becoming virtually unknown in England. Priests could no longer understand the Latin mass, much less study the works of Bede and the Latin Fathers. And the Anglo-Saxon language, which everyone knew, had only a very slender literary tradition behind it. Alfred himself described the decline of Latin in these words:

> So completely fallen away was learning now in the English race that there were very few on this side of the Humber who would know how to render their service book into English, and I doubt that there would be many

---

* i.e., Alfred's counselors

on the other side of the Humber. There were so few of
them that I cannot think of so much as a single one
south of the Thames when I took the realm.

The king may be exaggerating here, but probably not very much.

Alfred was determined to revive ecclesiastical culture in
his land, and he did what he could to create a literate priesthood.
The scholars whom he gathered around him created a notable
school at his court, and a few monastic schools were established,
but a general monastic revival seems to have been out of the
question in these turbulent times. Alfred's most original contribution to learning arose from his conviction that aristocratic
laymen should be educated – that his administrators and military commanders should have some knowledge of the civilized
heritage of Christendom. Such men were far too preoccupied
with the political and military hazards of their time to learn the
alien Latin tongue, but Alfred hoped that they might be taught
to read their native Anglo-Saxon. Accordingly, he and his court
scholars undertook to translate into the vernacular some of the
important Latin masterpieces of the day – Boethius' *Consolation
of Philosophy*, Bede's *History of the English Church and People*, and Pope Gregory's *Pastoral Care*, to name but three. A
copy of the vernacular *Pastoral Care* was sent to every episcopal
see in England in the hope that Alfred's bishops might be inspired by St. Gregory's wisdom and common sense.

Alfred himself participated in the work of translation, and
often added comments of his own to the original text. In his
translation of Boethius, Alfred injects the revealing observation,
"In those days one never heard of ships armed for war," and in
the preface to the *Pastoral Care* he speaks with sad nostalgia
of the time "before everything was ravaged and burned, when
England's churches overflowed with treasures and books." In
passages such as these, one is reminded forcefully of the enor-
mous disadvantages against which Alfred worked. Given the
desperate military circumstances of his time, his achievements
seem little less than heroic.

Associated with Alfred's reign is one further literary monument in the English vernacular: the *Anglo-Saxon Chronicle*.[4]
This important historical project, although probably not insti-
gated by Alfred directly, was inspired by the general surge of
vernacular writing with which the king was so closely associ-

---

[4] The *Anglo-Saxon Chronicle* is available in several modern English translations.
The best of these, in many ways, is D. Whitelock, D. C. Douglas, and S. Tucker
(ed. and tr.), *The Anglo-Saxon Chronicle* (1961).

ated. Around 892, an unknown Wessex chronicler wrote a year-by-year account of English history and its Roman and British background, running from the birth of Christ to 891. The account is based on earlier sources, most of which are now lost. The identification and reconstruction of these earlier ingredients have occupied several generations of scholars, and many aspects of the problem remain obscure. In general, the early entries are characterized by extreme verbal economy:

> 634. In this year bishop Birinus preached Christianity to the West Saxons.
> 635. In this year Cynegils was baptized by Birinus, bishop of Dorchester, and Oswald [king of North-umbria] stood sponsor for him.
> 636. In this year Cwichelm was baptized at Dorchester, and the same year he passed away. And bishop Felix preached the faith of Christ to the East Anglians.
> 639. In this year Birinus baptized Cuthred at Dorchester and stood sponsor for him.

Copies of the 892 Chronicle were sent to a number of important ecclesiastical centers of the time, and in some instances the early entries were expanded to include facts and traditions available in other portions of England. One manuscript was sent to Northumbria where the entry for 634, for example, was elaborated as follows:

> 634. In this year Osric, whom Paulinus had baptized, succeeded to the kingdom of the Deirans; he was the son of Elfric, Edwin's paternal uncle; and to Bernicia succeeded Ethelfrith's son, Eanfrith. Also in this year Birinus first preached Christianity to the West Saxons under king Cynegils. That Birinus came thither at the command of pope Honorius, and was bishop there until his life's end. And also in this year Oswald succeeded to the kingdom of Northumbria, and he reigned nine years....

At several ecclesiastical centers the 892 Chronicle was continued thereafter on a year-by-year basis. In subsequent years copies continued to be exchanged and taken from one monastery to another, with the result that the *Anglo-Saxon Chronicle* is a very complex document indeed. To be precise, it is not one document at all, but a series of several related documents. Altogether, seven distinct manuscripts of the *Anglo-Saxon Chronicle* are now extant, representing four more or less separate chronicles. Of these chronicles, three end in the later eleventh century—between 1066 and 1079—while the fourth continues to the accession of King Henry II in 1154.

The various versions of the *Anglo-Saxon Chronicle*, being written by many different chroniclers in several religious houses over a number of generations, are exceedingly uneven. At times they fail to rise above the level of bare annals; at others, they provide fairly comprehensive accounts of the events of their day, sometimes even attempting a degree of historical interpretation. The chroniclers, like modern journalists, tended to pass over periods of peace and cultural creativity with a few bare allusions to royal deaths and accessions but became positively eloquent in times of upheaval and disaster. So little is made of the fruitful reigns of Alfred's successors and King Canute, so much is made of the second Danish invasions and the Norman Conquest, that some readers of the *Chronicle* have been misled into regarding Anglo-Saxon England as one vast, sterile bore relieved by occasional cataclysms. But whatever its shortcomings, the *Anglo-Saxon Chronicle* is a unique phenomenon in the European vernacular literature of its day and provides the modern student with an invaluable if sometimes aggravating narrative of later Anglo-Saxon history. It is appropriate that from the reign which witnessed the genesis of the English monarchy should come this remarkable national history in the Old English tongue.

In many respects, therefore, Alfred's reign is the great watershed in the history of Anglo-Saxon England. It represents the turning point in the Danish invasions, the climax of the age-long trend toward political unification, and the all-important first stage in the development of the English royal government. Alfred once described himself modestly as one who works in a great forest collecting timber with which others can build. He was alluding to his efforts toward intellectual revival, but the metaphor is equally relevant to his military, administrative, and political achievements. As architect of the English monarchy, he gathered the wood and also provided the blueprint which would guide his successors in constructing a spacious and durable political edifice.

Chapter 3

𝕷𝖆𝖙𝖊 𝕾𝖆𝖝𝖔𝖓 England

The Reconquest of the Danelaw

KING Alfred's great work of reconquest and political consolidation was carried to its climax by his talented successors
during the first three quarters of the tenth century.[1] At Alfred's
death in 899, Wessex passed to his son Edward (899–924), whom
later historians called Edward the Elder in order to distinguish
him from a subsequent monarch of the same name. Edward
the Elder joined with his sister Ethelfleda, Lady of Mercia, in
pursuing an aggressive military policy against the Danelaw,
strengthening Alfred's burghs and founding a number of new
ones in the midlands to consolidate their conquests. One of the
new burghs of this age was Oxford, a significant commercial
and intellectual center in later years, whose name betokens its
humble origin. By 918, all the Danish settlers south of the
Humber had submitted to Edward the Elder's rule, and the death

---

[1] The works cited in Chapter 1, Footnote 3, are relevant also to the present chapter.
Another excellent general study is Peter Hunter Blair, *An Introduction to Anglo-
Saxon England* (1962), now available in paperback. Christopher Brooke, *The
Saxon and Norman Kings* (1963), is illuminating and a delight to read. Professor
Brooke has also written Volume II of the Nelson History of England: *From Alfred
to Henry III, 871–1272* (1961), which is both authoritative and interesting.

of Ethelfleda in that year resulted in the permanent unification of Wessex and Mercia under Alfred's dynasty.

Edward the Elder was succeeded by his able son, Athelstan (924–939), a brilliant military leader who, turning back a major invasion of Yorkshire by Norse Vikings from Ireland, extended his sway across Northumbria to the Firth of Forth. By the time of Athelstan's death, virtually all England was under his control. His successors consolidated the conquest, put down revolts, and repulsed invasions until, by 954, England stood united under the Wessex dynasty of English kings.

Still, the word "united" is perhaps too strong to describe accurately England's situation in 954. The country was united politically (although with much local autonomy remaining), but not socially or culturally. The Old English inhabitants of northern Northumbria, who had managed to retain a precarious independence during the age of Danish invasions, had long been isolated from their brethren to the south and remained a people apart. And the numerous Danish settlers in Yorkshire, East Anglia, and the Five Boroughs remained socially and culturally distinct. The process of amalgamation between Dane and Englishman was exceedingly slow and required several centuries to complete.

The immediate effect of reconquest and political unification was a generation of peace, well-being, and fruitful activity in the areas of royal administration and ecclesiastical reform. Anglo-Saxon England's happiest years coincided with the reign of King Edgar the Peaceable (959–975). In the words of the *Anglo-Saxon Chronicle:*

> His reign was marked by greatly improved conditions, and God granted that he lived his days in peace; he did his duty, and labored zealously in performing it; he exalted God's praise far and wide, and loved God's law; he improved the security of his people more than all the kings before him within the memory of man.

Such is the flattering but stereotyped picture of Edgar the Peaceable and his reign as disclosed in the *Anglo-Saxon Chronicle*. From another source we learn that Alfred's navy had developed by Edgar's time into an impressive fleet that maintained a constant series of coastal patrols, suggesting that Edgar was not only a man of God but also a vigorous and intelligent military strategist who took strong measures to protect his land from Viking assaults.

Edgar's reign witnessed an impressive movement of monastic reform which paralleled the reform movements that were occurring concurrently on the Continent. Medieval monasticism followed a pattern of ebb and flow—decline and reform. Like all human institutions, it tended to decay with the passage of time from simplicity and fervor to luxury and complacency, yet over the centuries it proved itself capable of periodic revitalization through successive waves of reformist enthusiasm. The reinvigoration of continental monastic life brought about by the Carolingian Renaissance had run its course by the tenth century, but the laxity of tenth-century monasticism was challenged by a new religious movement centering on the new Burgundian monastery of Cluny. Founded in 910, Cluny developed, under the leadership of dedicated and long-lived abbots, into a vital center of ecclesiastical reform. The Cluniac monks followed an elaborated version of the Benedictine rule, but they abandoned the traditional Benedictine principle of autonomy. Instead, Cluny became the mother house of an ever growing congregation of monasteries, subject to the direction and discipline of a single abbot, which spread the ideal of the uncompromising religious life across Europe.

The great champion of monastic reform in King Edgar's England was St. Dunstan, abbot of Glastonbury, who became archbishop of Canterbury in 960. St. Dunstan took up the cause of monastic reform independently, but some of the other English reformers of his day were deeply influenced by the example of Fleury, a Cluniac daughter house on the Loire. The English reformers worked with considerable success toward the strict enforcement of the Benedictine rule in English monasteries, but had no wish to associate formally with the Congregation of Cluny. As a result of their efforts old monasteries were reformed and reorganized and a number of new ones were built. Women were expelled from monastic houses, and clerical celibacy underwent a general revival. The pious King Edgar cooperated fully with his ecclesiastical reformers, evidently recognizing, as Alfred and Charlemagne had recognized long before, that a vigorous Church could contribute much to the political and social welfare of the realm. Nor should it be thought that Edgar was merely harnessing ecclesiastical reform to his own secular purposes. A faithful Christian no less than a talented monarch, he doubtless regarded the purification of the Church as a good in itself.

Anglo-Saxon Institutions

Edgar's reign was followed by a second round of Danish invasions, the accession to the English throne of the Danish king, Canute (1016–1035), the reestablishment of the Wessex dynasty under Edward the Confessor, and, finally, the Norman Conquest of 1066. Before turning to these momentous events it will be well to pause for a time in order to examine the development of political, social, and economic institutions in Anglo-Saxon England.

The Anglo-Saxons, like the later Danes, came to England as small war bands. During the centuries following their first settlements, they gradually elaborated their institutions, transforming their primitive military organization into a hierarchy of *territorial* units. The old Germanic *comitatus*, for example, seems to underlie the medieval and modern English county or shire. *Comitatus* became the medieval Latin word for "county," and our word "shire" is based on the Old English term, *scir*, which originally meant the local war band or "fyrd" led by its lord, the ealdorman, who was subject only to the king. In other words, the territorial county or shire seems to have had its origin in the perambulatory war band of an earlier day.

By the tenth century, the shire had emerged clearly as a territorial district. The fyrd of each shire was led by the shire lord – the ealdorman – who was by now not only the leader of a military unit but the territorial lord and administrator of a geographical district. Such was the situation in Alfred's Wessex, and with the reconquest of Mercia and the Danelaw these districts, too, were organized into shires on the Wessex model. Some of the new tenth-century shires corresponded to old kingdoms or subtribal districts – Norfolk, Suffolk, Kent, Sussex, and Essex, for example. Others were organized around important towns after which they were named: Bedfordshire, Northhamptonshire, Cambridgeshire, etc. Four of the Five Boroughs – Lincoln, Leicester, Derby, and Nottingham – became nuclei of new shires. The process of shiring the Danelaw was progressing rapidly in the late ninth and early tenth centuries and was virtually complete by Athelstan's reign.

The shires of Alfred's time still sent warriors to the fyrd under the command of their ealdormen, as well as submitting to his administrative jurisdiction. The ealdorman was at once a royal official and a local aristocrat. He led the fyrd and governed the shire in the king's name, and only at times when the monarchy was weak did he assert a dangerous degree of independence. As time went on, the ealdorman began to exert authority over several shires; administrative and military command of an individual shire then passed to another royal official known as the "shire reeve" or "sheriff."

The lord of the shire, whether sheriff or ealdorman, presided in the king's name over the shire court which convened twice yearly to try important legal cases on the basis of Germanic law. The personnel of the shire court consisted of im-

THE ENGLISH SHIRES: *LATE Saxon England*

1 Northumberland
2 Cumberland
3 Westmorland
4 Durham
5 Lancashire
6 York
7 Anglesea
8 Carnarvon
9 Denbigh
10 Flint
11 Cheshire
12 Derby
13 Nottingham
14 Lincoln
15 Merioneth
16 Montgomery
17 Shropshire
18 Stafford
19 Leicester
20 Rutland
21 Cardigan
22 Radnor
23 Hereford
24 Worcester
25 Warwick
26 Northampton
27 Huntingdon
28 Cambridge
29 Norfolk
30 Pembroke
31 Carmarthen
32 Brecknock
33 Glamorgan
34 Monmouth

35 Gloucester
36 Oxford
37 Buckingham
38 Bedford
39 Suffolk
40 Cornwall
41 Devon
42 Somerset
43 Wilts
44 Berks
45 Hertford
46 Essex
47 Dorset
48 Hampshire
49 Middlesex
50 Surrey
51 Sussex
52 Kent

SCOTLAND

ISLE OF MAN

York

Lincoln

Bath

London

ISLE OF WIGHT

portant freemen of the district who supplied relevant evidence and declared ancient custom. Guilt or innocence, however, was determined neither by the members of the court nor by the presiding sheriff or ealdorman but rather by the solemn oath of the accused (often assisted by the sworn testimony of kinsmen or friends known as oath helpers) or by recourse to one of the ancient ordeals (above, p. 19). Run by local freemen and presided over by an official of the king, the shire court was at once a royal and a popular institution—an assembly in which monarchy and local freemen joined to provide justice (of sorts) to the land.

The late-Saxon shire was normally divided into smaller territorial units called hundreds. Like the shires, the hundreds too were probably military in origin, representing a group of 100 warriors which served within the larger *comitatus*. By the tenth century the hundred had been territorialized and was developing into an administrative district centering on a hundred court. Similar in purpose and organization to the shire court—and presided over by a royal appointee—the hundred court met more frequently, normally once a month, and played a more intimate role in the affairs of the average freeman. Ordinarily, the hundred court, like the shire court, represented a mixture of royal and popular justice, but as time progressed, jurisdiction over many hundred courts passed into the hands of great private lords, both lay and ecclesiastical. These powerful landholders were granted by royal charter the rights of jurisdiction in their districts (contemporary charters refer to these jurisdictional rights as *sac* and *soc*), and their representatives took the place of royal officials as presidents of the hundred courts which they controlled.

The hundred was typically (although by no means always) composed of 100 hides. We have already encountered the hide in connection with the Mercian Tribal Hidage and the Wessex Burghal Hidage, and have seen that originally it was regarded as an estate sufficient to support the family of an individual warrior. The late-Saxon hide was not a unit of standard size; rather it was an assessment unit on which fiscal and military obligations were based. Of two estates of identical area, one might be more productive than the other and therefore assessed at more hides than the other. Moreover, hidage assessment was often erratic and unfair. Some districts were assessed more severely than others, and sometimes, through royal generosity, an estate might have its hidage assessment diminished. A forty-hide estate might be reduced to a twenty-hide estate without losing so much as an inch of land.

Thus, the shire, the hundred, and the hide represent the territorial equivalents of the large tribal war band, the subgroup of 100 warriors, and the individual warrior. The military institutions of the old invasion days had changed considerably by the tenth century, but their outlines were still visible. Now, however, the legal and administrative responsibilities of shire, hundred, and hide assumed great significance alongside their older military functions.

There is no evidence that the hundreds retained any significant role in the tenth-century fyrd, but the shires and hides remained basic to it. Ealdormen continued to summon the fyrds of their shires and to lead them into battle. And the hide remained the basis of military recruitment. By the tenth century, and perhaps long before, the one-hide estate had come to be regarded as insufficient to provide the necessary economic support for a properly equipped warrior and was replaced by the estate of five hides. The profession of arms was the supreme aristocratic vocation in all Germanic societies, and the typical Anglo-Saxon aristocrat – the holder of a five-hide estate – was known as a thegn. In time of war, every five-hide unit was obliged to provide a fighting man for the army (or sometimes the navy), and although the owners of small estates within a five-hide unit might occasionally pool their resources to send a particularly well-equipped freeman as their representative to the fyrd, the normal five-hide warrior was a member of the thegnly aristocracy. The almost universally accepted relationship between status and arms in this violent age insured that the society of Anglo-Saxon England – influenced so deeply by the hard necessities of war – would be profoundly aristocratic.

Still, the varying military requirements of tenth- and eleventh-century England required, on occasion, the service of other groups than the thegns. In time of invasion every freeman was obliged to take up arms in defense of his locality. These ordinary freemen formed a motley but massive force around the nucleus of the five-hide warriors. At other times, the territorial five-hide fyrd proved insufficiently flexible or battle-ready, and was augmented or replaced by full-time professional warriors. These might be simple mercenaries, or they might be landless household soldiers maintained on a permanent basis by the king or some great lord. In the course of the eleventh century these landless professionals became increasingly important. One such group, the "housecarles," who were instituted by King Canute and retained by King Edward the Confessor, formed the nucleus of the Anglo-Saxon army at Hastings in 1066.

Five-hide thegns, ordinary freemen, and landless professional warriors – these were the components of the Anglo-Saxon army. But a mere review of this organizational scheme fails to do justice to the powerful emotional factors which underlay the military structure of this age. In the tenth century, the ideology of the old Germanic *comitatus* was still very strong. Military prowess, absolute loyalty to lord, and honor among warriors remained the supreme aristocratic virtues. Indeed, in all Germanic literature the *comitatus* ideology is nowhere more powerfully illustrated than in a late tenth-century Anglo-Saxon poem, the *Song of Maldon*, describing a fierce battle in 991 in which an invading Danish host defeated the fyrd of Essex led by its lord, the ealdorman Byrhtnoth.[2] Toward the battle's end, Ealdorman Byrhtnoth was killed and the English nearly defeated. At this desperate moment,

> Byrhtwold spoke and seized his shield — he was an old follower of the earl; he took his ash-wood spear and boldly exhorted the men: "Thoughts must be braver, hearts more valiant, courage all the greater as our strength diminishes. Here lies our lord, cut down — the hero in the dust. Long may he mourn who now considers turning from the play of battle; although old in years, I will not leave the field, but think to lie beside my lord, the man I hold so dear."

Byrhtwold's speech is followed by others in a similar vein. Inspired by these appeals to the traditional heroic ideal, the Anglo-Saxons attack the Danes, and in the midst of the fray the *Song of Maldon* comes to an abrupt end. The author was doubtless embroidering his data. Byrhtwold was surely not so eloquent as he is described. Nevertheless, the story reflects with perfect accuracy the highest aristocratic ideals of a people still tied to their bellicose past and dominated by the concept of lordship.

The development of Anglo-Saxon institutions must be understood as the gradual evolution of a Germanic warrior society toward territorial stabilization and administrative coherence. The fundamental element in this evolution was the rise of a centralized monarchy. Among a people to whom loyalty to one's lord was an almost holy virtue, the king endeavored to secure for himself the pledged allegiance not only of his ealdormen, sheriffs, and personal thegns, but of all freemen in England. In the dooms of King Edmund (939–946) it is commanded "that all, in the name of God . . . shall swear fealty to King Ed-

---

[2] A modern English translation of the *Song of Maldon* is contained in Margaret Ashdown (tr.), *English and Norse Documents Relating to the Reign of Ethelred the Unready* (1930).

mund, as a man should be faithful to his lord, without dispute or treachery, in public and in private, loving what he loves and shunning what he shuns. . . ." Thus, the powerful bond of allegiance between an ealdorman and his thegns and household followers – attested so vividly in the *Song of Maldon* – was subordinated to the still higher duty of all free Englishmen to render loyalty to their monarch.

This principle of universal allegiance to the king was essential to the maintenance and progressive extension of royal control over England. The ealdormen must be royal officers, not independent potentates, and when they lead the fyrd of their shire they must do so – as Byrhtnoth did – in the king's name and in the king's service. Indeed, when the fyrd was summoned on a regional or national scale its normal leader was the king himself. As lord of the Anglo-Saxons, he was necessarily the supreme war leader of the people in arms.

In time of war, the king was expected to be braver and fiercer than any of the warriors whom he led, but in time of peace he sought to temper the violence of his people. In his coronation oath, King Edgar the Peaceable makes these commitments:

> In the name of the Holy Trinity I promise three things to my Christian subjects: First, that God's Church and all the Christian people of my realm shall enjoy true peace; second, that I forbid robbery and wrongful deeds to all ranks of men; third, that I exhort and command justice and mercy in all my judgments, so that the gracious and compassionate God who lives and reigns may grant us all His everlasting mercy.

In effect, Edgar is appealing from the militarism of Germanic culture to the pacifism of the Christian tradition. The Germanic king must lead his folk in war, but the Christian king must keep the peace.

The concept of the king's peace developed slowly. Crimes of violence normally fell under the jurisdiction of the popular courts of shire and hundred, but almost from the beginning there existed the concept that violations of the peace committed in certain special places or at certain special times were subject to a direct royal fine. At first the king's peace extended only to the limits of the royal household, but in time it came to cover the shire and hundred courts, major roads and rivers, and churches and abbeys. Since the royal household had no permanent headquarters but was constantly on the move, the king's peace moved, too, sometimes protecting one area, sometimes another. By the time of King Henry I (1100–1135), the king's peace extended throughout the entire shire wherein the king was temporarily residing. And the king's peace was also gradually extended to cover all crimes of violence committed during the liturgical seasons of Christmas, Lent, Easter, and Whitsuntide. In the twelfth century, as we shall see, royal justice expanded significantly at the expense of popular and private justice and evolved ultimately into what Englishmen call the Common Law. The gradual spread of the king's peace in Anglo-Saxon times may be regarded as an early expression of this momentous legal concept of direct royal jurisdiction.

As the scope and functions of the Anglo-Saxon monarchy expanded, the royal administrative machinery became steadily more elaborate. In the earliest days, the retinue of an Anglo-Saxon monarch would normally include a goodly number of military followers or "companions" and some servants to look after the stables, maintain the royal wardrobe and bedchamber, supervise the food supply, and prepare meals. The king's income was derived chiefly from the rents of tenant farmers on his own vast estates—his *demesne*—and since money was in short supply in early medieval England, these royal demesne rents were paid in kind. Rather than transporting the food to a central royal residence, the king traveled from estate to estate in his demesne, consuming as he went. Under the circumstances, the minimal administrative duties of the royal household could easily be handled by the chief servants.

With the passage of time royal fines increased, the royal treasure grew, royal military organization became more elaborate, and royal documents—particularly charters granting land —became ever more numerous. The king's secretarial duties were assumed by the royal chaplain and his priestly subordinates who were to be found in every royal household after the Conversion. In the eleventh century the head of the king's chapel-secretariat came to be known as the chancellor (from *chancel*, the space in a church reserved for the officiating clergy), and rose to become one of the chief officers of state.

The other departments of the royal bureaucracy developed out of various branches of the household serving staff. The master of the stable—the *constable* of later times—supervised the royal hunt and eventually became a leading officer in the king's army. The chief servant of the royal bedchamber and wardrobe evolved into the later *chamberlain*, and since the king customarily kept his treasure in his wardrobe (or sometimes under his bed), the chamberlain assumed important financial responsibilities. In the course of the eleventh century the monarchy adopted the policy of leaving the bulk of its treasure at Winchester, the chief town of Wessex, and carrying on its travels only enough money to meet current expenses. The royal officer in charge of the Winchester treasure chest came to be known, appropriately, as the treasurer. He and his staff constituted the first sedentary department of the royal government.

The chancellor, the constable, the chamberlain, and other household officials such as the steward and the butler—although not known by those names until after the Norman Conquest—rose in importance with the growth of the Anglo-Saxon monarchy to become dominant figures in the royal administration. Besides performing their own special functions, they served the king collectively as a trusted and intimate advisory body. Accompanying him on his endless perambulations through the country, they functioned as a pocket council, administering the king's justice and attending to the varied and ever-growing business of royal government.

Occasionally, when unusually important business arose such as the issuing of a series of dooms or the undertaking of a major military campaign, an Anglo-Saxon monarch would call many of the great magnates of the realm, both lay and ecclesiastical, to join his normal household advisers in counseling him or giving their formal support to his policies. We have already encountered references to large councils of this sort on the occasion of King Edwin's conversion in 627 (above, p. 36) and in King Alfred's statement that he had shown his laws "to all my *Witan* who declared that they were all pleased to observe them" (above, p. 55). The terms *Witan* or *Witenagemot* (council) might apply to either the small household group or the larger and more formal assembly of magnates. Both the small and the large *Witenagemot* undoubtedly had their roots in the primitive Germanic tribal assemblies, but the limitations of our sources prevent us from tracing the evolution of the *Witenagemot* with any precision until the tenth and eleventh centuries. We know from occasional references that it existed in early Anglo-Saxon England, but we can say little of such matters as its normal size, composition, or functions. Indeed, as the fuller sources from the late-Saxon period disclose, the *Witenagemot*, whether large or small, was an exceedingly flexible and informal institution. It was in no sense, of course, a representative assembly. It possessed no formal right of veto over royal policy, but was strictly advisory. It had no *ex officio* members so far as we can tell, but simply included whatever important household officers happened to be available and, on the more significant occasions, a miscellaneous group of great lords. Still, the sources make clear that the *Witenagemot* played a crucial role in Anglo-Saxon government. Many historians today, in endeavoring to dispel the romantic myth of certain nineteenth-century scholars that the *Witenagemot* was a protodemocratic national assembly, have tended to underestimate its importance. To be sure, no Anglo-Saxon king was legally bound to follow his *Witan*'s advice, but few monarchs were so foolish as to flout it. In an age lacking precise definitions of constitutional relationships, the deeply ingrained custom that the king was to govern in consultation with his *Witan*, a custom that is implicit in almost every important royal document of the period, is sufficient to make the *Witenagemot* one of Anglo-Saxon England's most fundamental political institutions.

The expanding monarchy of late-Saxon England was able to draw on an increasing variety of financial resources. The royal demesne remained the chief source of revenue, and since the growing towns were normally regarded as belonging to the king's demesne, exactions from burghers now poured into the royal treasury along with the dues from the royal estates. The monarchy delegated responsibility for the fiscal exploitation of its demesne estates and towns to royal officials called reeves who were assigned a fixed tax quota or "farm" to be collected from the districts which they supervised. Any dues in excess of the quota belonged to them. As commerce gradually quickened, it became increasingly common for the monarchy to receive a portion of its demesne dues in coin rather than in kind, for during the last several decades prior to the Norman Conquest, Anglo-Saxon England enjoyed a circulation of currency that was remarkably brisk by continental standards. Nevertheless, it was not until the early twelfth century that payment in coin became the norm on royal estates.

With the growth of royal jurisdiction, fines became a significant factor in the royal revenue. And conversely, the impulse to increase the profits of justice prompted the monarchy to expand its judicial activities. This tendency will be particularly evident in the twelfth century, as we shall see.

Finally, what began as a symptom of military weakness and the monarchy's endeavor to purchase security from Viking marauding ultimately became one of the most lucrative and important sources of royal income. In 991 King Ethelred, appropriately described as the Unready, imposed a comprehensive land tax, known as the danegeld, to raise protection money against the Danes. This tax, like military service, was assessed on the basis of hides.* It was not restricted to the royal demesne but embraced all the lands of England. At first a symbol of national weakness, it eventually became a significant source of strength to the English monarchy. For in later years the funds from the

---

* Often at the rate of two shillings per hide.

danegeld tax were employed to hire soldiers in defense of the realm and to meet various other royal expenses. As the first general land tax in Western Europe since Roman times, the danegeld illustrates perhaps more vividly than anything else Anglo-Saxon England's unparalleled progress toward royal centralization and administrative sophistication.

Continental monarchs, like English monarchs, were employing agents to collect dues from demesne estates. And on the Continent, as in England, central administrative bureaucracies were slowly evolving out of household staffs. But the late Anglo-Saxon royal administration was more coherent in its organization, broader in its scope, and therefore considerably more powerful than any other contemporary government of Western Christendom. In the centralization of its administrative structure, as in the efficiency of its tax system, England stood in the vanguard of a momentous movement which, during the coming centuries, would see the transformation of loosely structured Germanic monarchies across the length and breadth of Christendom into well-organized sovereign states.

Town and Field

The century or so prior to the Norman Conquest was a period of accelerating commercial activity, a product of the general political stability of the age. With commerce came the rise of towns, far smaller at first than those of Roman times — and far dirtier, too — but from the economic standpoint, far healthier. For unlike the administrative and military towns of the Western Roman Empire which functioned as economic leeches on the countryside, the towns of late-Saxon England — and their continental counterparts — produced more than they consumed. It has already been suggested that many of the late-Saxon towns evolved out of the military burghs or boroughs of Alfred and his successors, but the rise of towns was nevertheless an economic phenomenon, a product of England's unusual wealth and vigorous commerce. A vast amount of urban development still lay in the future — in the decades and centuries following the Norman Conquest — but our evidence suggests that the elaborate guild systems of a later day were already in their formative stage in the late-Saxon period, and that borough courts may have been functioning as early as the tenth century. As parts of the royal demesne, the towns were a source of wealth to the monarchy, and, in later years particularly, the English kings favored them in numerous ways. Their emergence and growth were accompanied by slow but profoundly significant changes in the social and economic order. A nearly natural economy gave way to a money economy, and the parochialism of the early Middle Ages was eroded by the rise of international commerce. And in the High Middle Ages — the twelfth and thirteenth centuries — the towns would become the foci of a rich, vibrant culture. Perhaps the greatest glories of high medieval civilization were the cathedral and the university, and both were characteristically urban phenomena.

In the tenth century, however, one could hardly be expected to see that the struggling, unprepossessing urban communities had such a future before them or that they would one day be agents of such momentous social change. For as yet they were mere specks on an otherwise unrelieved agrarian landscape. The townsmen went about their apparently humble tasks; the aristocracy fought, trained, and dreamed of war; but the chief business of the Anglo-Saxons remained what it had been for generations gone by, and what it would be for centuries to come: the raising of crops.

Among the fascinating myths of nineteenth-century historical scholarship was the legend of the stalwart, gritty Anglo-Saxon freeman, communing with the good earth, fighting against invaders like a Massachusetts Minute Man, and laying the foundations of democracy by participating fearlessly and intelligently in village councils and hundred courts. Historians have since concluded that most Anglo-Saxon agricultural workers were probably slaves or inarticulate, semi-servile tenants. Men such as these were virtually ignored in contemporary documents, but without question they represented the majority of Englishmen in late-Saxon times and long thereafter. They played no real role in local or hundredal administration, nor were they permitted to bear arms, for the possession of weapons was by long tradition a mark of free status. Their influence on English constitutional development was minimal, but their contribution to the economy was vital. Through their labor the food was produced by which Anglo-Saxon society was sustained.

Not all farm workers lacked personal freedom. At the top of the peasant hierarchy was a class of free farmers known as *ceorls*. It was this class that the nineteenth-century scholars had in mind when they made their allusions to Anglo-Saxon grass-roots democracy. It seems quite certain, however, that the ceorls were neither as "democratic" nor as numerous as was previously believed. Rather than being "typical Anglo-Saxon peasants," the ceorls were a peasant elite. They bore arms and, on occasion, fought in the fyrd alongside the aristocratic thegns. They usually owned their own farms, and most of them owned slaves. They enjoyed a status before the law and were assigned a wergeld of 200 shillings. Beyond these few generalizations we cannot go, for the contemporary sources disclose very little about the free peasantry except to make clear that the term ceorl was applied rather loosely to agrarian free-men of widely differing economic levels.

At the next level in the social hierarchy one encounters the thegns, sharply differentiated by their 1,200-shilling wer-geld but otherwise just as heterogeneous as the ceorls. The thegns, as we have seen, constituted a warrior aristocracy, yet there is clear evidence that many of the lesser thegns were little better off economically than the wealthier ceorls. Some of them, at least, seem to have labored on their own fields as a matter of course, but ordinarily their involvement in agriculture was limited to supervising the labor of their subordinates.

Both ceorls and thegns participated in local administra-tion and in the popular courts, and such experience was doubt-less useful in later centuries in providing these classes a certain degree of political sophistication. But they made their chief contribution to the realm by defending it in battle and partici-pating in the humble but essential task of food production.

The development of Anglo-Saxon agriculture was almost imperceptibly slow yet immensely significant. Over the genera-tions and centuries of the Anglo-Saxon age the momentous work of land clearing, begun by the Celts and pushed ahead by the Romans, gradually resulted in the conquest and ex-ploitation of vast districts of lowland England. Over these wide areas the Anglo-Saxons placed the indelible imprint of their long strip fields. The Celtic family farm was superseded throughout nearly all of England except Kent by the Anglo-Saxon village, a nucleus of many families living in a small agrarian community surrounded by fields. These strips of land were not held in common by the village, but were held by indi-vidual tenants. But since the various fields comprised a single agrarian unit it was necessary for a village council (perhaps dominated by a local thegn) to make decisions on such matters as crop rotation, labor-pooling, and boundary disputes.

Accordingly, the village was the fundamental agrarian unit of medieval England. Alongside it there existed another, more artificial unit—the estate of the thegn or higher noble, which in later days was known as a *manor*. Normally the manor and the village were identical, but it was by no means unusual for a single manor to include several villages or a single village to include parts of several manors. Basically, the village and manor differed in that the former was a tangible agrarian entity—an actual village surrounded by fields, whereas the latter was a unit of ownership—an estate controlled by a single thegn.

Let it be said at this point that the details of agrarian or-ganization and class structure varied bewilderingly from one district to another. Kent remained throughout the Middle Ages a land apart, with family farms taking the place of the more normal village community. Throughout much of the Danelaw there were far more freemen than elsewhere. In Northumbria the manor was exceedingly slow in developing. And numerous other local variations existed which the limitations of space preclude our discussing. Whatever the details, however, the remarkable agricultural achievement of the Anglo-Saxons cannot be gainsaid: they transformed forests into fields, established the village community, fixed the peasant on his plot, and vastly augmented the bounty of their land.

The Second Danish Invasion

Precisely a century after Alfred turned the Danish tide at the battle of Edington, disaster struck England. It was a disaster that few at the time could have recognized as such, for in the year 978 England was apparently just as prosperous and secure as it had been for the previous generation. Under Alfred and his able descendants the monarchy and the kingdom had achieved notable progress, but now, in 978, the crown passed to an incompetent heir—Ethelred the Unready (978–1016). The cataclysmic events that followed his accession proved once again the importance of adequate military and political leadership to a medieval state.

Ethelred was timid, banal, and indecisive. He fell heir to the throne as a boy of ten, and although he reigned for thirty-eight years, he remained a child at heart to the end. Like Peter Pan, he never really grew up. The kingdom which he inherited was wealthy and well-governed by contemporary standards, but the long process of amalgamating the Scandinavian settlers of the Danelaw into the fabric of Anglo-Saxon society had barely begun, and the loyalty of these Anglo-Danes to the English monarchy was still rather tenuous. Without external pressures Alfred's dynasty would doubtless have survived Ethelred's reign, but the age of the Vikings was not yet passed, and within a couple of years of Ethelred's accession the raids resumed.

The early years of the reign were marked not only by Danish raids but also by the rising power of the Anglo-Saxon ealdormen at the expense of the centralized royal government—an inevitable consequence of weak rule. As this trend toward decentralization progressed, the Danish raids steadily increased in intensity. These new raiders were organized in many instances into tight military brotherhoods—war bands along the lines of the old *comitatus* but with stricter rules and more predatory goals. The Viking brotherhoods of this era seem to have been modeled on a warrior community which, according to Norse legend, was founded at Jomsburg near the mouth of the Oder in Germany by King Harold Bluetooth of Denmark. The Vikings of Jomsburg – the Jomsvikings as they are often called – had strict regulations regarding membership and conduct which they enforced in their own military court. Under the general direction of the Danish monarchy, they often displayed fierce independence, undertaking plundering expeditions on their own or selling their services to the highest bidder. One of the most savage and bloodthirsty Danish raiders in Ethelred's reign, Thorkell the Tall, seems to have been a Jomsviking, and for a time Ethelred himself was able to purchase the services of Thorkell's band against the attacks of other Danes.

Nevertheless, England's second Viking invasions were far more closely governed by the Danish monarchy than were the first. In Scandinavia, as in England, royal power had made impressive gains in the tenth century, and when the invasions reached their climax they had become, in effect, an integrated effort on the part of the Danish monarchy to conquer England.

It would be a serious mistake to ascribe the success of the second Danish invasions, as is sometimes done, to an inherent weakness in the Old English state. The failure of the Anglo-Saxon military effort at this time resulted from the disloyalty of the Anglo-Danes combined with the ill fortune of being ruled by an incompetent king. Contemporary writers dwell repeatedly on the wavering loyalty and outright treason of the Anglo-Danish aristocracy, and the utter futility of Ethelred's leadership is illustrated vividly in the *Anglo-Saxon Chronicle:*

> And when they [the Danes] were in the east, the English army was kept in the west, and when they were in the south, our army was in the north. Thereupon all the counselors were summoned to the king, and it was decided how the country should be defended. But if anything was decided then, it did not last even a month. Finally there was no leader who would collect an army, but each fled as best he could, and in the end no shire would even help the next.

Desperate to forestall total disaster, Ethelred adopted the hopeless expedient of appeasing the Danes with bribes. In 991, the very year that Ealdorman Byrhtnoth scorned the Danish demand for tribute at Maldon, King Ethelred paid the first danegeld. In later years danegelds were paid repeatedly, serving merely to dramatize to the fierce seamen the extent of England's weakness. Still later, Ethelred used the danegeld to temporarily seduce the allegiance of Thorkell the Tall, and eventually, as we have seen, this humiliating tribute became a great source of royal strength, providing the monarchy with income long after the Danish invasions had ended.

In 1013, King Swein of Denmark, son and successor of Harold Bluetooth, threw all his resources into a campaign of conquest, and Anglo-Saxon England, now badly demoralized, fell quickly into his hands. The old Danelaw gave Swein its firm support, and the English, thoroughly disgusted with Ethelred the Unready, offered only mild resistance. Ethelred fled to Normandy. His son, a skillful and courageous young prince named Edmund Ironside, fought on bravely for a season, but Prince Edmund was killed in 1016 and the *Witan* concurred in the accession of a Danish king to the throne of Alfred. Swein having died in 1014, his son Canute became the new king of England.

The Reign of Canute (1016–1035)

No savage barbarian, Canute was a product of the momentous new forces that were then in the process of transforming the Norse world.[3] By 1016 Viking states from Iceland to Russia were in the process of embracing Christianity, and in Scandinavia itself the rise of royal power was bringing political coherence to the northern lands of Denmark, Norway, and Sweden. Accordingly, Canute ascended the Anglo-Saxon throne as a civilized man and a dedicated Christian. Alfred's dynasty was temporarily unseated, but in Canute's reign security and prosperity returned to England and the monarchy continued to grow in strength.

As it happened, Canute ruled Norway as well as Denmark, and his accession to the Old English throne made him master of a great empire girding the North Sea. It was an ephemeral empire, to be sure, held together by the fragile bonds of allegiance to a single man, but while he lived, Canute was the dominant political figure in northern Europe.

England was far the wealthiest and most civilized land in his empire, and there Canute spent most of his reign. Aware of the valuable achievements of his Anglo-Saxon predecessors, he ruled in the Old English tradition, respecting old customs, issuing dooms, and supporting the Church. He won the vigor-

---

[3] On the reign of Canute and his Anglo-Scandinavian "empire" see L. M. Larson, *Canute the Great* (1912).

ous support of the clergy by granting them land and treasure and providing them with an environment of peace in which to do their work. In the words of one contemporary observer, "Merry sang the monks of Ely as Canute the king rowed by."

This able Danish king succeeded far better than his Anglo-Saxon predecessors in bringing unity to the land. Englishmen and Anglo-Danes supported him with almost equal enthusiasm. Indeed, it was perhaps only a king such as he who could win for the English monarchy the unquestioned loyalty of the Danelaw. At a council at Oxford in 1018, Canute is described as formally declaring peace between Danes and Englishmen and bringing an end to their former strife. The king's *Witan* swore to uphold Christianity, to love Canute, and to observe the laws of King Edgar.

King Canute was a Dane—of that there could be no question. He divided his kingdom in Danish fashion into several large districts ruled by earls (a name derived from the Old Norse *jarl*), and he brought to his court a bodyguard of Scandinavian housecarles, a sizable group of trained warriors organized along the lines of the Jomsvikings, with their own elaborate regulations and their own judicial assembly. But in most other respects Canute ruled much as an able Anglo-Saxon might have done. Hundred courts and shire courts continued as before, towns grew even more rapidly through the stimulus of an increased North Sea commerce, and agrarian life proceeded unaffected. Indeed, Canute carried his Anglo-Saxon traditionalism to the bedchamber by marrying Ethelred's widow, a lively Norman princess named Emma, who quite clearly preferred her second husband to her first.

On Canute's death in 1035, his empire was divided between his two sons, who ruled England briefly and badly in turn. When the last of them died without heirs, the *Witan* chose as its new king a member of the old Wessex dynasty, the long-exiled son of Ethelred and Emma. In 1042 the dynasty of Alfred was reestablished peacefully on the English throne in the person of Edward the Confessor.

The Reign of Edward the Confessor (1042–1066)

Edward, paradoxically, was less an Englishman than Canute. Between the ages of twelve and thirty-six he had lived in exile in Normandy, the homeland of his mother, and in these years he had become deeply Normanized. A pious man and rather weak, he spoke French by preference and installed Norman favorites in his court. In a sense, it can be said that the Norman Conquest of England, although consummated on the field of Hastings in 1066, had its beginning in 1042. Such, at least, were the feelings of many Englishmen of the time who loved the pious Edward but despised his Norman favorites and resented his importation of Norman customs.

Under Canute, the earls had been kept under strict control, but under the weaker Edward they began to assert a dangerous degree of autonomy. Some of the great English earls became foci of the growing Anglo-Saxon resentment against Norman infiltration. The most powerful of these magnates was Earl Godwin of Wessex, who managed to place his sons in several of the other great earldoms and even engineered a marriage between his daughter Edith and King Edward the Confessor. The rise of Godwin and his fellow earls represents an ominous retrograde development in the evolution of the Old English state.

The political tensions of the Confessor's reign reached their climax in 1051–52 when Earl Godwin and his allies turned momentarily against the king in open rebellion. The affair began with an incident at the port of Dover, an important town in Godwin's Wessex earldom. As a distinguished French lord was passing through Dover on his return from a visit to the royal court, the townsmen rioted and killed some of the knights in his retinue. King Edward demanded that Earl Godwin punish the rebellious townsmen. Godwin refused, but discovering that Edward had the backing of the great earls outside the Godwin family, he and his sons were forced to cross the Channel into exile. In 1052, however, Godwin and his sons returned, rallied support to their cause, overawed Edward with a show of military power, and forced him to reinstate them.

The Godwin clan had won an important bloodless victory. Edward was humiliated and, bowing to the wishes of the earls, sent home most of his Norman supporters. Among these Normans was Robert of Jumièges, archbishop of Canterbury, who was forced to abandon his see. Archbishop Robert was replaced by a creature of the Godwins named Stigand—a vainglorious popinjay of a man who presided over the English Church with a singular lack of distinction. Thenceforth Edward was a virtual figurehead. Real power was exercised by Earl Godwin and, after Godwin's death in 1053, by his son, Harold Godwinson, who succeeded to the earldom of Wessex.

Harold emerges from the writings of his age as a more attractive, less crassly ambitious figure than his father. Between 1053 and Edward's death in 1066, the king and the earl seem to have worked together on reasonably good terms. Harold behaved with the proper deference toward Edward, did most of the necessary frontier campaigning, and left the monarch to his favorite pastimes of hunting and churchgoing. Harold proved himself a man of political talent and exceptional generalship, and in the years of his power the kingdom flourished.

By the standards of mid-eleventh-century Western Europe, England on the eve of the Norman Conquest was remarkably prosperous and well-governed. The Church was thriving, the military organization was strong and efficient, towns and commerce were growing, and money was circulating to a degree unknown on the Continent. Despite the enduring diversities in law and custom between one region and another, Anglo-Saxon England had achieved a genuine sense of national unity which contrasted sharply with the state of political chaos and endemic private warfare that persisted throughout most of contemporary France. A vivid illustration of England's growing feeling of national cohesion is to be found in a passage from the *Anglo-Saxon Chronicle* under the year 1052. On Godwin's return from exile, both he and King Edward had large military forces behind them, and for a time there seemed every possibility of open battle. But, as the *Chronicle* explains, the chief military leaders on both sides decided against a test of arms: "It was hateful to them that they should fight against men of their own race, because very few worthy men on either side were not Englishmen." As this crucial passage makes clear, Bede's lofty vision of the English as a single people was at last shared by the laity.

The Reign of Harold and the Norman Conquest

King Edward the Confessor died childless in 1066. He is reputed to have remained chaste throughout his marriage to Godwin's daughter, Edith, and whether this is a fact or merely a pious excuse for a childless marriage, his death at once created a serious problem in the royal succession.

There were three serious candidates for the Confessor's throne: (1) Harold Godwinson had been the most powerful man in England for the previous thirteen years and had proven his capacity. Edward is alleged to have designated Harold his heir on his deathbed, and on the day after Edward's death the *Witan* chose Earl Harold as king. In the absence of a royal son, Harold's position as heir designate of King Edward and his selection by the *Witan* gave him an exceedingly strong claim. Harold was not of royal blood, but he did have a certain tenuous connection with the throne through his sister Edith, who was Edward's widow.

(2) Duke William the Bastard of Normandy, a powerful

feudal magnate, was also vaguely related to Edward. Emma, the Norman wife of Ethelred the Unready and Canute, was William's great aunt. And William claimed that when he had visited England in 1051 during Godwin's exile, Edward had designated him heir to the English throne. It is quite possible, incidentally, that Edward designated William in 1051 and Harold in 1066. Finally, William claimed priority over Harold Godwinson on the basis of a peculiar episode that occurred in 1064. Harold, visiting the Continent, had fallen captive to a petty lord who had released him, at William's bidding, into the duke's custody. William seems to have treated Harold as an honored guest, but it is by no means clear that the earl was free to leave the Norman court. At length, William obtained Harold's oath to support the duke's claims to the English throne on Edward's death. Hence, William and his supporters in 1066 regarded Harold as an oath-breaker, and by the ethics of the day the violation of one's pledge was regarded with profound contempt.

(3) Harold Hardrada, King of Norway, was an illustrious Norse warrior whose skill at arms had won him fame from Byzantium to Scandinavia. As ruler of Norway, he claimed the dominion over England that had formerly belonged to his predecessor, King Canute. Harold Hardrada's claim was perhaps the weakest of the three, but his immense military reputation must have made contemporary Englishmen deeply apprehensive. It was clear that Harold Godwinson would have to fight for his new crown.

Besides the rivalry of Harold Hardrada and William the Bastard, Harold Godwinson had two additional liabilities. In 1066 the papacy in Rome was undergoing a momentous reform and was in the process of reasserting its authority over the European Church. As a jealous guardian of proper canonical processes, the papacy could not accept the deposition of Robert of Jumièges as archbishop of Canterbury in favor of Stigand. The appointment of a new archbishop before the old one was dead was a flagrant violation of canon law. Hence, the papacy was hostile toward Harold Godwinson who supported Stigand and whose father had engineered his usurpation. Duke William exploited this hostility, winning full papal support for his projected conquest of England. William's invading army was privileged to carry the papal banner which, together with the Norman claim that Godwinson was a perjurer, placed the duke in an exceedingly strong moral position.

Harold Godwinson's second liability was his brother, earl Tostig of Northumbria. Tostig was an unpopular lord who was overthrown by a Northumbrian revolt in 1065. The revolt appeared to have strong popular backing and was therefore condoned by Harold. Tostig never forgave his brother for this act. The Northumbrians chose as their new earl an important magnate named Morcar, brother of Earl Edwin of Mercia, and totally unrelated to the Godwin clan. Harold's passive role in this affair seems to have won him the gratitude of the two powerful brothers, Edwin and Morcar, but Tostig, now in exile, was bitterly hostile. In the months following his coronation Harold was reasonably secure at home but he had far more than his share of dangerous enemies abroad.

Normandy, on the eve of the battle of Hastings, was a well-organized feudal state whose duke controlled his great vassals to a degree unmatched elsewhere in France.[4] During the century and a half since its establishment in 911, the Viking state of Normandy had embraced Christianity, absorbed French culture, adopted the French language, and based its military and political organization on the principles of French feudalism. Normandy in 1066 was a land of feudal castles and of feudal knights whose cavalry tactics contrasted sharply with the infantry tradition of the Anglo-Saxon fyrd.

Our evidence relating to pre-Conquest Norman history is far from abundant, but it is sufficient to suggest that the high degree of ducal control and centralization that Normandy enjoyed in 1066 was to a considerable extent a product of William the Bastard's own statesmanship. Winning a significant victory over his rebellious barons in 1047, he spent the years thereafter subordinating the Norman nobility to the ducal administration and working toward the elimination of private warfare which had long been endemic among the feudal baronage.

But strong as William was, he was not strong enough to win for Normandy a position of hegemony in northern France that would provide him with the necessary security to undertake a major invasion of England. He achieved this hegemony quite by accident when his two chief rivals, the count of the neighboring feudal state of Anjou and the king of France, both died in 1060. France fell to a child king, and Anjou entered a long period of disputed succession. And in the meantime William had insured the support of the prosperous neighboring county of Flanders by marrying the daughter of its count in 1053.

On Edward the Confessor's death, therefore, William was in a position to make good his claims to the English throne. Good fortune provided the opportunity, and William had the courage, the imagination, and the greed to grasp it.[5] The

---

[4] A thorough, if highly technical and slightly outdated, account of eleventh-century Normandy is C. H. Haskins, *Norman Institutions* (1918).

[5] Much has been written on the Norman Conquest of England. Sir Frank Stenton, *Anglo-Saxon England* (see Chap. 1, note 3), contains a good summary. More

barons of Normandy agreed to the daring enterprise at a great council early in 1066, and William thereupon set about to augment his Norman force with volunteers from all over Europe. Adventurous knights flocked to his standard from all quarters — from Brittany, Maine, Flanders, Aquitaine, central France, and even southern Italy — drawn by William's already formidable military reputation, by the generous wages that he promised, and by the hope of treasure and estates in the conquered land. But despite the support of his duchy, the growing size of his army, and the moral backing of the papacy, William's projected invasion was nevertheless an audacious gamble. England was far larger and wealthier than Normandy, and it was ruled by a warrior-king of ability and resolution.

Harold Godwinson, however, had a staggering task before him. Beset by an overabundance of enemies, he could predict neither the place, the time, nor the source of the first attacks against his kingdom. As it happened, the initial assault came from his brother Tostig. In May 1066, Tostig emerged from exile to begin harrying the coasts of southern and eastern England with a sizable body of followers. Tostig's men were turned back by local contingents of the fyrd, and he was obliged to retire to Scotland. Obviously incapable of doing serious damage on his own, he entered into an alliance with Harold Hardrada and merged his forces with those of the Norse king.

By midsummer, Duke William's army was ready for the invasion and only the persistence of contrary winds prevented his crossing the Channel. Godwinson had meanwhile assembled the fyrd in southern England to defend against the Norman invasion and had stationed a large fleet off the Channel shore. But week after week the winds remained contrary for William and the English watched their coasts in vain.

Midway through September Godwinson was forced to dismiss his army and fleet. According to custom, service in the fyrd was not to exceed two months, and by the middle of September the term had expired, provisions were exhausted, and the warriors wished to return home for the harvest. The contrary winds had served William after all, for Harold now had only his housecarles to guard the shore.

Immediately after disbanding his army, Godwinson received news that Harold Hardrada had invaded Yorkshire in northern England. Hardrada's army was exceedingly powerful, consisting of some 300 shiploads of Norse warriors to-

recent works are C. W. Hollister, *Anglo-Saxon Military Institutions* (1962), especially pp. 147–52, C. H. Lemmon, *The Field of Hastings* (2nd ed., 1960), and H. R. Loyn, *The Norman Conquest* (1965).

gether with Tostig and his own considerable following. The combined force moved toward the key northern city of York. On September 20, 1066, Hardrada's host encountered the northern fyrd led by the two earls, Edwin and Morcar, at Fulford Gate, two miles south of York. The battle of Fulford raged for the better part of a day, and in the end the local fyrd broke before the invaders. Receiving the submission of York, Hardrada then apparently conceived the idea of incorporating a number of Anglo-Danish Yorkshiremen into his army. He withdrew to a strategic crossroads called Stamford Bridge, seven miles east of York, to await hostages from the conquered city.

Meanwhile Godwinson had reassembled his army as best he could on short notice, and was rushing northward. Five days after Fulford, on September 25, Godwinson's army arrived at Stamford Bridge, caught the Norwegian host by surprise, and after a long and savage battle succeeded in crushing it. Tostig and Hardrada were both killed in the fray, and the battered survivors of the great 300-ship host returned to Norway in twenty-four ships. Stamford Bridge was a tremendous victory for Harold Godwinson—perhaps the greatest military triumph in Anglo-Saxon history. An ominous Scandinavian threat of twenty years' standing was removed, and the mightiest Viking warrior of the age lay in his grave.

Two days after the battle of Stamford Bridge the Channel winds changed at last and the Norman invasion began. At nine A.M., Thursday, September 28, the Norman Fleet entered Pevensey Bay in Sussex and William's army disembarked at leisure on an undefended shore. Immediately thereafter the Normans occupied the important port of Hastings and proceeded to build a castle there to protect their avenue of escape should the fortunes of war turn against them. Modern historians, with the inestimable advantage of hindsight, have sometimes assumed quite wrongly that the Norman victory at the battle of Hastings was inevitable. Duke William, lacking the gift of foreknowledge, was far from certain of the outcome. Indeed, he could hardly have known at the time whether his enemy would be Harold Godwinson or Harold Hardrada.

On news of the Norman landing, Godwinson acted with almost frenzied speed. Within thirteen days he settled affairs in Yorkshire, pulled together his tired and decimated army, and marched 240 miles from York to Hastings. From the standpoint of military strategy, Harold's haste was a serious error. There was no real reason for it, since William was too cautious to proceed far from the Sussex shore until he had done battle with the English. Perhaps Godwinson was overconfident after his phenomenal victory at Stamford Bridge; perhaps he was solicitous of the defenseless people of his former earldom of Wessex

Detail from the Bayeux Tapestry (late eleventh century): The appearance of Halley's Comet frightens King Harold (center, on throne) and his subjects. Harold's fear of Normans crossing the Channel is depicted on the lower border beneath the king.

who were being cruelly ravaged by the Normans. Whatever his reasons, he was obliged to face William's host with an exhausted army that was far below normal strength.

On Friday, October 13, William's scouts sighted King Harold's army, and on the following day there occurred the most decisive battle in English history. The battle of Hastings was fought on Saturday, October 14, from dawn to dusk. For the English, it was the third major battle in less than four weeks, and the two previous ones—Fulford and Stamford Bridge—had taken their toll. Edwin and Morcar and their troops had been too badly mauled by the Norsemen to join Harold on his southward march, and there had been insufficient time to summon the full complement of the southern fyrd.

Harold's army, depending on the traditional infantry tactics of the Anglo-Saxons to turn back William's feudal cavalry, took a strong defensive position on the crest of a low hill, the forward line standing shoulder to shoulder in the form of a shield wall. Numerous Norman cavalry charges were repulsed by this shield wall during the course of the day, and although the arrows of Norman archers took their toll, the Anglo-Saxon position remained firm. At one point in the battle the Normans fled in panic until their duke rallied them and ordered them to turn on the pursuing English, who were then savagely cut down. There is some evidence—perhaps inconclusive—that on one or two later occasions the Normans feigned flight in order to draw more of the English out of their impenetrable shield wall. At

Normans and English do battle at Hastings. In this second detail from the Bayeux Tapestry the English footsoldiers, shown atop their hill, are repulsing a charge of mounted Norman knights.

length King Harold himself seems to have been killed by a random Norman arrow,* and in the gathering dusk the shield wall broke at last. The English fyrd, now leaderless, fled into the Sussex forest.

William's momentous triumph marks the end of Anglo-Saxon England and the beginning of Norman England. It remained for William to consolidate his conquest and to establish his firm rule over the kingdom, but with the battle of Hastings behind him, the completion of his task was only a matter of time.

It has been necessary to describe the great battle and its background in some detail in order to refute the popular view that Hastings represented the inevitable victory of an up-to-date continental feudal state over an effete, insular culture, exhausted of its inspiration and militarily antiquated. On the contrary, the Anglo-Saxon army gave a splendid account of itself under almost unbelievably adverse conditions, and Anglo-Saxon civilization retained to the end its remarkable political coherence and its rich cultural vitality. On the sturdy foundation constructed at such effort by Theodore of Tarsus, Alfred the Great, Edward the Elder, Edgar the Peaceable, and others of their sort, the Norman kings would build the most efficiently organized Western European state since the days of the Romans.

---

* This detail, like others in the battle, is uncertain and subject to dispute.

Chapter 4

𝕹𝖔𝖗𝖒𝖆𝖓 ENGLAND

The Conquest Consolidated

WILLIAM the Conqueror was an immensely gifted warrior-statesman, tenacious in the pursuit of his objectives, cruel or magnanimous as it suited his purposes, phenomenally energetic, and possessed of a superb strategic imagination.[1] Having won his gamble at Hastings, he moved unerringly toward the consummation of his conquest. London, as William shrewdly recognized, was the key to England, and shortly after the great battle he advanced toward the city. Finding the south end of London Bridge sufficiently well defended to prevent his crossing the Thames and assaulting the city directly, he led his army westward, devastating the countryside as he went, until he reached the town of Wallingford in Berkshire. Here he crossed the Thames and advanced eastward toward London. Before he reached the city he was met by a number of London citizens and other notables, such as Archbishop Stigand and earls Edwin and Morcar, who made their submission to him and surrendered the city. On Christmas Day, 1066, Duke William was crowned king of England with all the pomp and ceremony

---

[1] One biography of William the Conqueror stands out above all others: D. C. Douglas, *William the Conqueror* (1964). This study also provides the most satisfactory recent account of pre-Conquest Normandy.

that traditionally accompanied Anglo-Saxon coronations. All present, both Norman and English, promised their allegiance to the new king, and William, for his part, undertook to abide by the laws in effect during Edward the Confessor's reign and to rule in the tradition of the Wessex kings.

Generally speaking, William abided by his promises, but it soon became clear to him that more than words would be required to pacify his new kingdom. In the months and years following the coronation many Englishmen continued to resist him or revolted against his rule at the first opportunity. And the Scandinavians, despite their calamitous defeat at Stamford Bridge, continued to risk new invasions of England. To complicate matters, the kingdom of France and the county of Anjou were gradually recovering their former coherence, and William was obliged to devote much of his energy to continental campaigning in order to protect his Norman duchy. In short, William's vast new Anglo-Norman state was threatened by many hostile forces, both internal and external, and his boundless energy was taxed to the limit in the defense of his far-flung domain.

For some five years following the Conquest, William and his lieutenants were kept occupied by a series of English rebellions, some of them coordinated with amphibious attacks from Scandinavia. The historian William of Malmesbury, writing several decades later, comments on the savage measures which the Conqueror took in defense of his crown:

> Perhaps the king's behavior can be excused if he was at times quite severe with the English, for he found scarcely any of them faithful. This fact so irritated his fierce mind that he took from the greater of them first their wealth, then their land, and finally, in some instances, their lives.

In the course of these revolts Edwin and Morcar both turned against the Conqueror and both lost their lives. A lusty ruffian named Hereward entrenched himself against William on the Isle of Ely and plundered the surrounding countryside until he was at last suppressed by the Normans. Despite his savage sack of Peterborough Abbey, Hereward became in later years a glamorous figure in English patriotic legend.

William used both kindness and cruelty in consolidating his new realm, but in retrospect it was his cruelty that predominated. Having been obliged to besiege the town of Exeter, he allowed its citizens to surrender on very generous terms, but he replied to a major revolt in the north by undertaking a campaign of ruthless devastation through Yorkshire, transforming vast areas of that once-prosperous county into sterile waste-lands.

During these restless years William's task was rendered all the more difficult by the fact that he had to divide his time between England and Normandy. His ultimate success in sub-duing England was due to several interrelated factors: (1) En-glish opposition was never properly coordinated. Almost from the beginning William was able to summon substantial por-tions of the English fyrd to fight in his behalf against English rebels. (2) While William was rising to power in pre-Conquest Normandy he had won the firm support of a rising new feudal aristocracy; after the Conquest he could usually depend upon these powerful Norman aristocrats to defend his interests both in Normandy and in England. Having been given vast estates in the conquered land, they had both the power and the motiva-tion to uphold the interests of the Norman monarchy. (3) Wil-liam himself exhibited remarkable energy and resourcefulness in these years and demonstrated an almost uncanny ability to buy off his enemies, win their loyalty through generous terms, or terrorize them with his cruelty, as the occasion might demand. (4) Both William and his aristocratic followers built numerous castles in England. These fortresses, long a characteristic feature of the Norman landscape, were smaller, tougher, and far more numerous than the Old English burghs. Although crude by later standards, normally consisting merely of an earthen mound surrounded by a wooden palisade and sur-mounted by a square wooden tower, they were nevertheless exceedingly difficult to capture by assault. Accordingly, they became bastions of Norman power and stark symbols of Nor-man authority in the conquered realm.

As it happened, the Anglo-Saxon revolts ended around 1071. Thereafter, the English were remarkably loyal to William and his successors, and in later years the Norman kings often employed Englishmen to help suppress rebellions by Norman barons. Nevertheless, even if the Conqueror had intended in 1066 to allow members of the Anglo-Saxon aristocracy to share the wealth and governance of England with his Norman fol-lowers, the revolts of 1066–71 forced him to adopt a thorough-going policy of Normalization. As a consequence, the Old English aristocracy was virtually disinherited, and the spoils of the Conquest passed almost entirely to the king, his great Norman nobles, and other continental lords who had supported his invasion of England. Not only was the Anglo-Saxon secular aristocracy dispossessed; the great abbeys and bishoprics of England also passed, with few exceptions, into the hands of Norman prelates.

The effect of the Norman Conquest upon England has long been one of the most hotly contested issues in English medieval scholarship. That it resulted in a transformation of aristocratic society there can be no question, for it brought to power a French-speaking nobility, accustomed to knightly cavalry warfare and castle building, and different in many respects from the aristocracy of Anglo-Saxon times. But the aristocracy, powerful though it was, constituted only about one percent of the population. What of the rest?

The towns were growing in size and economic importance before the Conquest and continued to grow thereafter; on the whole they seem to have been little affected by the dynastic and aristocratic revolution. If Scandinavian commerce declined, commerce with the Continent increased. It is quite true that the century or two following William's invasion witnessed a momentous growth in towns and commerce, but this economic expansion was a product not of the Norman Conquest so much as of vast economic changes that affected all Europe.

Peasant life, too, went on much as before. In the long run, the Norman Conquest probably tended to make the peasantry more uniform than in Anglo-Saxon times, raising the status of slaves and lowering that of freemen. Gradually, both tended to become absorbed into the vast middle range of dependent farmers or serfs, bound to a manorial lord, tied to their land, obliged to give a portion of their produce to their lord and to work certain days of the week on their lords' demesne fields. But such changes occurred quite slowly, and they are difficult to trace with certainty. And eventually the buoyant economy of high medieval Europe seems to have resulted in a gradual elevation of serfly status, both in England and on the Continent.

It must never be forgotten that the Norman Conquest occurred at the beginning of a notable epoch of European expansion—economic, political, military, religious, cultural, and intellectual.[2] This profound creative upsurge has been termed "the renaissance of the twelfth century," but in fact it affected the entire period from the mid-eleventh century to the end of the thirteenth—the period which is conventionally called the High Middle Ages. France was the core of this remarkable cultural development—the source of Gothic architecture, the site of the great University of Paris, the home of many of medieval Europe's most distinguished scholars and writers, and the

---

[2] The bibliography on the High Middle Ages is immense. See in particular C. H. Haskins, *The Renaissance of the Twelfth Century* (1927); R. W. Southern, *The Making of the Middle Ages* (1953); and Friedrich Heer, *The Medieval World: Europe, 1100–1350* (J. Sondheimer, tr., 1962).

birthplace of Crusaders and military adventurers who expanded the frontiers of Western Christendom. It has been suggested that since the culture of the High Middle Ages was preeminently French, the conquest of England by a French duchy had the effect of making England much more susceptible to the great creative trends of the era. This is an attractive theory, but it is also a dangerous one. Ties with the Continent had been strong ever since the conversion of England to Christianity, and with or without the Norman connection England would surely have been deeply influenced by the culture of high medieval Europe. The effect of the Norman Conquest in this respect must remain an imponderable.

We should bear this in mind as we turn to the problem of Norman influence on the English Church. William came to England with the blessing of the reform papacy on his head and holy relics around his neck. Harold's archbishop, the usurper Stigand, was offensive to the papacy, and in time William deposed him. Stigand's successor was a brilliant ecclesiastical statesman named Lanfranc—a noted scholar, abbot of the great Norman monastery of Bec, and one of William's most trusted advisers. Under Archbishop Lanfranc the English Church began a thoroughgoing reform in keeping with the policies of the reform papacy. Simony, the buying or selling of ecclesiastical offices, was proscribed; and the marriage of clergymen, long uncanonical but widespread nevertheless, was expressly forbidden. New monasteries were founded and old ones reformed, and cathedral clergy began to follow more stringent rules. Finally, William permitted the Church to disentangle itself from the traditional Anglo-Saxon judicial system of shire and hundred courts and to establish its own separate system of ecclesiastical courts.

One might well conclude that the Norman Conquest had a momentous effect on the English Church, bringing its practices closely in line with the notions of continental reformers. It could be argued, on the other hand, that Church reform would soon have come to England even without the Norman Conquest. The greatest of the eleventh-century reformers, St. Gregory VII, did not become pope until 1073, and it was not until his pontificate that the reform movement attained its full momentum. The reform ideas of Pope Gregory VII were bound to affect England, and the most that can be said of the Norman Conquest in this respect is that it hastened the process by perhaps a decade or two.

It should be added that King William and Archbishop Lanfranc were by no means as advanced in their concepts of Church reform as was Gregory VII. Pope Gregory and many of the reform cardinals who surrounded him were convinced that such evils as simony and clerical incontinence were products of a far more basic flaw in Christian society. To them, it was profoundly wrong that the appointment of clergymen should be in the hands of lay lords, as had long been the case in Western Europe. In the tenth and eleventh centuries it was customary for kings and dukes to select their archbishops, for counts to select their bishops, and even for manorial lords to select their parish priests. Indeed, until the 1050s it was by no means uncommon for the Holy Roman Emperors to appoint popes. To lay lords, control of the Church seemed essential to their power since the Church held such vast amounts of land and since churchmen often occupied key positions in the administrative and military systems of secular governments. To Gregory VII and his supporters, however, it seemed necessary that the Church should assume its proper position at the head of society. Spirit, they argued, is greater than matter, and the spiritual authority of the Church ought to take precedence over the worldly authority of kings and magnates. Accordingly, churchmen should judge laymen, not the reverse, and the Church should be supreme in the Christian commonwealth. Only then could Christian society assume its rightful order.

The vast gulf between papal and secular opinion on this crucial matter resulted in a protracted and often violent struggle between Church and state. Pope Gregory VII, who had long been contending against simony and incontinence, raised the explosive issue of lay control in 1075 by issuing a formal ban against lay investiture. This ban, and the bitter Investiture Controversy that followed in its wake, were focused on the ceremony by which a bishop was invested in his see. Traditionally, a lay lord formally bestowed upon the initiate bishop a ring, symbolic of his marriage to the Church, and a staff, symbolic of his pastoral duties as shepherd of his Christian flock. Symbols had profound meaning in the Middle Ages, and in forbidding laymen to invest new bishops with the ring and staff Gregory VII was in fact striking at the vital principle of lay control of the clergy.

Since Gregory VII's chief opponent in the Investiture Controversy was Henry IV, king of Germany and prospective Holy Roman Emperor, the fiery pope was not in a position to press the issue in England or Normandy. He could not fight all Europe at once. William the Conqueror, who would not have dreamed of loosening his grip on the Anglo-Norman Church, was nevertheless treated quite deferentially as a friend of the papacy and a sincere opponent of ecclesiastical corruption. The issue of lay investiture exploded in England a generation later, to be sure, but during the Conqueror's reign it remained dormant.

Nevertheless, certain tensions were bound to arise in

Anglo-papal relations. William and Gregory VII were both dedicated to Church reform, but the two men had radically different
ideas on the question of lay *vs.* ecclesiastical supremacy in Christendom. Gregory VII, for example, seems to have assumed that
the supreme spiritual position which he claimed for the papacy
carried with it broad secular powers as well. He succeeded in
getting a number of important Christian princes to acknowledge
that they were papal vassals—that the pope was their overlord.
Indeed, he demanded the allegiance or "fealty" of the Conqueror
himself, along with a request for the resumption of a papal tax
known as Peter's Pence. William replied politely but firmly:

> Your legate, Hubert, Most Holy Father, coming to me on
> your behalf, has admonished me to profess allegiance
> to you and your successors, and to think better regarding
> the money which my predecessors were wont to send to
> the Church of Rome. I have consented to the one but
> not to the other. I have not consented to pay fealty, nor
> will I now, because I never promised it, nor do I find that
> my predecessors ever paid it to your predecessors.*

With this assertion, the issue was abruptly closed. William and
Archbishop Lanfranc continued to work toward the reform of
the English Church, but the good work was accomplished under
strict royal supervision.

The Problem of Feudalization

At the present moment, the most vigorously contested
scholarly problem relating to the Norman Conquest is the question of whether William the Conqueror introduced a "feudal
revolution" into England—whether the new Norman aristocracy
established a network of feudal institutions in a previously nonfeudal land.[3] Many nineteenth-century scholars were inclined
toward the view that feudalism developed gradually in eleventh-

---

* From the translation in *English Historical Documents*, II, edited by David C.
Douglas and George W. Greenaway (London, 1953), p. 647.

[3] On this issue see C. W. Hollister, *The Military Organization of Norman England*
(1965), and M. R. Powicke, *Military Obligation in Medieval England* (1962). The
classical account of the Norman Conquest as "feudal revolution" is Sir Frank
Stenton, *The First Century of English Feudalism, 1066–1166* (2nd ed., 1961).
Radically different views are expressed in H. G. Richardson and G. O. Sayles, *The
Governance of Mediaeval England* (1963), pp. 22–135.

and twelfth-century England, and that the Norman Conquest merely hastened somewhat a development that was basically inevitable. During most of the present century, however, the opposite view has prevailed—that feudalism was introduced by the Normans quite suddenly—that pre-Conquest England was fundamentally unfeudal and that without Norman intervention it would probably have remained so. At present, this "feudal revolution" hypothesis is under strong attack by some scholars and is being stoutly defended by others.

In order to understand the problem we must explore carefully the nature of medieval feudalism. At heart, feudalism consisted of a complex of personal and territorial relationships between members of a warrior aristocracy. It combined the old Germanic notion of the loyalty of a *comitatus* member to his lord with the early medieval concept of service in return for land tenure. In its developed form, feudalism involved a relationship between two aristocratic warriors—a lord and a vassal. The lord granted a parcel of land to his vassal and undertook to protect the vassal's interests. The vassal, in return, gave his allegiance (homage and fealty) to his lord and agreed to render him services of various sorts—most notably, knightly military service. The estate granted by the lord to his vassal was known as a fief or *feudum*—from which our word "feudal" is derived.

Feudalism was emerging in Frankland during the eighth and ninth centuries, at a time when traditional Frankish infantry tactics were giving way to cavalry warfare. The cavalryman, or knight, was a far more elaborate and expensive soldier than his unmounted predecessor. He required a fine horse, better arms and armor and, above all, a great deal of training in the art of mounted combat. In short, the rise of cavalry necessitated the creation of an important and fairly numerous military elite. But this tactical revolution occurred at a time when money was in relatively short supply. Some knights were simply fed and maintained in their lord's household, but gradually it became customary for a king or a great magnate to "pay" his knights by granting them land in return for their service.

The practice of paying for service with land was by no means limited to the military sphere. The tenure-service relationship extended also to the fields of administration, justice, and even farming. A great landholder was expected, in return for his wealth in land, to assume the essential functions of public administration and to operate courts of law, as well as to provide knights for the army of his overlord. A peasant farmer, in return for his right to farm a particular plot, was required to contribute his labor on certain days of the week to the tilling of his lord's demesne land. Thus, in a money-poor society, wage service was secondary in importance to tenure service.

With the decline of central authority in Carolingian Frankland during the Viking age, the desperate need for local defense against the lightning raids of the Norsemen resulted in an expansion and intensification of the lord-vassal relationship. Independent freeholders were forced to seek the protection of local lords, often becoming their vassals and giving them their lands. The lord would then return the land to his new vassal to be held as a fief in return for homage and fealty and knightly service. Or if the freeholder was of the humbler sort and owned only a small farm he might find himself sinking into the ranks of the dependent peasantry. It should be understood that the fief-holding vassal did not ordinarily labor on his own lands but rather drew his wealth from the obligations of his serfs to pay him a proportion of the yield of their fields and to work on his own demesne fields. There existed, therefore, an immense social chasm between the vassal and the serf, and the latter was not directly involved in the network of relationships which we call feudal. But on the other hand, the feudal aristocracy depended ultimately on the toil of its serfs, and the entire feudal system rested on the economic foundation of peasant labor. For without serfs, a fief would be valueless.

During the Viking age there was a growing tendency for fiefs to become hereditary. This was particularly true of the extensive fiefs held by the great vassals of the Frankish kings — the dukes and counts. And although a powerful monarch like Charlemagne might well expect the devoted loyalty of his chief vassals, it was far from certain that the sons, grandsons, or great-grandsons of these vassals would be equally loyal to Charlemagne's descendants. It is one of the characteristics of feudalism that loyalty tends to become attenuated with the passage of generations. This centrifugal characteristic was aggravated during the Viking age by the fact that the French kings often seemed helpless in defending their realm and that the great vassals were, from the military standpoint, thrown on their own. Hence, the ninth and tenth centuries witnessed a steady disintegration of public authority. Administrative and judicial responsibilities and royal revenues passed increasingly into the hands of dukes, counts, and local warlords who built castles, fought the Vikings, and ignored the sovereignty of the king. And with the fractionization of sovereignty and the rise of small, semi-independent feudal states, it became increasingly common for feudal lords to fight one another when they were not fighting the Vikings. Private war became a characteristic curse of feudal society.

Every important feudal lord, even though a vassal of a higher lord, aspired to have a large army of his own. Hence, a vassal frequently divided a portion of his fief into smaller fiefs which he granted to subvassals. This process, known as sub-infeudation, sometimes went down through as many as twenty degrees, with subvassals functioning as lords of sub-subvassals who, in turn, were lords of sub-sub-subvassals, and so on down to the lowly vassal who held a single "knight's fee." And even the rear vassal was a lord of sorts—a landlord over the serfs on his fee. Every vassal, therefore, was a lord as well, and every lord, except the king of France himself, was a vassal of some higher lord.

This description may seem sufficiently complex for the taste of even the most ardent reader, yet it remains an over-simplified abstraction of the actual situation. Often a vassal might have two or three lords, each for a different part of his holdings, and should two of his lords go to war with one another he was faced with the perplexing question of which one to serve. Occasionally a lord might not be satisfied with his vassal's service, or a vassal might not be satisfied with his lord's protection, in which case lord and vassal might wage war against one another. There are even cases of a lord's receiving a fief from his own vassal, and thereby becoming his vassal's vassal. The following charter may suggest some of the fantastic complexities that might occur in the feudal "system":

> I, John of Toul, affirm that I am the vassal of the Lady Beatrice, countess of Troyes, and of her son Theobald, count of Champagne, against every creature living or dead, excepting my allegiance to Lord Enjourand of Coucy, Lord John of Arcis, and the count of Grandpré. If it should happen that the count of Grandpré should be at war with the countess and count of Champagne in his own quarrel, I will aid the count of Grandpré in my own person, and will aid the count and countess of Champagne by sending them the knights whose service I owe them from the fief which I hold of them.

By the eleventh century, feudal France was beginning to regain a measure of coherence. The power of the French crown remained restricted to a modest territory in north central France embracing Paris and Orleans, known as the Île de France, and the French monarchs exerted little or no authority over the states of their vassals. But these great vassal states themselves were gradually becoming centralized and well governed. The counts and dukes of such feudal principalities as Anjou, Champagne, Blois, Flanders, and Normandy were succeeding in bringing their own vassals under control. If they could not eliminate private war in their states, they could at least reduce it considerably, and through their establishment of networks of castles and their exploitation of various feudal and nonfeudal revenues they acquired the strength and wealth to dominate their lands.

It was only in the eleventh century that the obligations which a vassal owed his lord became explicit. In Normandy, at least, the number of knights which a vassal owed from his fief came to be specified exactly. In addition to the service of a stipulated number of knights, a vassal was ordinarily obliged to join his lord's retinue on important ceremonial occasions and to serve in his lord's court. Every important lord had a feudal court in which he exercised jurisdiction over his vassals and heard appeals from subvassals. The vassal also owed his lord certain monetary payments known as aids, rendered on special occasions such as the marriage of the lord's eldest daughter, the knighting of his eldest son, or the paying of his ransom should he be captured by an enemy.

The lord's authority over his vassal was further emphasized in four additional privileges: (1) the right to veto the marriage of a vassal's widow or an heiress to his fief, (2) the right to occupy a fief during the minority of a deceased vassal's son and to serve as guardian of the young heir, (3) the right to collect a payment known as "relief" when the fief passed from a deceased vassal to his heir, and (4) the right to repossess the fief should the vassal die without heirs. These rights are characteristic of the highly developed feudalism of the eleventh and twelfth centuries. Although far from universal in their application, they are of particular interest to us because they became customary in post-Conquest England.

During the later eleventh and twelfth centuries, feudal obligations were becoming increasingly exact. A vassal was now understood to owe his lord a certain number of knights to be used within a specified area (say, within the frontiers of Normandy) for a specified number of days per year (usually forty). Paradoxically, this tendency toward legal coherence and systematization occurred concurrently with two other tendencies that would ultimately prove subversive to feudalism: the emergence of strong centralized states, and the rise of a money economy. As states grew in strength, feudal autonomy declined, and the authority of feudal courts was slowly undermined by the growth of royal justice. And with the expansion of commerce and monetary wealth, tenure service was gradually giving way to wage service and a new economic order was coming into being. From the standpoint of legal definitions the later eleventh and twelfth centuries are the "classical age of feudalism," but from the political and economic standpoints they mark the beginning of feudalism's decline.

Prior to the Norman Conquest, the feudal customs which

we have described were limited by and large to northern France. Even there, a bewildering degree of diversity prevailed, and a significant amount of territory remained outside the feudal structure altogether, being held unconditionally by free land-owners. On the other hand, feudal institutions were already beginning to spread — into parts of southern France, into eastern Spain, and into the lands which Norman military adventurers were beginning to bring under their control in southern Italy. In the century after 1066 feudalism made its way into Germany, the Crusader States of the Holy Land, and many other districts of Western Christendom, each region exhibiting its own peculiar feudal characteristics. Most scholars would add that the post-Conquest century witnessed the advent of feudalism in England. It is beyond doubt that post-Conquest England was a feudal state, but scholars still differ as to whether the genesis of English feudalism was sudden or gradual, and whether or not post-Conquest English feudalism was anticipated significantly in the development of Anglo-Saxon institutions.

At first glance, one is struck by the fundamental differences between Anglo-Saxon England and feudal France. The shire and hundred courts, the danegeld, and the five-hide fyrd were all, basically, *public* institutions of a sovereign monarchy, whereas the feudal armies, feudal courts, and feudal aids were *private* in nature — products of a system in which privileges and responsibilities once exercised by a royal government had fallen into private hands. But it is unsafe to stress this dichotomy too strongly. The public orientation of Anglo-Saxon institutions had been strongly modified by the spread of private lordship. Great magnates and prelates received royal land charters granting not only extensive territories but also important jurisdictional rights. Many of the lords of Anglo-Saxon England operated the hundred courts within their territories and led their own contingents of the fyrd. But even so, the courts continued to function as units of a national legal system that remained fundamentally public, and the fyrd was still, both in theory and in practice, a national or royal army whose role was limited to the defense of the realm and the service of the king. One might cite certain exceptions to this statement, such as the military confrontation between Earl Godwin and King Edward in 1052, but in general, Anglo-Saxon lords did not lead their fyrds against one another; pre-Conquest England was remarkably free of private war. And even in Edward the Confessor's final years, when Harold Godwinson attended to the defense of the realm, the chroniclers often took the trouble to point out that Earl Harold led the fyrd "by the king's order."

The lord-vassal relationship of feudal France undoubtedly existed in essence in pre-Conquest England. The practice of thegns and other men promising their loyalty—"commending themselves"—to lords was widespread, and the intensity of such relationships is clearly demonstrated in the devotion of Ealdorman Byrhtnoth's men at Maldon. No French lord could ask for better vassals than these. In short, the personal relationship of lord to man was derived from a Germanic tradition shared by both England and France. But although the Anglo-Saxons had their own equivalent of the feudal vassal, it is doubtful that they possessed anything resembling the fief. The *personal* aspect of feudalism existed in Anglo-Saxon England, but the *territorial* aspect probably did not.

Even here, however, there is room for argument. Beginning in the tenth century, the bishops of Worcester are known to have granted "loan lands" to be held by tenants for life—or sometimes for "three lives"—the life of the tenant, his heir, and his heir's heir. In return for the tenure, the recipients were obliged to perform a rather miscellaneous group of services to their lord, the bishop of Worcester. Among their obligations was military service, to be rendered at the normal rate of one man per five hides. The Worcester tenants were not knights in the strict sense of the word: they were not trained in cavalry warfare, they were ignorant of the art of castle building, and of course the bishop of Worcester would not dream of leading them against some local enemy unless in the service of the king. Still, these loan lands might perhaps be described as fiefs if one is willing to define the word rather broadly. Whatever their differences from French vassals—and they were many—the Worcester tenants did, after all, hold their lands conditionally from their lord in return for service. It has been argued that the Worcester loan lands were not typical of Anglo-Saxon landholding, but some scholars would reply that the existence of loan lands elsewhere in England is hidden from us by the disappearance of relevant records. Thus the argument goes on and on. It is interesting up to a point, but ultimately the question of whether Anglo-Saxon England was feudal depends on how broadly one is willing to define the word. "Feudalism," like "democracy," is a useful term in some respects, but it is nevertheless dangerously fuzzy.

One might wish to say that William the Conqueror established feudalism in England, or perhaps simply that he instituted a far more thoroughgoing feudal regime than England had known before. He and his great barons covered England with castles and introduced the private feudal court alongside the older courts of hundred and shire. He introduced the highly significant concept, unknown in either Anglo-Saxon England or pre-Conquest Normandy, that all the land of England belonged either directly or indirectly to the ruler. Operating on this philosophy, and angered by the protracted English rebellions, he undertook vast confiscations of land. Much of this land he added to the royal demesne – the territory controlled directly by the crown. The remainder he granted as fiefs to his trusted military followers. In the course of this vast process of redistribution, the lands of several thousand thegns, each of whom had been a direct tenant of the Old English monarchy, were consolidated into large fiefs held by about 180 great Anglo-Norman barons – tenants-in-chief who held their land directly of King William. Most of these fiefs consisted of widely scattered estates rather than compact territorial blocks, and although the scattering of baronial estates had the effect in later years of attenuating local particularism, William had no such object in mind as he distributed the lands. On the contrary, the scattering was quite accidental, arising from the fact that pre-Conquest estates themselves tended to be scattered, and the further fact that the distribution was made in piecemeal fashion as the estates of one rebellious Anglo-Saxon lord after another fell successively into the king's hands.

By the 1070s William had assigned arbitrary quotas of knights' service on virtually all the lands outside the royal demesne, whether held by secular or ecclesiastical vassals. These quotas were sufficient to provide the king with a total force of some 5,000 knights. Aside from a handful of exempt abbeys, every English tenant-in-chief now owed a specific number of knights to the crown and was also obliged to perform many of the additional feudal duties which we have already noted in northern France. And in the years that followed, William's great vassals undertook to support the knights whom they owed the crown by creating smaller fiefs from portions of their larger ones. Thus, the process of subinfeudation occurred in England much as it had at an earlier time in France. English aristocratic society soon took the form of a complex chain of lord-vassal relationships.

The arbitrary nature of William's knight quotas, which were only approximately related to the size or value of the baronial fief, stands in sharp contrast to the systematic five-hide recruitment system of the fyrd. The English feudal army, which William and his successors assembled by summoning the tenants-in-chief to appear with the knights whom they owed, was the product of a vast number of individual feudal contracts. The fyrd, on the other hand, was based upon a standard relationship between land and service.

Feudalism in Norman England, being the product of a single will, was far more orderly and thoroughgoing than its French counterpart. Above all, it was rigorously subordinated to the interests of the ruler, who was at once sovereign king and chief lord at the apex of the feudal pyramid. This lord-king—*dominus rex* as he was called in contemporary documents—exerted a control over his potentially turbulent vassals such as feudal France had never known. In part, this remarkable authority was a product of the Conqueror's own forceful personality, but it owed much to his skillful use of Anglo-Saxon traditions. He preserved the danegeld, as we might expect, and exploited it thoroughly as a unique and highly lucrative source of royal revenue. He also preserved the Old English fyrd and summoned it to his service on numerous occasions. He tempered the centrifugal forces of feudalism by calling upon the Old English custom of universal allegiance to the crown. In England, the subvassal owed primary loyalty not to his immediate lord but to the supreme overlord—the lord-king. In 1085, William summoned the more important landholders of England to a great assembly at Salisbury in order to receive their oaths of allegiance. In doing so, he was following a venerable English tradition which had been exemplified long before in the oath which King Edmund demanded of his subjects (above p. 66). Again, William permitted his great vassals to build castles as they had been accustomed to do in Normandy, but recognizing that these fortresses were potential centers of insurrection as well as strong points in England's defensive system, he allowed them to be built only by royal license. Finally, and still following Anglo-Saxon tradition, he took much of the fun out of feudalism by refusing to countenance private war. The knights of England, like the soldiers of the Anglo-Saxon fyrd, were to serve the king alone.

In many ways, therefore, William employed the Anglo-Saxon tradition of royal centralization to establish iron control over the feudal system which he introduced. Indeed, the establishment of a highly systematic and centralized feudal regime in England had significant repercussions on post-Conquest Normandy. Norman feudalism, itself largely a product of forces operating during the earlier years of William's rule as duke, was comparatively coherent in 1066 but far less so than post-Conquest English feudalism. It was probably only after the Conquest, and owing to the English example, that the system of knight quotas and the concept of conditional tenure came to be universally accepted in Normandy. Thus, the Norman Conquest resulted not only in a Norman impact on England but also in a far from insignificant English impact on Normandy.

Norman England was deeply influenced by the royal centralization achieved by the Anglo-Saxons, yet it was more cohesive under William the Conqueror than it had ever been in Anglo-Saxon times. In a very real sense, the Anglo-Norman monarchy was greater than the sum of its parts, for the English and Norman traditions on which it was built were strengthened and enlarged by the creative statesmanship of the Conqueror himself. William's claim to ultimate ownership of all English land, which went far beyond the claims of any lord in feudal France, was equally unprecedented in England. It is by no means certain that fiefs were normally regarded as hereditary under William the Conqueror, and even though they were usually passed on from father to son, the Norman kings denied their vassals the security of *legally* hereditary tenure by charging arbitrary and exceedingly high reliefs when the fief passed to an heir. In effect, these monarchs allowed a son to succeed his father only by royal sufferance, and at an exorbitant price.

There is something rather artificial – even paradoxical – about the highly systematic feudal regime of post-Conquest England. Feudalism had arisen long before to meet the needs of a money-poor, intensely particularistic society. It was now adapted to a society ruled by a relatively strong monarchy – a society that enjoyed a vigorous commercial life and an expanding money economy. Thus, the feudalism of Norman England was compromised from the beginning, and gave way increasingly, as time went on, before the steady growth of royal government and the progressive substitution of wage service for tenure service. The Conqueror himself had made good use of mercenary soldiers in his great invasion, and as the decades passed, mercenaries became steadily more important to the English military system. Furthermore, before the end of the eleventh century it was becoming customary for some tenants to pay a sum of money to the crown in lieu of their feudal military obligation, and this military tax – known as scutage – was usually employed by the post-Conquest kings to pay the wages of mercenaries. With the development of scutage, the fundamental feudal obligation of knightly service to a lord was converted into a new source of royal revenue. The feudal structure remained, but the basic principle of tenure service was gradually dissolving. At the same time, another primary characteristic of feudalism – private jurisdiction – was being steadily eroded by the expanding authority of the royal courts and the royal administration.

This is not to say that England was never really feudal, but rather that from the Conquest onward, English feudalism was being subjected to dynamic political and economic forces which were changing it perceptibly from generation to generation. Far into the later Middle Ages the English "feudal" aristocracy remained powerful, but scholars are unanimous in recognizing that by the fourteenth century tenure service was utterly dead. It had been replaced by a system of lords and hired retainers – a system dominated by cash, which has been called "bastard feudalism." It may be useful to suggest that the feudalism of William the Bastard, with its distinct fiscal overtones, was already a bastard feudalism of sorts.

The Administrative Contributions of William the Conqueror

With a vastly augmented royal demesne, with danegeld revenues flowing in regularly, and with a tight control over a loyal feudal aristocracy, William ruled England with unprecedented authority. And like his Anglo-Saxon predecessors, he ruled with the advice of a royal council. The council of the Norman kings — the *Curia Regis* — represents a drawing together of two parallel institutions: the ducal court of Normandy and the Anglo-Saxon *Witenagemot*. William's counselors are described in the *Anglo-Saxon Chronicle* as his *Witan*, and like the Old English *Witenagemot*, the Anglo-Norman *Curia Regis* could be either the small and more or less permanent council of household officials and intimate friends or the larger and more formal council of great magnates. But it would be both hazardous and profitless to argue that the *Curia Regis* was more English than Norman. The councils of England and Normandy were evidently quite similar, and William's large, formal councils, attended by the greater tenants-in-chief, were predominantly Norman in personnel and feudal in mood. They represent neither a violent break with the Anglo-Saxon past nor a conscious accommodation to it.

While on their numerous visits to Normandy, the Norman kings left the administration of England in the hands of some trusted subordinate who was necessarily empowered to act in the king's name. William the Conqueror delegated his authority to different men at different times — to loyal magnates, to some trustworthy household official, or to a powerful churchman such as Archbishop Lanfranc. In later reigns this vice-regal authority came to be assigned permanently to a particular individual who, by the early twelfth century, had assumed the title *justiciar*. But the Conqueror, with his boundless energy, preferred to rule for himself or to delegate authority on an *ad hoc* basis. With the possible exception of Lanfranc, no one person shared William's authority for any significant time.

The power and vigor of English royal government under William the Conqueror, unmatched in Western Christendom, is illustrated vividly in William's greatest administrative achievement: the Domesday survey. As the *Anglo-Saxon Chronicle* describes it, the king had important deliberations and deep discussions with his council about this country, how it was peopled and with what sorts of men. Then he sent his men all over England into every shire and had them determine how many hundreds of hides there were in each shire, and how much land and cattle the king himself had in the country, and what annual dues he ought to have from each shire. He also had recorded how much land belonged to his archbishops, his bishops, his abbots, and his earls, and – though I relate it at too great length – what and how much everybody had who was a landholder in England, in land or in cattle, and how much money it was worth. So very thoroughly did he have it investigated that there was not a single hide or virgate * of land, or even (it is shameful to record but it did not seem shameful to him to do) one ox or one cow or one pig which was omitted from his record; and all these records were afterwards brought to him.

The Domesday survey, later consolidated into two large volumes known as Domesday Book, would have severely taxed any modern government. For its age it was altogether unique. Although not entirely free of errors and omissions, it is nevertheless an essentially trustworthy and immensely valuable historical source. It is organized by shires, and, within each shire, by the estates of the royal demesne and the fiefs of royal vassals. Although cows and pigs were omitted from the final record, Domesday Book undertakes to list the name of every manor, its assessment in hides, its value both in 1066 and at the time of the survey (1086), and the number and social status of its tenants. Nothing, unfortunately, is said about the knight quotas which the tenants-in-chief owed to the crown, but virtually everything else is covered. Any social, economic, or institutional history of Saxon or Norman England must begin with this astonishing survey.

The Conqueror died in 1087. Incapacitated while in the midst of a continental campaign, he was brought to Rouen, the chief city of Normandy, where he settled his affairs, made his last confession, and expired. Having devoted his career to the establishment of an Anglo-Norman state, he was nevertheless forced to divide the state at his death. The eldest of his three sons, Robert Curthose, was the obvious heir, but he had rebelled against his father on several occasions and was, indeed, in

---

* A virgate is a quarter of a hide.

rebellion at the time of the Conqueror's death. Robert inherited Normandy by virtue of the feudal custom of primogeniture, but William refused to allow him to succeed to the hard-won English throne. England passed to the Conqueror's second son, William Rufus, who became King William II. To his youngest son, Henry, the Conqueror granted scattered estates and an immense treasure. The struggles of these three sons over the next two decades resulted finally, as we shall see, in the reunification of England and Normandy.

Of William the Conqueror's ability there can be no question, but judgments of his character have varied widely. He enforced justice and kept the peace, but he was avaricious and sometimes savagely cruel. His most recent biographer describes him as "admirable; unlovable; dominant; distinct." * A similar ambivalence is to be found in the judgment of a well-placed contemporary observer:

> He was gentle to those good men who loved God, but stern beyond all measure to those who resisted his will. . . . And he was such a stern and violent man that no one dared go against his will. Earls who resisted him he placed in fetters, bishops he deprived of their sees, abbots of their abbacies, and thegns he imprisoned. . . . Among other things we must not forget the good order he kept in the land, so that an honest man could traverse his kingdom unharmed with his bosom full of gold. No one dared kill another however much he had wronged him, and if any man raped a woman he was immediately castrated.†

The Reign of William Rufus (1087–1100)

As the Conqueror lay dying at Rouen, William Rufus — William the Red — left for England with his father's blessing and, through the good offices of Archbishop Lanfranc, received the customary approval of a council of magnates and was crowned in Westminster Abbey.[4]   Rufus was even a greater puzzle than

---

* D. C. Douglas, *William the Conqueror* (London, 1964), p. 376.

† From the *Anglo-Saxon Chronicle*, A.D. 1087.

4 For the period from William Rufus through John, see A. L. Poole, *From Domesday Book to Magna Carta*, the most readable volume in the Oxford History of England. The Pelican History volume for this period stresses social and economic developments: D. M. Stenton, *English Society in the Early Middle Ages (1066–1307)* (2nd ed., 1952). A comprehensive selection of sources in English translation is to

his father. He scorned religion and ruthlessly exploited the Church (except at such times as he feared imminent death) and therefore earned the hostility of the monkish chroniclers. Their hostility may have been heightened by his probable homosexuality. Many of his barons, fearful of a situation in which their Norman and English fiefs were held of two different lords, were inclined to support the claims of his elder brother, Duke Robert of Normandy, to the English throne.

But Rufus was not without friends. He was an excellent soldier and was as loyal to his trustworthy vassals and his knightly followers as he had earlier been to his father. Although remorseless in his financial exploitation of the English Church and people, he was exceedingly generous to his military companions and prodigal in the wages and bounties which he gave to his numerous mercenary knights. Greedy and unchivalrous, he nevertheless demonstrated a deep moral commitment to the ancient Germanic notion of loyalty among men-at-arms. His saving virtue was the strength of his iron rule, for by inspiring fear in the hearts of his subjects and maintaining the devotion of his soldiers he managed generally to keep peace in his land. The *Anglo-Saxon Chronicle* was perhaps overly prejudiced when it branded Rufus as a man "hated by almost all his people and odious to God," but other writers of the period were scarcely more sympathetic. The twelfth-century historian William of Malmesbury described him as a man much pitied by churchmen for losing a soul that they could not save, beloved by the mercenary soldiers for his innumerable gifts, but unlamented by the people because he brought about the plundering of their property.

Rufus's reign had scarcely begun when, in 1088, he was faced with a general baronial rebellion. The rebellious barons cast their lot with Duke Robert of Normandy, a far weaker, more chivalrous man than his royal brother, and sought through armed force to reunite the Anglo-Norman state under Robert's genial rule. But Rufus kept the loyalty of the English Church, a few of the barons, and the articulate classes of the English people. In view of the above appraisals of his character, it may well be wondered why the Church and the English stood by him. They did so for two reasons. First, the reign was young, and Rufus had yet to make his abhorrent impression. He won the English with lavish promises of just taxes and good government which he did not keep. Second, the Church and the English

---

be found in D. C. Douglas and G. W. Greenaway (tr.), *English Historical Documents, 1042–1189* (1953). The best of several fine contemporary historians is William of Malmesbury, *History of the Kings of England* (J. A. Giles, tr., 1847).

consistently favored strong government, however harsh, over the terrible prospect of baronial anarchy. Accordingly, the English fyrd, the military tenants of the bishoprics and monasteries, and the knights of the remaining loyal barons rallied to Rufus's side and enabled him to crush the rebellion. A feudal insurrection of 1095 suffered a like fate, and thereafter Rufus reigned over a sullen but undefiant land.

As the Anglo-Saxon chronicler observed, Rufus, even more than his father, claimed ultimate control of all the English lands—"he claimed to be the heir of every man, cleric or lay." Accordingly, he denied the security of a normal succession to laymen and churchmen alike. A baronial heir could succeed to his father's estates only after paying the king, as a relief, whatever sum he might demand—and Rufus's reliefs were notoriously high. Again, the king exploited the feudal privilege of vetoing the marriage of a vassal's widow or female heir by literally selling the hand of this noble lady to the highest bidder or forcing her to pay him generously for the privilege of selecting a husband of her choice. He abused the right of wardship by taking possession of the estates of minor heirs and milking them dry before the heirs came of age. He behaved in much the same way toward Church lands, keeping abbacies and bishoprics unfilled for scandalously long periods after the deaths of their former incumbents and diverting their revenues into the royal treasury.

Indeed, he was not ashamed to deal in this manner with the archbishopric of Canterbury itself. At Lanfranc's death in 1089, Rufus took the vast archiepiscopal lands into his own hands and left the archbishopric empty for some four years. It might well have remained vacant still longer had it not been that in 1093 Rufus suffered a near-fatal illness. Fearing death, he responded to the pressures of his lay and ecclesiastical subjects—pressures which had been building up ever since Lanfranc's death—and appointed to the archbishopric of Canterbury the saintly and scholarly Anselm, a distinguished Italian churchman who had previously succeeded Lanfranc as abbot of Bec.[5]

It is ironic that such a despised king should appoint such a notable archbishop. St. Anselm was not only a man of profound piety; he was the supreme intellectual of his age, and quite possibly the greatest Christian scholar since St. Augustine of Hippo. St. Anselm's philosophical and theological works constitute the initial achievement of the momentous intellectual awakening that liberated the European mind in the High Mid-

---

[5] R. W. Southern, *Saint Anselm and His Biographer: A Study of Monastic Life and Thought* (1963), is a thoughtful and perceptive recent study.

dle Ages. As the first great scholastic philosopher he stood at the beginning of a remarkable intellectual movement that culminated in the works of such men as St. Bonaventure and St. Thomas Aquinas.

We are concerned here, however, not with Anselm the philosopher but with Anselm the ecclesiastical statesman. A man of absolute integrity, fully sympathetic with the revolutionary notions of papal supremacy and ecclesiastical independence that had been pioneered by Pope Gregory VII, St. Anselm brought the Investiture Controversy to England. A man in his early sixties at the time, he accepted the archbishopric reluctantly, remarking sadly that he was like a weak old sheep being yoked to an untamed bull. But as archbishop of Canterbury he was far from sheepish in his defense of the new reform ideology. King and archbishop soon found themselves at odds on a multitude of issues. Anselm wished to go to Rome to receive the pallium — the symbol of his spiritual authority — from the reform pope, Urban II. Rufus refused to let Anselm out of the kingdom and, for a time, even refused to recognize the claims of Pope Urban over those of an antipope supported by the Holy Roman Emperor. At length, late in 1097, these and other difficulties forced Anselm to flee the kingdom for exile in Rome, and Rufus resumed his control of the revenues of the Canterbury archbishopric. Anselm returned to England early in the next reign, but for the time being, the Norman monarchy was rid of its troublesome saint.

Rufus's ruthless financial exactions were carried out by a loyal subordinate and thoroughly unscrupulous churchman, Rannulf Flambard, whom the king had raised from a lowly station to become first the royal chaplain and later bishop of Durham. Flambard was Rufus's man Friday. He was the ubiquitous agent of the royal administration whom Rufus employed for a variety of executive and legal tasks. He served as the king's regent in England when Rufus was overseas. His primary function, however, was the raising of revenues for the king, and he performed this task with such ruthless ingenuity that he was soon as roundly hated as his master. On one occasion, for example, he summoned the English fyrd to Hastings for service overseas, then collected ten shillings from every soldier and sent them directly home.

Rufus was a man of inordinate ambitions who needed every penny that Flambard could collect for the fulfillment of his lofty plans. Once secure in his kingdom he undertook to conquer Normandy, but his campaigns and machinations against Duke Robert Curthose met with only middling success. In 1095, however, Duke Robert was seized with crusading fervor in the wake of Pope Urban II's powerful appeal to the warrior nobility of Western Christendom to drive the Moslems from the Holy Land. Having determined to participate in this First Crusade, Robert was hindered by a lack of money to support a worthy knightly retinue on the immense journey. Accordingly, a bargain was struck between the two brothers in 1095: Robert pawned Normandy to Rufus for three years in return for 10,000 marks of silver which the king obtained by levying a double danegeld on his kingdom. Robert was enabled to go crusading well financed, and William Rufus had Normandy at last.

The red king quickly transformed Robert's casually governed duchy into a centralized and tax-ridden state on the English pattern. He defended Normandy's frontiers and endeavored to expand them, and shortly before his death he seems to have been bargaining to receive Aquitaine in pawn from its crusade-bound duke. One contemporary writer suggests that Rufus even aspired to the throne of France.

These vast schemes were destined, however, to go unfulfilled. On August 2, 1100, Rufus was fatally wounded by an arrow while hunting in the New Forest—a vast royal hunting preserve in southern England which the Conqueror had established by cruelly evicting a great number of peasants. The New Forest had become a symbol of Norman tyranny, and it was regarded as fitting that the most tyrannical of the Norman kings should meet his death there.

The Reign of Henry I (1100–1135)

Rufus was in his early forties when he was killed. His abrupt death brought about a crisis in the royal succession. Since he had left no sons, the kingdom would normally have passed to his elder brother, Robert Curthose. But Robert was only now returning from the Crusade whereas the Conqueror's youngest son, Henry, was right on the scene. Henry had been a member of Rufus's fatal hunting party; some historians have suggested that Rufus was deliberately murdered at Henry's instigation. In the absence of the slightest hint of fratricide in the contemporary sources Henry must stand acquitted, but a lingering doubt remains.

However this may be, from the standpoint of Henry's interests the accident was ideally timed. A few weeks' delay would have found Robert in Normandy ready to claim his inheritance. As it was, Henry dashed immediately to Winchester, seized the royal treasure, won the approval of a rump royal council, and was crowned at Westminster Abbey on August 5, a mere three days after the shooting. In preparation for Robert's return,

Henry did everything in his power to win the support of his subjects. He sought to appease the barons and the Church by issuing an elaborate coronation charter in which he promised to discontinue the predatory practices of his predecessors. Among other things, Henry promised to "neither sell nor put at farm nor, on the death of an archbishop, bishop, or abbot, take anything from a Church's demesne or from its vassals during the interval before a successor is installed.... If any of my barons or earls or other tenants shall die, his heir shall not redeem his land as he did in my brother's time, but shall henceforth redeem it by a just and lawful relief.... And if the wife of one of my tenants survives her husband ... I will not give her in marriage unless she herself consents...." Henry did not keep the promises which he made in his Coronation Oath. It has been estimated that they would have cost him four or five thousand pounds a year—perhaps a quarter of the total royal revenue under Rufus—and Henry was no less avaricious than his predecessors. The Oath was neither a prelude to constitutional monarchy nor an open act of royal generosity, but simply one of several gambits which Henry employed to draw needed support in the oncoming crisis.

In order to win Anglo-Saxon backing, the new king married Princess Edith of Scotland, a direct descendant of the Old English royal family, while at the same time he bowed to Norman prejudice by obliging his bride to assume the Norman name Matilda. He courted popular opinion still further by imprisoning the detested Rannulf Flambard.

Early in 1101, Flambard escaped from the Tower of London and crossed to Normandy to join Robert Curthose, who had now returned from a distinguished career on the First Crusade and was eager to wrest England from his upstart brother. Alarmed by the growing threat, Henry sent letters into every shire confirming his Coronation Oath and requesting that all his free subjects swear to defend the land against all men and especially against Duke Robert of Normandy.

In August 1101, Robert Curthose led a large force across the Channel to Portsmouth, where he was joined by many barons of England who longed for the reunion of the two lands and the soft rule of the Norman duke. Meanwhile Henry had assembled a sizable army of his own, consisting chiefly of episcopal contingents, common knights, and a large force of native Englishmen. Some barons were present in the royal army, but the loyalty of most of them was uncertain. Henry seems to have placed his greatest confidence in the English, and we are told that he took pains to instruct them in the techniques of fighting against mounted knights. One contemporary writer asserts that Henry's army would have quickly driven Robert's forces out of the country, but as it happened the issue was settled by negotiation. "The more discreet on each side" — evidently the barons — arranged a truce, realizing perhaps that a decisive royal victory would weaken their own position. Henry, for his part, was only too happy to avoid the uncertainty of battle, and Robert, evidently at a military disadvantage, was glad to settle for what he could. The duke recognized Henry's royal title in return for an annuity of two thousand pounds (which Henry discontinued two years thereafter).

With the settlement of 1101 the great crisis of the reign had passed and Henry's throne was secure at last. One further rebellion, centering on the earldom of Shrewsbury on the Welsh frontier, was put down without great difficulty in 1102, and thereafter Henry ruled England unchallenged until his death in 1135. Indeed, the vast confiscations of land which Henry made in the wake of the Shrewsbury rebellion served as an invaluable source of royal revenue in the years to come.

Having secured England, Henry turned his attention to the conquest of Normandy. Paving his way with bribes to Norman barons, he campaigned in Normandy for two successive years. At length, in 1106, his army met Duke Robert's in open battle at Tinchebrai and won an overwhelming victory. Robert himself was captured and was allowed to languish in prison until his death in 1134. Tinchebrai, the antithesis of Hastings, constituted an English conquest of Normandy. It made Henry the Norman duke and reunited the Anglo-Norman state that the Conqueror had forged. Thenceforth King Henry spent the greater part of his time campaigning along the Norman frontiers against the king of France and the count of Anjou and quelling baronial rebellions within the duchy. His administration in England was sufficiently stable so that the kingdom could be safely left to itself for extended periods of time.

By the time of Henry's victory at Tinchebrai, another great crisis of his early years was nearing resolution. At the beginning of his reign Henry, in keeping with his early conciliatory policy, had invited the exiled Archbishop Anselm to return to England. But Anselm's long exile had only served to sharpen his commitment to the papal campaign for a Church free of secular control. Henry and Anselm were at odds from the first. The king insisted on receiving the customary homage for the Canterbury estates (which owed him sixty knights), but the archbishop, who had earlier rendered homage to Rufus, had now come to regard homage to a lay lord as subversive to ecclesiastical freedom. St. Anselm also objected vigorously to the practice of lay investiture which still persisted in England. Neither party would relent, and at length, in 1103, Anselm returned to exile and Henry confiscated the Canterbury revenues. But negotiations continued through the period of exile, reaching a crisis in 1105 when St. Anselm threatened Henry with excommunication. Both sides were by now willing to compromise, and in 1107 an agreement was worked out between the king, the archbishop, and the pope. Henry agreed to relinquish lay investiture, but was permitted, reluctantly, to continue receiving homage from his ecclesiastical tenants-in-chief. The English Church was never again quite so completely under royal control, but the king's authority over his churchmen remained substantial and he was generally successful in supervising their appointment. He had agreed to allow his clergy the privilege of free canonical elections, but free elections and strict royal control were by no means incompatible, as is demonstrated by a royal writ of the later twelfth century from King Henry II to the monks at Winchester: "I order you to hold a free election, but nevertheless I forbid you to elect anyone except Richard, my clerk, the archdeacon of Poitiers."

Henry I was not the patron of ecclesiastical reform that his father had been. The Conqueror, although far from a saint, had been a faithful and devoted husband; Henry was flamboyantly unfaithful and sired upwards of twenty illegitimate offspring. A satyr of Henry's sort could scarcely be expected to be a serious proponent of clerical celibacy, and the great ecclesiastical reform movement which was transforming the moral quality of the twelfth-century European Church made only limited progress in Henry I's England. The king's most powerful and trusted administrator, Bishop Roger of Salisbury, made no secret of his mistress, and Roger's nephew, Bishop Nigel of Ely, had a wife. Henry fattened his treasury from the sale of church offices and, like Rufus, kept bishoprics and abbacies unfilled for prolonged periods in order to enjoy their revenues. St. Anselm was not obliged to endure for long these unedifying activities. He died in 1109, and Henry kept the archbishopric vacant for five years thereafter.

If the reign of Henry I is not noted for ecclesiastical reform, it is exceedingly significant from the standpoint of royal administration. Henry was known as the Lion of Justice, and although this title is hardly in keeping with his remorseless avarice, nevertheless Henry's rule was firm and, when not against his interest, just. He was not a kindly or easy man. Having repudiated Rannulf Flambard at the beginning of his reign, he found the wily minister too valuable a servant to dispense with, and soon had Flambard in the royal service once again. His ambitious military and diplomatic policies required an endless flow of revenue for the building of castles, the bribing of barons and neighboring feudal princes, and the hiring of mercenaries. Henry and his ministers exploited the wealth of England to the fullest, although perhaps with somewhat more prudence and less gusto than had been customary in Rufus's reign. Henry's severity is a recurring theme in the *Anglo-Saxon Chronicle:*

> 1104. . . . It is not easy to describe the miseries this land was suffering at the time because of various and different injustices and taxes that never ceased or diminished. . . .
> 1110. . . . This was a very severe year in this land because of the taxes that the king collected for the marriage of his daughter.
> 1116. . . . This land and people were also this year often severely oppressed by the taxes which the king collected both in and out of the boroughs.
> 1118. . . . England paid dearly . . . because of the various taxes that never ceased during the course of all this year.
> 1124. . . . It was a very troublous year; the man who had any property was deprived of it by harsh taxes and harsh judgments at court; the man who had none died of hunger. etc. etc.

In 1125, discovering that his minters were producing adulterated coinage, the king had them castrated and deprived of their right hands. Yet, paradoxically, the *Anglo-Saxon Chronicle* observed of Henry on his death, "He was a good man, and people were in great awe of him. No one dared injure another in his time." In short, despite all his ruthless severity—or perhaps because of it—he enforced justice and kept the peace.

Justice, as we have seen, could be lucrative to an English monarch. The "profits of justice" constituted an important portion of the royal revenue, and it evidently occurred to Henry that by extending the scope of the king's justice he could augment the flow of money to his treasury. Perhaps it would not be unduly naive to suggest, as a possible additional motive, that Henry regarded the maintenance of justice as an important royal duty and that he wished to be a good king.

Whatever the king's motives, his reign witnessed a notable growth in the royal judicial system and the royal administration. Henry's chief administrator was Roger, bishop of Salisbury, a less than exemplary churchman as we have seen but one of the great architects of the English medieval government. Roger is the first man known to have held the office of chief justiciar in England. It has been suggested that this office, whose holder was empowered to supervise the royal administration and act for the king in his absence, arose in consequence of Henry's victory at Tinchebrai, for thereafter the king was obliged to be away from England for extended periods and could not, therefore, rule his kingdom personally. Indeed, the emergence of the chief justiciar, together with related administrative innovations, has been regarded as marking the rise of *impersonal* government—of government capable of functioning without direct royal supervision. As such, it constitutes a highly significant step in the direction of administrative sophistication.

Concurrently with the rise of the justiciar there emerged in Henry I's reign two additional administrative institutions of the very highest importance: the itinerant justices and the Exchequer. The itinerant justices, or justices in eyre, were royal officials, often of high noble rank, who toured the countryside trying important cases in the shires and thereby greatly enlarging the scope of the king's justice. When one of Henry's itinerant justices was present, the shire court was transformed temporarily into a royal court and ordinary people of the countryside were for the first time brought face to face with the direct judicial authority of the crown.

The Exchequer was a royal accounting bureau, permanently stationed at Westminster regardless of where the king might be. It was therefore an important element in the "impersonal" government that was now emerging. The term "Exchequer" is derived from the table around which the officials worked. The surface of the table resembled a checker board, being divided into columns representing various denominations of money. Markers were placed on these columns to represent the accounts of sheriffs who reported their collection of royal revenues twice a year to the Exchequer officials. The method of accounting was based on the principle of the abacus and the decimal system of arithmetic which had only recently been introduced from the Islamic world. The Exchequer accounts were recorded on long rolls known as Pipe Rolls which are now exceedingly valuable historical sources. Unfortunately, only one of the Pipe Rolls from Henry I's reign has survived, but we have a continuous set of these annual records from 1156 onward.

The Exchequer served as an important control on the activities of the king's sheriffs. These royal agents were by no means faceless bureaucrats in the Anglo-Norman period. It required a person of wealth and stature to protect the royal interests in the turbulent countryside of early feudal England, and consequently the sheriffs were normally recruited from the ranks of the high Anglo-Norman nobility. Indeed, many sheriffs seemed to be growing too powerful for the king's good; often they abused their positions to enrich themselves and their families, and sought to make their shrievalties hereditary. The Exchequer audits restrained them to a degree, but Henry I was obliged to take further measures to insure his control over his local officials.   He deposed sheriffs on a large scale, replacing them with trusted subordinates, sometimes of relatively humble origins, who were frequently given responsibility for a consider-able number of counties.

Thus Henry I's reign marks the coming of age of the royal administration.   The functions of the royal household officials were growing in importance and degree of specialization.   The chief justiciar of England served as a supreme administrative executive under the king.   The Exchequer provided Henry with the first remotely modern accounting office known to the medie-val West.   And the tightly controlled sheriffs and itinerant justices provided the essential links between the royal adminis-tration and the countryside.   Northern Europe had known no such coherent administrative machinery since Roman times, and no northern monarch was so wealthy as Henry I.   For Henry had discovered that a positive relationship existed between the efficiency of his administration and the size of his revenues.   He was fully alive to the fact that strong government was good business.

Henry's regime contained many nonfeudal elements, and his powerful administration doubtless limited the scope of his feudal aristocrats.   Still, Henry cannot be described simply as an antifeudal king.   The disasters of the later reign of King John should be sufficient to convince anyone that a medieval English monarch could not succeed without some degree of support from his barons.   And as it happened, Henry proved himself exceed-ingly adroit in winning the allegiance of a number of English nobles.   This he accomplished through a kind of primitive patronage system.   For those who demonstrated their loyalty and won his favor, he provided tantalizing opportunities to ad-vance their careers and fortunes in the royal service.   Such men were given an inside advantage in acquiring forfeited lands, wealthy wives, lucrative wardships, danegeld exemptions, shrievalties, and the various other spoils at the crown's disposal. In this way a number of lesser aristocrats rose to high position, and men of still lower station ascended into the prosperous middle levels of the aristocracy.   To be sure, these royal favor-ites had to pay the king for every privilege that he gave them – in Henry's government nothing was cheap – and they seldom rose to high position overnight.   Nevertheless, they were fully aware that they owed their success to the king's favor, and that their future service in his behalf would continue to be rewarded.

It was with the lands and privileges confiscated from his enemies, not with his own demesne lands, that Henry rewarded his favorites.   He was in the happy position of giving (or rather selling) to others without appreciably diminishing his own in-heritance.   With his patronage he created a royalist core in the aristocracy. Royal patronage was to be a central and enduring element in English politics and society for many centuries thereafter; under Henry I it makes its first appearance as a fully articulated system.

Henry's government was complex, sophisticated, and to a degree impersonal, yet it depended ultimately on the existence of a strong, fear-inspiring king. Accordingly, Henry devoted much attention to the problem of the royal succession. Although he had a score of illegitimate offspring, he produced only two legitimate heirs: a daughter named Matilda and a younger son named William. One might hazard the guess that this monarch, who had grown up in an atmosphere of fraternal conflict, quite consciously refrained from siring potential rivals to his son William. If so, he was the victim of an ironic turn of fate. For William, who had been carefully groomed for the throne, was killed on the eve of his manhood, in 1120, by the sinking of a vessel that was carrying the prince and a distinguished but rather intoxicated party of aristocratic associates from Normandy to England. This catastrophe, known as the disaster of the White Ship, threw the royal succession into a state of chaos. Henry, whose first wife had died, promptly remarried, but the second marriage was childless. Finally, in 1127, Henry secured oaths from his barons that they would accept his daughter Matilda as the royal heir.

Matilda had earlier been married, at the age of eleven, to the Holy Roman Emperor Henry V, but by 1127 she was a widow. Having secured the pledges of his barons, Henry arranged a fateful marriage between Matilda and Count Geoffrey of Anjou. This was a bold stroke of policy, for it promised to end the age-long struggle between Normandy and Anjou for hegemony in northern France, but it also gave rise to a myriad of problems. For one thing, the Anglo-Norman barons, doubtless uneasy over the prospect of being ruled by a woman, were still more apprehensive over the possibility of acquiring a king from the traditionally hostile county of Anjou. For another, Matilda and Geoffrey were poor mates. Matilda was a widow of 25, whereas Geoffrey was a boy of about fifteen. Their personalities clashed, they separated for a time, and the endemic warfare between Normandy and Anjou resumed. At length, however, Geoffrey and Matilda were reconciled, and in 1133 Matilda bore her husband a son, the future King Henry II. For a brief time Henry I relaxed, enjoying the pleasures of being a grandfather and the security of having obtained at last a male heir. But the turbulent politics of northern France allowed him only momentary peace. In 1135 he was engaged once again in the task of repressing rebellion, and in the midst of these campaigns he died, a victim of acute indigestion.

The reign of Henry I was long and significant. He had re-united the Anglo-Norman state, kept the peace in England, suc-cessfully defended his far-flung frontiers, and instituted notable administrative advances. Further, he had prepared the way for a new Anglo-Norman-Angevin political configuration that was to dominate northern Europe during the second half of the twelfth century. A perceptive modern scholar speaks of the reign in these words: "Looking to the future, it is here, we feel, that the history of England begins — a history which is neither that of the Norman conquerors, nor that of the Anglo-Saxons, but a new creation." *

The Reign of King Stephen (1135–1154)

When Henry I died, his grandson was a child of two whose ambitions did not yet extend to duchies and kingdoms. The English barons had sworn to accept Matilda, but they had never promised to submit to the rule of Count Geoffrey. Hence, the great English landholder Stephen of Blois, a son of the Con-queror's daughter and nephew of Henry I, acting with the same dispatch that Henry I had demonstrated in 1100, was able to seize the throne. Matilda had perhaps the better hereditary claim, but hereditary right was not everything in the making of an English king. Indeed, it had been nearly a century since an English monarch had been succeeded by his eldest offspring, and the claims of all the Norman kings thus far had been heavily clouded.

Stephen's elder brother was Count Theobald of Blois and Champagne, a powerful magnate of feudal France. It was evidently to win Count Theobald's friendship and support that Henry I had showered Stephen with lands and privileges. At Henry's death, only one other English landholder could com-pete in wealth with Stephen of Blois. That person was Earl Robert of Gloucester, King Henry's favorite bastard son.

Stephen was unquestionably the most genial of the Nor-man kings. Chivalrous, erratic, and lacking in firmness, he was in many respects Henry's opposite. In the words of the *Anglo-Saxon Chronicle*, "he was a mild man, and gentle and good, and did no justice...." During the first two years of his reign he squandered Henry's treasure on lavish bribes and wages for mercenaries, and managed more or less to keep the peace. In

---

* R. W. Southern, "The Place of Henry I in English History," *Proceedings of the British Academy*, XLVIII (1962), 128–29.

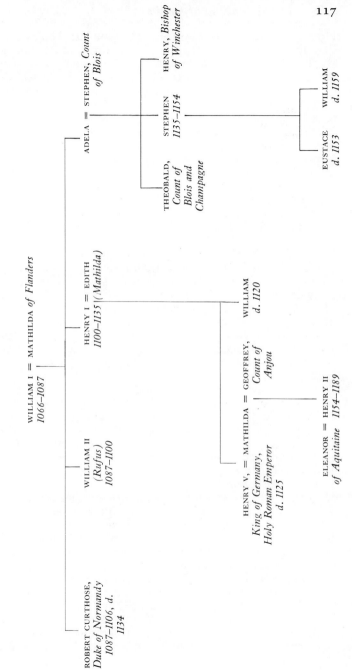

The Norman Kings

WILLIAM I = MATHILDA *of Flanders*
1066–1087

ROBERT CURTHOSE, *Duke of Normandy* 1087–1106, d. 1134

WILLIAM II (*Rufus*) 1087–1100

HENRY I = EDITH ((*Mathilda*)) 1100–1135

ADELA = STEPHEN, *Count of Blois*

HENRY V, = MATHILDA = GEOFFREY, *King of Germany, Holy Roman Emperor* d. 1125 *Count of Anjou*

WILLIAM d. 1120

ELEANOR = HENRY II 1154–1189 *of Aquitaine*

THEOBALD, *Count of Blois and Champagne*

STEPHEN 1135–1154

HENRY, *Bishop of Winchester*

EUSTACE d. 1153

WILLIAM d. 1159

117

1138, however, Count Geoffrey of Anjou attacked Normandy, Earl Robert of Gloucester rebelled in favor of his half sister, Matilda, and the king of Scots took up Matilda's cause by invading England. Stephen succeeded in defending himself against these threats, only to be faced with an invasion by Matilda herself in 1139. The next nine years witnessed a see-saw battle between Stephen and Matilda accompanied by a general state of baronial anarchy. The warfare and turbulence of these years was by no means universal—it was limited to particular areas at particular times—but it was terrifying nonetheless and left a deep impression on contemporaries. The twelfth-century historian Henry of Huntingdon, commenting on the horrors of Stephen's reign, remarks that "whatever King Henry had done, whether in the manner of a tyrant or that of a true king, appeared most excellent in comparison. . . ."

At length, the dynastic struggle settled into an uneasy truce. In 1148 Matilda retired from England in defeat, but in the meantime her husband, Count Geoffrey, had conquered Normandy. The two contending parties were separated by the English Channel, and baronial unrest diminished in England.

But now Henry I's grandson, Henry of Anjou or Henry Plantagenet, was approaching manhood and was preparing to undertake an energetic struggle to make good his inherited claims. Count Geoffrey died in 1151, and two years later the young Henry—Count of Anjou and Duke of Normandy—invaded England.

This ambitious young man of nineteen was already the greatest feudal magnate in France. In addition to Normandy and Anjou and their satellite provinces, Henry Plantagenet had won the extensive duchy of Aquitaine in southern France by marrying its vivacious heiress, Eleanor. He came to England as a man of great substance and significant resources, and as duke of Normandy he was in a position to terrify the English barons by threatening to confiscate their Norman fiefs. Henry's campaign in England progressed with moderate success, but Stephen resisted doggedly, not so much for himself, now, as for his son and chosen successor, Eustace. At Eustace's sudden death in August 1153, Stephen lost his spirit and submitted to the growing sentiment for compromise. He and Henry entered into an agreement known as the Treaty of Westminster. Stephen was to rule England unmolested until his death, but was to make Henry Plantagenet his heir. Baronial partisans on both sides were guaranteed their lands and were promised immunity from punishment. England was to return at last to a state of peace. Nine months after the Treaty of Westminster King Stephen died, and Henry Plantagenet acceded unopposed to the English throne. With his coronation the Norman age of English history came to an end, and the Angevin age began.*

The troubled reign of Stephen is traditionally described as an epoch of feudal anarchy, a reaction against the strong government of Henry I, an age when a good but pliable king was exploited unmercifully by greedy barons. As a result of recent research this interpretation requires modification. For one thing, Stephen was not so openhearted or simpleminded as he has sometimes been described. He was a cheerful man, by and large, but he could also be sly and treacherous. In particular, he had a habit of arresting his barons and administrators by surprise and without good cause. His arrest in 1139 of Henry I's great justiciar Roger of Salisbury, together with Roger's son and two nephews, made a shambles of the royal administrative machinery. His peremptory arrests of two of England's most powerful barons, Geoffrey de Mandeville and Earl Rannulf of Chester, prompted both of them, once released, to revolt against their king.

It should be clear from our discussion of the first three Norman reigns that the barons might well feel justified in rebelling against the whole autocratic tradition of the Norman monarchy, and the advent of a protracted period of disputed succession provided the opportunity. Throughout the Norman age hereditary feudal tenure had been persistently compromised by the royal doctrine of ultimate ownership, a doctrine that had been manifested repeatedly in arbitrarily excessive reliefs, royal abuse of the feudal rights of wardship and marriage, and widespread forfeitures. By Stephen's time a vast number of disputes had arisen over rights to land, and very often two contending claimants to a particular fief would be found fighting on opposite sides in the struggle between Stephen and Matilda. There was evidently a deep desire on the part of the feudal aristocrats to make their precarious holdings secure and to win the unquestioned right to hereditary succession on their fiefs. If their behavior in Stephen's reign was not particularly enlightened, neither was it entirely unjustified.

The Treaty of Westminster and the subsequent accession of Henry II constitute an epoch-making victory for the hereditary principle both on the royal and the baronial level. Henry succeeded in part by the approval of the council, in part by the designation of his predecessor—as kings had done over the past century—but above all, and unlike the Norman kings, he succeeded by hereditary right. And from that day to this, with very

---

* The "Angevin age" or "Angevin dynasty" is so called because King Henry II and his successors were descendants in the male line of Count Geoffrey of Anjou.

few exceptions, hereditary right has governed the succession of English monarchs.

It has also governed the inheritance of English lands. Henry II abandoned the principle that all the land was the king's land on which the barons were mere tenants. He and his successors recognized fully the right of an eldest son to succeed to his father's estates. Forfeitures to the crown became rare — only three are recorded in the half century following Henry's coronation. Stephen's own younger son was permitted to keep his vast estates, and most of the earlier baronial land disputes were settled by compromise. Thus, Henry II's succession marks a vital stage in the development of feudal land tenure into something approaching the modern concept of land ownership. In the words of one modern scholar, Stephen's magnates "demanded that the King should recognize their hereditary right in specific and unambiguous terms. . . . That is what the barons fought for in Stephen's reign, and that is what they won." *

* R. H. C. Davis, "What Happened in Stephen's Reign, 1135–54," *History*, XLIX (1964), 12.

Chapter 5

𝕳enrp 𝕴𝕴 AND HIS SONS

Henry II and the Twelfth-Century Renaissance

HENRY II reigned for thirty-five years—almost exactly as long as his grandfather, Henry I.[1] The two reigns are similar in many respects, for Henry II undertook quite deliberately to revive Henry I's policies and strove to rule in his imperious tradition. Yet the new king was a vibrant personality in his own right—an exuberant extrovert, short, powerful, and redheaded. His contemporaries regarded him as a fear-inspiring yet fundamentally trustworthy man—mercurial, lecherous, always on the move, and altogether overwhelming in personality. The contemporary scholar Peter of Blois, who spent some time at Henry's perambulatory court, describes it as a scene of fantastic confusion whose movement through the countryside depended on no prearranged schedule but on the royal whim. To Peter, Henry's court was "a perfect portrait of hell," and it is not surprising that the harassed scholar eventually elected to resign from the royal

---

[1] The first three works cited in Chapter 4, note 3, are useful for the period covered by this chapter as well. For a fairly detailed political narrative see Frank Barlow, *The Feudal Kingdom of England, 1042–1216* (1955). J. E. A. Jolliffe, *Angevin Kingship* (1955), presents a provacative thesis to the effect that the Angevin kings were essentially authoritarian and antifeudal. The argument is persuasively presented but has been widely criticized.

entourage: "I shall dedicate the remainder of my days," he concludes, "to study and peace."

But Peter of Blois' portrayal of a vast yet directionless royal effort is surely exaggerated. Henry knew where he was going, even if his followers did not. And it is significant that a scholar of Peter of Blois' sort should be in the royal household at all. Henry II was the first fully literate English king since the Conquest, and he delighted in consorting with scholars and patronizing their works.

In this respect, as in others, Henry II was a child of his age. The twelfth century had witnessed an impressive intellectual revival in England as elsewhere in Western Christendom. The University of Oxford was in the process of formation and was destined to develop within a century into one of Europe's most distinguished intellectual centers. Archbishop Theobald of Canterbury, whose archiepiscopate (1139–61) spanned the reigns of Stephen and Henry II, became the head of an important scholarly circle at Canterbury which included for a time such notable figures as the great twelfth-century English humanist, John of Salisbury, and the future archbishop, St. Thomas Becket. The English historian William of Malmesbury, writing in the first half of the twelfth century, practiced his craft with an elegance and insight almost worthy of Bede, and the historical works of William of Newburgh in the next generation are no less impressive. Nor were these historians isolated figures. Others only slightly less talented were writing at the same time.

The twelfth-century revival of historical writing was accompanied by a resurgence of philosophical and scientific thought. Adelard of Bath, a younger contemporary of Henry I, was a significant pioneer in bringing the Greco-Arabic scientific tradition into Western Europe. A great traveler, Adelard came into contact with Greek and Islamic science in Asia Minor, Greece, Sicily, and Spain. He translated several works of major importance into Latin—Euclid's *Elements*, for example—and he also wrote important philosophical and scientific treatises of his own. Adelard was by no means the only Western scholar of his age with keen scientific interests, nor even the only Englishman working in the fields of mathematics and science. He, and others like him, represent the genesis of the rich scientific tradition of medieval England which culminated in the works of Robert Grosseteste and Roger Bacon in the thirteenth century and William of Ockham in the fourteenth.

The revival of intellectual creativity was one of the essential factors underlying Henry II's fruitful reign. Another factor of equal importance was the growth of towns and commerce. Money was becoming more and more abundant, and town life, although still rustic and parochial by today's standards, was growing steadily more vigorous. Towns such as Bristol, Newcastle, Northampton and, above all, London, were becoming increasingly significant commercial centers. The monarchy, recognizing their importance, granted them charters containing valuable privileges such as the right to operate a borough court, freedom from customs and tolls, and various commercial monopolies. In general, the burghers were recognized as a class apart, free of the obligations and tenurial complexities of feudalism: "A burgher can give or sell his land as he pleases and go where he wishes, freely and undisturbed, . . ." *

The same creative vigor that the twelfth century devoted to learning and commerce is evident in the field of agriculture. The peasant's life remained grim by modern standards but it was steadily improving. The momentous work of the Anglo-Saxons in forest clearing and swamp draining reached its climax in the twelfth century, and with the growth of commerce and the increased circulation of money it became possible for farmlands to produce for a profit rather than for mere subsistence. The Cistercians, an austere monastic order that rose to great prominence in the twelfth century, established many abbeys in England, often in remote wilderness areas, and began to raise sheep on a large scale. Wool production had long been important to England, but it was now pursued at an unprecedented level of efficiency. As it happened, neighboring Flanders had developed a vigorous textile industry, and in the course of the twelfth century England became Flanders' chief source of wool. A large-scale trade developed between the two lands, and Henry II was able to turn the situation to his own diplomatic advantage by threatening the count of Flanders with suspension of the trade if he did not cooperate with English royal policies.

Grain production also became significantly more efficient. The traditional system of dividing manors into two fields, farmed in alternate years, gave way to a more complex and far more productive three-field system of rotation. Concomitantly, the horse was gradually beginning to replace the less efficient ox as the typical beast of burden on English farms. This gradual revolution in animal power rested on a series of earlier technological inventions: the horseshoe, a vastly improved horse collar, and the tandem harness. English agriculture was also benefiting from the increased use of mechanical power. Water mills were widely used in Anglo-Saxon times—over 5,000 are recorded in Domesday Book—and before the end of Henry II's reign the windmill had made its debut in the English countryside. These innovations are exceedingly difficult to trace—the historians of

---

* From the customs of Newcastle at the time of Henry I.

the age give them scant attention—yet their importance is incalculable. For despite the upsurge of commercial activity, grain production remained the fundamental economic enterprise of medieval England, and significant improvements in agrarian technology were bound to have a momentous effect on the prosperity of the realm. These innovations were by no means the products of English inventive genius but were appearing concurrently on the Continent. Hence the economic buoyancy of twelfth- and thirteenth-century England was shared by France, Germany, and indeed virtually all of Western Christendom.

Military, Administrative, and Legal Reforms

Still, in certain aspects of the twelfth-century upsurge England was in the vanguard. This was particularly true in the area of political administration. Under Henry II, as under Henry I, England was more thoroughly and efficiently governed than any other state in the West.

Henry II began his reign by endeavoring to revive in all its fullness the royal authority exercised by his grandfather. This he was not always able to do. The principle of hereditary feudal succession, for example, was now established beyond question. Nevertheless, Henry II undertook to undo insofar as possible the disintegrative work of Stephen's reign. He destroyed a great many of the unlicensed castles that barons had hastily erected during the height of the anarchy, and was exceedingly stingy in granting further licenses for baronial castle building. And he worked energetically, first to rebuild the powerful government of Henry I and later to expand it. Three areas of the royal government received Henry II's particular attention: the military organization, the administrative system, and, above all, the legal structure.

Henry II's military reforms are well illustrated by two important documents from his reign: the *Cartae Baronum* (Baronial Charters) of 1166 and the Assize of Arms of 1181. The first of these sources is a series of written statements from all the tenants-in-chief of the realm, both lay and ecclesiastical, in response to a royal inquest relating to knights' service. The tenants-in-chief were required to tell the king how many knights they had enfeoffed prior to Henry I's death in 1135, how many they had enfeoffed between 1135 and 1166, and to what degree —if any—the enfeoffments fell short of the knightly military quotas which the monarchy had imposed on them. The knights which the tenants-in-chief had enfeoffed were to be identified by name. Surprisingly enough, the *Cartae Baronum* of 1166 constituted the first general survey of knights' service to be undertaken by the king since the establishment of the quotas by William the Conqueror. So far as we can tell, however, Henry II was not particularly interested in discovering the extent of his feudal military resources as such, but proceeded with the inquest for two quite different reasons. First, he wished to identify all the knightly subvassals of England who had not yet rendered him their formal allegiance so that he might secure their oaths in the near future. Second, on the basis of the data supplied by the *Cartae Baronum,* he demanded higher scutage payments * from all his vassals whose enfeoffments exceeded their royal quotas. Thus the first feudal survey to be conducted at a national level was undertaken for purposes that were, strictly speaking, subversive to traditional feudalism — and expensive to the feudal aristocracy as well.

The Assize of Arms of 1181 was far more radical in its implications than the *Cartae Baronum.* Coming at a time when the Anglo-Saxon fyrd had ceased to function and the feudal military obligation was tending to become a mere excuse for the levying of scutage, the Assize of Arms marked the first of a series of attempts — running through the thirteenth century — to reorganize the English military obligation on the basis of wealth.

Henry II divided the English military force into four categories. The first corresponded to the feudal army: the holder of each knight's fee was to have a shirt of mail, a helmet, a shield, and a lance. The second and third categories corresponded to the old five-hide fyrd, but the basis of the obligation was shifted from the number of hides in a man's possession to the annual income from his land and the total value of his movable possessions: every free layman with movables and rents of sixteen marks or more was to have a shirt of mail, a helmet, a shield, and a lance (i.e., the equipment of a knight); and every free layman with movables and rents of ten marks or more was to have a hauberk, an iron cap, and a lance. The fourth category embraced all freemen with chattels and rents of less than ten marks: they were to have quilted coats, iron caps, and lances. Finally, all four of these groups were to swear fidelity to Henry II and bear their arms in his service according to his command.

The Assize of Arms established a graded hierarchy of military obligations based on a single recruitment system extending from knightly service down to the general military duty of all

---

* i.e., payments in lieu of knightly military service. See above, p. 10.

freemen. It preserved the knight's fee of earlier times but equated it with an estate of sixteen marks or more. This equation between a knight's fee and an estate of some specified monetary value constitutes the beginning of a long process that tended to incorporate the older system of arbitrary private feudal tenures into a larger and radically different structure – a standardized national system of military assessment. This new scheme, although based on annual income rather than on hides, bears an unmistakable resemblance to the national five-hide recruitment system of the Anglo-Saxon fyrd. For both were geared to a universally recognized ratio between land value and military service.

Henry II's Assize of Arms of 1181 was merely the first of a series of such ordinances. Similar ones were issued by King Henry III in 1230 and 1242 and by Edward I in his Statute of Winchester in 1285. These later ordinances increased the number of categories of nonknightly military service from three to five, incorporated the nonfree peasantry into the military system, and provided for new military classes such as archers and light horsemen. And beginning in the thirteenth century, the monarchy sought to bring knights' service still more closely in line with the new system by requiring all men with estates of a certain annual value (usually twenty pounds) to become knights. The nineteenth-century historian William Stubbs recognized clearly the implications of these policies when he spoke of the military provisions of the Statute of Winchester as "a monument of the persistence of primitive institutions working their way through the superstructure of feudalism and gaining strength in the process."

The shift from hides to annual income as the basis of land assessment is just as evident in the tax system as in the military system. By Henry II's reign the ancient hidage assessment was becoming anachronistic, for it no longer served as an adequate indication of changing land values and it failed to reflect the growing wealth of the townsmen. Thus, the danegeld, which had served so long as a lucrative land tax based on hides, was replaced under Henry II by a new tax assessed at some percentage of a subject's annual rents and chattels. Taxes levied on this new basis continued through the subsequent reigns of Richard I, John, Henry III, and long thereafter, paralleling the fundamental changes in the military recruitment system which were initiated by the Assize of Arms. From the standpoint of both taxation and military service Henry II's age marks the beginning of an epoch.

In other aspects of royal administrative development the reign of Henry II constitutes a revival and elaboration of Henry I's policies rather than a new beginning. As the functions of the household staff became gradually more specialized, separate administrative departments were beginning to emerge. The increasing efficiency and professionalization of the Exchequer is attested not only by an unbroken series of annual Pipe Rolls but also by a treatise—*The Dialogue of the Exchequer*—which explains in detail the duties and procedures of the Exchequer officials. Administrative records were increasing both in number and in sophistication, and would continue to do so during subsequent reigns. In brief, the royal coterie of servants, advisers, scribes, and cronies was evolving gradually into a bureaucracy of professional administrators.

Henry II, like Henry I, was seriously concerned with the administrative links between court and countryside. He revived his grandfather's system of itinerant justices and made it more systematic. In 1170 he undertook a thoroughgoing inquest of his sheriffs' activities and followed it up by replacing most of them with more trustworthy royal nominees. The sheriffs were obliged to execute royal orders—orders that were usually in writing—and to serve as local representatives of an increasingly literate royal administration. Hence, an efficient sheriff had to be literate himself, and it has been justly observed that the remarkable authority which Henry II exercised over the English countryside was made possible only by a significant rise in lay literacy. Government by the written word demanded local officials who could read.

It was in the field of law, above all else, that Henry II made his unique contribution.[2] Indeed, he has been called, perhaps without excessive exaggeration, the father of the English Common Law. Here again he followed in the tradition of Henry I, but many policies which Henry I had merely begun Henry II carried to consummation.

First of all, Henry II addressed himself to the perplexing problem of maintaining local law and order without a police force. In his Assize of Clarendon of 1166, augmented by the Assize of Northampton of 1176, he ordered that inquest juries of twelve men from each hundred and four men from each town be required to meet periodically. These juries were obliged to report the names of notorious local criminals to the king's sheriff or itinerant justice. The accused criminals were then forced to submit to the ordeal and were suitably punished if they failed to pass it. The ordeal was a crude and ancient procedure of

---

[2] The standard general work is F. Pollock and F. W. Maitland, *History of English Law before the Time of Edward I* (2nd ed., 2 vols., 1898). A recent and compact summary is Bryce Lyon, *A Constitutional and Legal History of Medieval England* (1960).

Germanic law * which was passing out of favor in the twelfth-century Church and was banned altogether by the Lateran Council of 1215. Henry II employed it as a traditional method of determining guilt or innocence, but he evidently did so with some hesitation, taking the precaution of providing that even if the denounced criminal should pass the ordeal he was nevertheless subject to banishment from the kingdom.

It should be clear that the juries established by the Assize of Clarendon were fundamentally different from the modern trial jury. The task of the modern jury, to decide whether the accused is guilty or innocent, was performed in Henry II's system by the ordeal. His juries were closer in spirit to our present grand juries; they were indictment juries rather than trial juries and their chief purpose was to supply information. Similar juries had been employed in the Anglo-Norman period not only to identify criminals but to provide local data of various kinds to the royal administration. They were used, for example, during the Domesday Inquest to supply the hard facts on which the Survey was based. Henry I used them on occasion to denounce law breakers, but it was only under Henry II that they became a part of a regular legal system. As such, they mark a notable extension of royal jurisdiction into areas traditionally reserved for the local courts of hundred and shire.

Henry II was as sensitive as his grandfather to the fact that an expansion of the scope of royal justice would inevitably result in augmented royal revenues from fines and court fees. Hence, he undertook the policy of extending royal jurisdiction systematically into the vast and bewildering area of land disputes. We have already noted the importance and complexity of landholding in medieval England. Although the Norman kings — most notably Henry I — adjudicated disputes among their great tenants-in-chief and occasionally intervened in lesser conflicts over land, these matters were customarily handled in the private baronial courts. It was only in Henry II's time that the full authority of royal jurisdiction was brought to bear on this crucial area of law.

The procedures of the baronial feudal courts were slow, antiquated, and otherwise unsatisfactory, and the traditional machinery of the royal courts was very little better. Henry II determined to provide a swift and rational method of settling land disputes which would not only improve the quality of justice but also bring an immense amount of lucrative new business into the royal courts. Thus, he instituted a series of "possessory assizes" — forms of legal action which were designed

---

* Above, p. 19.

not to determine who had the best *right* to the land in question but whether a plaintiff had been *forceably* dispossessed or disinherited. In this way he hoped to reduce the violent aspects of land rivalry by preventing a claimant, even one with a just claim, from taking possession of an estate by force.

The most important of Henry II's possessory assizes was the *Assize of Novel Disseisin.* It provided that a landholder who claimed to have been violently dispossessed could purchase a royal writ ordering the local sheriff to summon a jury and inquire of it whether or not the plaintiff had been driven from his land. If its decision was affirmative, the sheriff, with the full weight of royal authority behind him, was to restore the disputed land to the plaintiff. Here we find a jury being used in a somewhat different manner than in the Assize of Clarendon. The *Novel Disseisin* jury did not indict, rather, it testified — thereby performing, roughly, the function of the modern witness.

Novel Disseisin was only one of several possessory writs established by Henry II. Of the remainder, one is of particular interest: the writ of *Mort d'Ancestor*. This writ required the sheriff to ask the jury whether the plaintiff's father held the land in question when it last passed to an heir. If so, and if the plaintiff was the eldest son, he was to be given the land. The writ of *Mort d'Ancestor,* when understood in the context of the vague and insecure inheritance arrangements of the Anglo-Norman age, illustrates vividly Henry II's willingness to support the principle of normal inheritance. Indeed, it constitutes a crucial stage in the acceptance of the hereditary concept by the English monarchy.

Toward the end of his reign, Henry II instituted a legal action known as the Grand Assize which addressed itself not to the question of violent dispossession but to the more fundamental question of who had the best title to the land. As in the case of the possessory assizes, the question was answered by a local jury consisting of men who were likely to know the situation well. Previously, questions of rights to land were settled in feudal courts by the violent custom of trial by battle; the two disputants, or their representatives, simply fought it out. The new procedure was bound to commend itself to an age in which reason and logic were coming into high regard, and the ultimate effect of the royal land assizes was to make the royal courts the chief adjudicators of land quarrels of all kinds. Englishmen now learned to turn to the king for quick, modern, rational justice, and the feudal courts were hopelessly outclassed in the competition.

Henry I and Henry II, between them, achieved an enormously significant extension of royal jurisdiction at the expense of feudal and local justice. The various local peculiarities in legal custom—Kentish law, Northumbrian law, Danelaw—were giving way to a uniform royal law, a *common* law shared by all Englishmen. Thus, the political unification of the Wessex kings had its counterpart and consummation in the legal unification achieved by the two Henrys and their successors.

The emergence of a national legal system under Henry II, and its dependence on literate laymen, is illustrated perfectly by the appearance of England's first systematic legal treatise, written under the direction of Henry II's able lay justiciar, Rannulf Glanville. Glanville's treatise is practical and utilitarian rather than philosophical—Englishmen were not yet ready to speculate on the fundamental nature of their jurisprudence—but it is nevertheless indicative of the rise of a coherent body of royal law.

As the common law was evolving under Henry II a profoundly different legal tradition was developing on the Continent. Henry's law, precocious though it was in many respects, had its roots in Germanic custom, whereas continental law was gradually passing under the influence of the Roman legal tradition, which was undergoing a notable revival in the twelfth-century universities. Roman law is fundamentally constitutional in nature, resting on the concept that ultimate political authority inhered in the Roman people. But it passed into the twelfth-century West in the rather autocratic form which it had acquired at the hands of Justinian. For it was above all Justinian's *Corpus Juris Civilis* that was studied and expanded by the continental Roman lawyers of the twelfth century. The legal concepts of the Roman Republic and early Empire were deeply colored by the absolutism of sixth-century Byzantium, and when these concepts began to influence Western Europe once again in the High Middle Ages they tended to make continental governments not only more rational but also more autocratic.

Roman law had a far greater influence on the Continent than in England. This was due in part to geography, for England was remote from Italy where the study of Roman law centered. More important, however, is the fact that in the mid-twelfth century, when the revived Roman law was first making its impact on European politics, France and other continental states were still relatively disunited and amorphous, whereas the English monarchy already had a powerful administrative and legal tradition behind it. To continental monarchs Roman law seemed an ideal tool with which to build strong, centralized political structures, but a king such as Henry II would quite naturally prefer to rely upon the Germanic traditions of the Anglo-Saxon and Norman kings which had already

carried the monarchy so far. Hence, although the Roman law
of the Continent made a distinct mark on English legal development, its influence was not decisive. The common law remained essentially an indigenous phenomenon.

Henry II and the Church

For all its achievements in the realms of commerce, agriculture, administration, and thought, the twelfth century remained fundamentally an age of faith. Indeed, a great deal
of the immense creative originality of the period was devoted,
in one way or another, to the service of Christianity. The best
historians of the age regarded historical development as the
progressive unfolding of a divine plan. Scholars such as St.
Anselm and John of Salisbury were interested primarily in God
and God's relationship to man. Architects devoted their talents
to the building of abbeys and cathedrals. By the time of Henry
II the powerful Romanesque style had reached its fullest development and had spread across the length and breadth of Western Europe, and in the course of his reign a stunning new style,
the upward-reaching Gothic, was making its appearance.

The creative upsurge of high medieval Europe was accompanied by a major effort to reform the Church and by a profound
intensification of piety at all levels of society. The struggles
over lay investiture left the twelfth-century papacy and episcopacy more powerful than ever before, and the holders of high
ecclesiastical offices were often men of sanctity as well as
practical wisdom. Kings and noblemen retained a voice in
ecclesiastical appointments, and the universal Church was
still plagued with unworthy, time-serving bishops and abbots
and incompetent or even licentious priests. Still, there can be
little question but that the moral calibre of the clergy was gradually rising. And the papacy was steadily extending its control
over the Church through its wide-ranging legates and its expanding administrative organization.

The high medieval Church succeeded in bringing the Faith
to the ordinary Christian as never before. A fully elaborated
system of dioceses and parishes covered the entire European
countryside, and through the system of the seven sacraments,
fully elaborated only in the twelfth century, the ordinary Christian believer received the grace of the Christian God, through
priestly intercession, at every important juncture in his life.
At birth, *baptism* cleansed him from the inherited taint of sin
and initiated him into the community of the Church. At pu-
berty, the sacrament of *confirmation* reinforced the grace

received at baptism and gave him the spiritual strength with which to enter adulthood. His wedding was blessed by the sacrament of *marriage*. If he chose a priestly vocation, he received the sacrament of *holy orders*. Throughout his adult life he periodically received absolution from his sins through the sacrament of *penance*—confessing his transgressions fully and sincerely and with a firm intention of amendment. His relationship with God was intensified at regular intervals through the sacrament of the *eucharist* in which he consumed the body and blood of Christ in the form of bread. And at his death his spirit was strengthened and purified for the last journey through the sacrament of *extreme unction*. Through the sacraments, through regular attendance at the Mass, and in countless other ways the life of the average medieval Christian was deeply influenced by the Church. Cruelty, avarice, lust, and violence continued to afflict society as they always have, yet religious awareness was never far from the center of men's minds.

Henry II, in his effort to extend the royal jurisdiction not only at the expense of local and feudal courts but also at the expense of ecclesiastical courts, was undertaking a policy that ran directly counter to the steady growth of ecclesiastical jurisdiction. But the papacy at the time was deeply involved once again in a struggle with the Holy Roman Emperor, and had Henry enjoyed the full cooperation of the English episcopacy he might well have succeeded in carrying out his policies unhindered. As it was, however, his effort to limit the jurisdiction of the ecclesiastical courts encountered the violent opposition of the new archbishop of Canterbury, Thomas Becket, and resulted in a fateful struggle between the king and his primate.

The public career of Thomas Becket was divided into two phases of approximately equal length. For eight years, from 1154 to 1162, he served as Henry II's chancellor and boon companion. In 1162 Henry appointed him archbishop of Canterbury to succeed Theobald (who died in 1161), and for the following eight years, until his dramatic murder in 1170, he was Henry's most implacable foe. Much has been written of the transformation in Becket's character from the roistering, worldly chancellor to the stern and uncompromising archbishop. The complexities of Becket's personality will doubtless always remain obscure. All that one can say is that he was an exceedingly talented person who, as chancellor, served his king faithfully and skillfully, and as archbishop fought with equal ardor for what he conceived to be the interests of the Church. The perfect chancellor, and one of England's most famous archbishops, he has sometimes been described as an actor—a person of few personal convictions but with a flair for the dramatic, who was capable of playing to the hilt each of his two roles. This viewpoint is superficial and contrived. More probably, the heavy responsibilities which he assumed at his elevation to the archbishopric of Canterbury caused him to undergo a genuine religious conversion. Archbishop Thomas was no play actor but rather a fervent ecclesiastical reformer in the tradition of Pope Gregory VII and St. Anselm, and a late-blooming saint on the pattern of Augustine of Hippo. If the stern archbishop was lacking in Christian charity and generosity, one must nevertheless concede that his later years were made infinitely more difficult by his uncompromising dedication to the Church. We must grant him the honesty of his convictions.

Henry, of course, could not have anticipated Becket's conversion. He must surely have assumed that in appointing Becket to the archbishopric he was installing a royal agent at the apex of the ecclesiastical hierarchy. But almost immediately Becket asserted his independence and began to treat Henry not as his master but as his spiritual son. Henry, quite naturally, was surprised and resentful, and hostility soon developed between the two men. Early in 1164 Henry forced Becket and the other English bishops to consent to a list of customs relating to Church-state relations known as the Constitutions of Clarendon. These customs were, of course, strongly pro-royal. Henry II maintained that they represented common practice in the days of Henry I, and with one or two possible exceptions they did. Yet for several reasons they were difficult for reform churchmen to accept. For one thing, although Henry I had acted contrary in many ways to the new spirit of ecclesiastical reform, he had never been so bold—or perhaps so foolish—as to commit his practices to writing. He may have wronged the Church, but he never asked his churchmen to give their formal sanction to his abuses. Moreover, the English Church had achieved a fair measure of independence during Stephen's reign and had attained a position much more in harmony with the contemporary reform ideology. Certain of the provisions in the Constitutions of Clarendon must have appeared to reform churchmen as distasteful retrograde steps. This was particularly true of the provision forbidding appeals to Rome without royal permission and the provision establishing a degree of royal jurisdiction over "criminous clerics" who had traditionally been subject to Church courts alone.

The proper treatment of criminous clerics was the most bitterly disputed issue in the Henry-Becket controversy. Some clerics, particularly those in minor orders, engaged in crimes of violence, then threw themselves on the mercy of the ecclesiastical courts and were often given relatively light punishments. Frequently they were defrocked and released without further penalty. The monarchy quite naturally resented such soft treatment of criminals and sought to punish secular crimes in secular courts. Moreover, the Constitutions of Clarendon, in asserting that "If a cleric has confessed or been convicted, the Church shall protect him no further," was implying that the defrocked cleric was to be arrested and tried for his crime in a royal court. Becket objected that no man should be tried and punished twice for the same crime.

The issue of the criminous clerics symbolized a far deeper controversy. The twelfth century witnessed a rise in the centralized power of the English royal administration and a concurrent expansion of ecclesiastical administration. In the Becket dispute we are seeing two worlds in collision: the secular world of the royal bureaucracy and the spiritual world of the international Church. Two radically different kinds of government – royal and ecclesiastical – were in conflict. Similar disputes occurred off and on throughout high medieval Europe and were, indeed, merely particular manifestations of a single fundamental conflict inherent in the divergent ideals of the epoch. It was basically a power struggle – a struggle for precedence between the universal Church and the rising secular states. The rivalry between Henry II and Becket was one of its most dramatic episodes.

Shortly after subscribing to the Constitutions of Clarendon, Becket reversed himself and appealed to the pope for support. The papacy, having its hands full with Germany, sought to compromise, wishing neither to offend King Henry nor to repudiate its faithful servant Becket. Henry had by now lost all patience with Becket and toward the end of 1164 ordered him to stand trial in the king's court for various offences which he was alleged to have committed while serving as chancellor. Becket claimed clerical immunity from royal jurisdiction and fled the country to appeal his case to the pope. In so doing he was challenging one of the basic articles of Henry's Constitutions of Clarendon – the prohibition of unlicensed appeals to Rome.

There followed a protracted struggle between the fiery king and the exiled archbishop. The papacy managed for nearly six years to placate the archbishop while at the same time restraining him sufficiently to avoid a complete break between England and Rome. The crisis reached its climax in June, 1170. Henry II, anxious to protect the hereditary principle of royal succession, wished to have his eldest son crowned. Since the archbishop of Canterbury was obviously unavailable, Henry turned to Canterbury's ancient rival, the archbishop of York. When Becket heard that the archbishop of York had presided over a royal coronation he was furious at the affront to the dignity of Canterbury and, with papal backing, threatened to lay

England under the ban of interdict. Deeply alarmed at this threat, which would have had the result of closing all of England's churches, Henry II worked out a temporary reconciliation with Becket which left all major issues unresolved but allowed the archbishop to return to England.

A truce that failed to resolve any of the conflicts was perhaps worse than no truce at all. Just before returning to England, in the late autumn of 1170, Becket shocked Henry by excommunicating all the bishops who had participated in the coronation. Henry was beside himself with anger. Four of his knights, responding to their king's fury, forced their way into Canterbury Cathedral on December 29, 1170, and brutally murdered Becket in the presence of numerous observers.

The deed had a momentous impact on public opinion in England and the Continent. Becket was immediately hailed as a martyr, and his tomb at Canterbury became an immensely popular pilgrimage center. He was quickly canonized, and his bones were reputed to be a source of miraculous cures. To Henry, of course, Becket's murder was a source of profound embarrassment. The king denied that the four knights had acted under his orders, and we can well believe that Henry would not have been so foolish as to deliberately undertake such a violent and self-defeating policy. Nevertheless, Henry was not absolved of all responsibility. He had been Becket's arch-enemy, and if the four knights were not acting on his command they were at least responding to his anger. The king was obliged to do penance by walking barefoot through the Canterbury streets and undergoing a flogging by the Canterbury monks. He was also compelled to repudiate the Constitutions of Clarendon, to permit appeals to Rome without specific royal license, and to refrain from subjecting criminous clerics to capital punishment. On the surface of things, the martyred archbishop would seem to have won a total victory.

In reality, however, the expansion of royal justice at ecclesiastical expense suffered only a partial and temporary interruption. Although the Constitutions of Clarendon were withdrawn, most of their provisions remained effective in fact if not in law. Henry continued to place trustworthy royal servants in high ecclesiastical offices, and in the later years of his reign he succeeded in keeping tight control over the Church without any dramatic violations of canon law or harsh conflicts with the papacy. His earlier policy of flamboyant aggression, symbolized by the Constitutions of Clarendon, gave way to a far more effective policy of subtle and silent maneuvering. The Becket affair notwithstanding, Henry II succeeded in ecclesiastical affairs, as elsewhere, in advancing his realm toward administrative and legal centralization.

The Angevin Empire

In emphasizing the development of England under Henry II we must never overlook the fact that Henry's authority extended far beyond his island kingdom. Many of his legal and administrative policies in England were applied also to some of his continental domains – Normandy in particular. The Norman ducal court and the Norman Exchequer paralleled those of England; Henry issued a military ordinance for his French lands that was quite similar to the English Assize of Arms and undertook a feudal survey of Normandy in 1172 that paralleled the *Cartae Baronum* of 1166. Nevertheless, one can separate England from the remainder of the Angevin Empire without excessive violence to historical reality. Henry's constellation of territories was in reality no empire at all; each territorial unit which he controlled had its own separate government – its own distinct customs – and the heterogeneous lands were held together solely by their allegiance to a single individual. There was no central "imperial" government, no unified body of "imperial" law, but rather a myriad of separate administrations of varying efficiency held together by the intelligence and tremendous energy of Henry II. Still, from the military and diplomatic standpoint, if not from the standpoint of law and administration, the Angevin Empire must be regarded as a single entity. England was its most tightly administered district and its chief source of wealth, whereas the continental territories required the bulk of Henry's military efforts in subduing their rebellious nobles and guarding them against the growing pressure of the French monarchy.

In the years of Henry II's reign the French monarchy was coming of age. Ever since 987 the crown had been in the hands of the Capetian family. This dynasty had managed to secure its hold on the French throne by producing male heirs at the proper time, but until the twelfth century its actual power had remained exceedingly limited. Its direct authority was restricted to a relatively small area of north-central France embracing Paris and Orleans, known as the Île de France, and even here it was plagued by a host of recalcitrant minor barons. To be sure, the great dukes and counts of France – even the duke of Normandy himself – were crown vassals, but on the whole they ignored their obligations to their feeble lord unless it was in their interest to ally with him.

In the twelfth century, however, the power of the Capetian monarchy was growing. King Louis VI (1108–37) succeeded in taming the robber barons of the Île de France, thereby providing the monarchy with a secure, if limited, territorial base. His successor, Louis VII (1137–80), was a genial and pious man

The ANGEVIN *Empire*

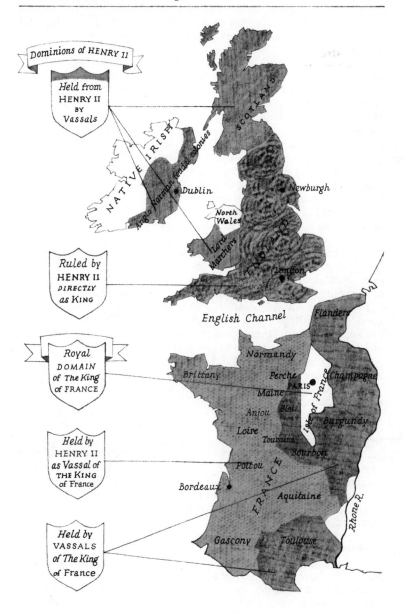

Dominions of HENRY II

Held from HENRY II BY Vassals

Ruled by HENRY II *DIRECTLY* as KING

Royal DOMAIN of *The King* of FRANCE

Held by HENRY II as Vassal of THE KING of France

Held by VASSALS of *The King* of France

SCOTLAND

NATIVE IRISH

Anglo-Norman feudal colonies

Dublin

Newburgh

North Wales

Lord Marchers

ENGLAND

London

English Channel

Flanders

Normandy

Brittany

Perche

Champagne

PARIS

Maine

Isle of France

Anjou

Blois

Loire

Touraine

Burgundy

Bourbon

Poitou

FRANCE

Bordeaux

Aquitaine

Rhone R.

Gascony

Toulouse

who extended the prestige of the monarchy by serving as a rallying point for the French nobility against the immense power of the Angevin Empire. More and more, the French nobles outside Henry II's dominions looked to Louis VII for leadership and submitted their disagreements to the court of this self-effacing, honest king.

To Louis VII, the growth of the Angevin Empire was an ominous development. From his diminutive territorial base in the Île de France he faced a vast configuration of territories controlled by his nominal vassal, Henry II. England, Normandy, Maine, Anjou, Brittany, Touraine, and Aquitaine had all been joined together in an empire that dwarfed the French royal domain. On the other hand, the Capetian monarchy had the advantage of a nominal overlordship over Henry II's French territories, and the further advantage that these territories were exceedingly heterogeneous – too extensive to defend easily, and in some cases quite loosely governed. Aquitaine in particular had a long tradition of baronial independence, and outside the northern Aquitainian province of Poitou the ducal authority tended to be nominal.

Thus, the Angevin Empire had serious weaknesses which the French monarchy might exploit. Under Louis VII the exploitation was only halfhearted, consisting largely in a policy of fomenting rebellion among Henry II's sons and his abused wife, Eleanor of Aquitaine. Henry left himself open to such tactics. He alienated his wife by his infidelities and annoyed his sons by giving them titular authority over various districts of his Empire while reserving actual political authority for himself. Urged on by the French king, and resentful of their father's authoritarian policy, Henry II's three eldest sons, Henry, Richard, and Geoffrey, rebelled against the king in 1173–74. They were supported by their mother and by a portion of the continental nobility but were able to win the backing of few English barons. In the end the rebellion collapsed, and Henry II sought to prevent future ones by keeping his wife in comfortable imprisonment and placating his sons with greater responsibility and authority. All this did little good. Young Henry and Geoffrey both died in the midst of plots or insurrections, Henry in 1183 and Geoffrey three years thereafter. At King Louis VII's death in 1180 the French crown passed to his shrewd and ruthless son, Philip II, "Augustus" (1180–1223), who adopted a far more aggressive anti-Angevin policy than his father had pursued.

Consequently, Henry II's final years were deeply troubled ones. The great king could keep the peace everywhere except within his own family, and Philip Augustus was able to exploit to the fullest the rebelliousness of Henry's offspring. In the late

The Angevin Kings

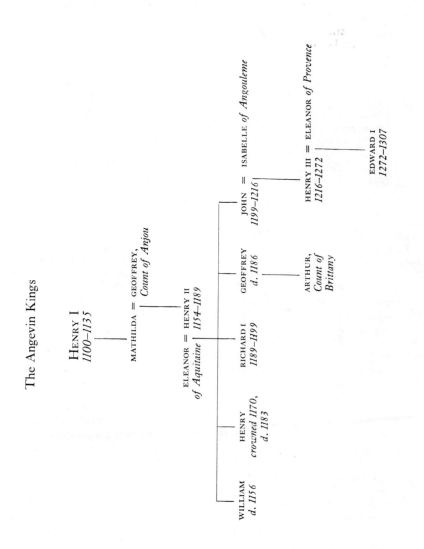

1180s both of Henry's surviving sons, Richard and John, were in league with Philip Augustus and in rebellion against their aging father. On the eve of his death in 1189 Henry was forced to make a humiliating submission to this hostile coalition, and tradition has it that his dying sentence was one of bitter self-reproach: "Shame, shame on a conquered king."

But Henry II's defeat in 1189, although a personal tragedy, had little effect on French or English history. For despite the involvement of King Philip Augustus, the rebellion was fundamentally a family affair, and on Henry II's death the Angevin Empire passed intact to his eldest surviving son, Richard the Lion-Hearted. Philip Augustus's machinations had done him little good. The French monarch, however, was both patient and persevering. He was intent on the destruction of the Angevin Empire and was prepared to devote his whole life to the task if necessary. Henry II had held grimly to his continental lands. It remained to be seen whether his sons could do as well.

Richard I, the Lion-Hearted

King Richard the Lion-Hearted (1189–99) was a profoundly admired and almost legendary figure in his own age. He has fared less well at the hands of modern historians. He made no personal contribution to English constitutional and legal development and, indeed, spent less than six months of his ten-year reign in England itself. This statistic is enshrined in every textbook, and we have no intention of neglecting it here. Still, some modern historians, in describing Richard as a poor king, are guilty of judging him by anachronistic standards. We now know that the Angevin Empire was ephemeral and that the crusading movement was ultimately a failure, and we are therefore prone to discount Richard's activities in defending his French territories and in winning glory on the Third Crusade. Yet these are the very activities that won him fame among his contemporaries and thereby insured the success of his reign. His remarkable military prowess and chivalric reputation retained for him the loyalty of his vassals and subjects even when he himself was far away. Hence he preserved the integrity of the Angevin Empire and was never seriously threatened by internal rebellion.

Immediately after his coronation in 1189, Richard began preparing for a crusade. Jerusalem, which had fallen to the Christian warriors of the First Crusade in 1099, had been retaken by the talented Moslem leader Saladin in 1187. Beginning in 1190 a multitude of European warriors set off on the

Third Crusade with the goal of recapturing the Holy City. This Crusade was led by three distinguished European monarchs: Emperor Frederick Barbarossa of Germany, King Philip Augustus of France, and King Richard of England. Considering the magnitude of the effort and the distinction of its leaders, the Third Crusade must be regarded as a failure—but it was an exceedingly romantic failure which added much to the fame of Richard the Lion-Hearted. For, as it happened, Richard became the real leader of the movement. Frederick Barbarossa drowned while crossing a river on his way to the Holy Land and Philip Augustus—who was psychologically unsuited for crusading—abandoned the venture after cooperating with Richard in the capture of the important port of Acre. The French-Angevin conflict made the two monarchs natural rivals, and having quarreled with Richard, Philip left for France to plot against him. Richard was left in command of the campaign against Saladin.

In this great Moslem chieftain Richard found an adversary as chivalrous as himself. While fighting one another the two warriors developed a strong mutual admiration, and when, after many months of campaigning, Richard found it impossible to take Jerusalem, he entered into a treaty with Saladin which guaranteed the rights of Christian pilgrims in the Holy City. He then set out for home to take his revenge on Philip Augustus. On his return journey he had the extreme misfortune of being captured by the duke of Austria and handed over to his enemy, Emperor Henry VI of Germany, son and heir of Frederick Barbarossa.

Europe was outraged that a crusading hero should receive such treatment, but Henry VI refused to give up his valuable hostage until his terms were met. In the end England submitted to ruthless taxation in order to raise the immense sum of one hundred thousand pounds—literally a king's ransom—and Richard was obliged to grant Henry VI the overlordship of England, to hold his kingdom as a fief of the Holy Roman Empire. Only then was Richard set free.

On his return in 1194 Richard had several scores to settle. Philip Augustus had been doing what he could to subvert the Angevin Empire, which was held together only by the loyalty of its barons to their chivalric and ill-treated lord. Philip had even sought to persuade Emperor Henry VI to keep Richard in perpetual custody. Accordingly, the last half of Richard's reign was marked by endemic warfare against France, and it soon became clear that on the battlefield Philip Augustus was no match for his illustrious adversary. Richard more than held his own and at his untimely death from a battle wound in 1199 he was threatening the French throne itself.

In England, during Richard's absence, the bitter Angevin tradition of family discord had asserted itself in the person of Richard's fickle younger brother, John. When Richard departed from England for the Crusade he left the kingdom in the control of his chancellor, William Longchamp, bishop of Ely. Longchamp was an able but heavy-handed administrator whose low birth and imperious airs soon made him extremely unpopular. John attempted to place himself at the head of the movement against Longchamp with the ultimate goal of wresting England from Richard's control. He succeeded in having Longchamp removed from office but failed to win control of the Angevin Empire for himself. Thereupon he began to plot with the ever-willing Philip Augustus against his absent brother. The plotting was ineffectual, however, and on Richard's return John was obliged to beg his mercy and forgiveness. Richard is recorded as replying in a generous but patronizing tone: "Think no more of it, John; you are only a child who has had evil counselors."

In the years after Longchamp's fall, the administration of England passed into the hands of a brilliant and trustworthy royal official, Hubert Walter, who was raised in 1193 to the archbishopric of Canterbury. More an administrator than a pastor, Hubert Walter did not distinguish himself as a man of God. But he provided Richard with something that Henry II had always sought in vain: a trusted supporter at the head of the English Church. More than that, Hubert Walter, who dominated the English administration during the last half of Richard's reign and the first third of John's, presided over an era of immense significance in English administrative history. In addition to his exalted position as archbishop of Canterbury he served as Richard's justiciar and as John's chancellor. In his time the royal administration functioned with unprecedented efficiency (the hundred-thousand-pound ransom is merely one illustration of this), and royal records were preserved far more extensively than ever before.

Hubert Walter and his able administrative colleagues provided a degree of continuity between the reigns of Richard and John. The two brothers were so contrary in personality, however, that their reigns form two distinct epochs. Royal administration had made great progress in the twelfth century, but the quality of royal leadership remained of fundamental importance. And even more than the chivalrous Richard, John was to make his own distinctive impression on the development of the English state.

King John: An Evaluation

John's reign (1199–1216) is marked by three great conflicts: with the French monarchy, with the papacy, and with
the English barons.   Each of these struggles ended in failure
for John, and his failures were of momentous consequence in
the making of England.   They resulted in the disintegration of
the Angevin Empire, the establishment of papal lordship over
England, and the issuing of Magna Carta.[3]

John himself is an elusive, ambivalent figure.   In many
respects he was Richard's opposite – unchivalrous, moody,
suspicious, a mediocre general, yet highly intelligent and
deeply interested in the royal administration.   He is at once
unattractive and fascinating.   Historians of the nineteenth
century tended to regard him as a brilliant, unscrupulous villain;
J. R. Green describes him in these words:

> "Foul as it is, hell itself is defiled by the fouler presence
> of John."   This terrible view of his contemporaries has
> passed into the sober judgment of history . . . in his inner
> soul John was the worst outcome of the Angevins.   He
> united into one mass of wickedness their insolence,
> their selfishness, their unbridled lust, their cruelty and
> tyranny, their shamelessness, their superstition, their
> cynical indifference to honor or truth.[*]

Since these words were written, historians have tended to
modify their appraisal of John.   Some have ascribed his difficulties to mental illness: "It is our opinion that John Lackland
was subject to a mental disease well known to-day and described
by modern psychiatrists as the periodical psychosis. . . .   Among
his Angevin ancestors were fools and madmen. . . . [†]   Modern
psychology shares with medieval penance the happy quality

---

[3] King John has received much attention; two recent biographies are highly
recommended: Sidney Painter, *The Reign of King John* (1949), and W. L. Warren,
King John (1961).   The latter is somewhat more popular in approach and more
readable.   There is also a splendid biography of Queen Eleanor, whose career
encompassed the reigns of her husband, Henry II, and her sons, Richard I and
John: Amy Kelly, *Eleanor of Aquitaine and the Four Kings* (1950).   The fourth
king is Louis VII of France, Eleanor's first husband.

[*] J. R. Green, *History of the English People* (Special ed., Nations of the World
Series), I, 237.

[†] C. Petit-Dutaillis, *The Feudal Monarchy in France and England* (London,
1936), p. 215.

of forgiving all sins, and by portraying John as a psychotic it is possible to absolve him of his wickedness.

Other historians have sought to rehabilitate John in different ways. The mind of the twentieth century is skeptical of such concepts as the foulness of hell, corrupt inner souls, or masses of wickedness, and there has been a serious attempt to demonstrate that John was considerably maligned by his contemporaries. Many of the most delicious atrocity stories relating to his reign, for example, come from the writings of two thirteenth-century historians from St. Alban's — Roger Wendover and Matthew Paris — who have been shown to be biased and inaccurate on the subject. Roger Wendover was bitterly hostile to John and Matthew Paris copied from Wendover and elaborated his tales. From the works of these men comes the story that John ordered his soldiers to seize Archdeacon Geoffrey of Norwich, bind him with chains, cast him into prison, and torture him to death by crushing him beneath a leaden cope. This unedifying event is said to have occurred in 1209, yet there is proof that sixteen years later, in 1225, this same Archdeacon Geoffrey became bishop of Ely. It has been demonstrated that there were several Geoffreys connected with Norwich and that Roger Wendover may have gotten them confused but, if so, we can only accept the remainder of the anecdote with grave reservations. Again, Matthew Paris reports that at the death of Archbishop Hubert Walter in 1205 John made the disrespectful statement, "Now for the first time I am king of England." The same historian relates that when John's talented justiciar, Geoffrey Fitz Peter, died in 1213, the monarch exclaimed, "By the feet of God now for the first time am I king and lord of England." Unless we wish to add redundancy to John's numerous sins, we must view both tales with extreme skepticism.

Still, even though such stories as these may be exaggerated or even false, John was the sort of person about whom they could be believed. He was a repellent, unlovable man who almost certainly murdered his nephew in a drunken rage, killed his hostages, starved his prisoners, and broke his word with exuberant abandon. Such behavior fell far short of the standards which twelfth- and thirteenth-century England demanded of its kings, and John's behavior cost him the respect of his subjects and ruined his effectiveness as a political and military leader.

Richard was successful in preserving his patrimony because his barons and lesser subjects trusted and admired him. John, although his authority was not compromised by long absences, failed because he lost his barons' confidence. They did not demand a living saint as their monarch — many of John's predecessors had been ruthless and cruel men — but they did demand consistency of policy and military prowess.   And John was, above all, inconstant.   He was capable of almost senseless lethargy, excessive caution, even panic.   The barons, who were willing to forgive much in an able warrior king, gave John the humiliating nickname "Softsword," and right or wrong the image had a fatal effect on John's leadership.   His barons, regarding him as suspicious and untrustworthy, often refused to join his military expeditions or fight his battles.   And the more they did so the more suspicious and untrustworthy John became. In the generations since the Norman Conquest, monarchy and nobility had often been at odds, but never before was the cleavage so sharp or so complete.

John's reign was not without its triumphs.   His military and diplomatic policies toward Wales, Scotland, and Ireland succeeded as never before.   He undertook to give England what was by the standards of the time a strong, well-organized navy. He devoted much intelligent attention to the royal administration.   He enforced the law strongly and—unless it was against his interest—justly.   Indeed, his accession marks the beginning of a great new epoch in the administrative history of the realm. Three of medieval England's most notable administrators worked under him and evidently received his full support: the chancellor-archbishop, Hubert Walter;   the justiciar, Geoffrey Fitz Peter;   and the treasurer, William of Ely.   Royal records became more abundant and more exact;   copies of the royal charters and other correspondence issuing from the Chancery now began to be preserved for the first time.

Like his predecessors, John was keenly acquisitive, and the tightening of royal law and administration was accompanied by a distinct increase in taxation.   Many of the unpopular practices of the Norman age were now temporarily revived—arbitrarily high reliefs, abuses of the king's authority over wardships and marriages—and to these were added new fiscal expedients such as higher and more frequent scutage levies and a greater incidence of taxes on rents and chattels.   England was prosperous and could doubtless afford such exploitation, and John, who had inherited an empty treasury from Richard, was in desperate need of funds.   Nevertheless, the overall effect of John's financial policies was to increase still further his unpopularity and to heighten his reputation as an arbitrary tyrant.

The Collapse of the Angevin Empire

When John acceded to the throne of England and assumed the leadership of the Angevin Empire in 1199, he faced a multitude of difficulties.[4] His reputation was already damaged, not so much by his earlier machinations against his crusading brother (filial disloyalty was by no means unprecedented) as by their utter futility. He inherited from Richard an effective but expensive and demanding military policy in France and an exhausted treasury. Moreover, he was confronted from the first with a dangerous rival to the throne in his nephew, Arthur of Brittany—son of his late brother Geoffrey, and grandson of Henry II. Since John managed to win England and most of the continental territories, Arthur quite naturally received the full support of the persistently troublesome Philip Augustus of France.

King Philip and Richard the Lion-Hearted had been at war when Richard died, and the hostilities continued into the early months of John's reign. In 1200 a truce was arranged, but Philip continued to await his opportunity to shatter the Angevin inheritance. The opportunity came a mere three months thereafter when John, on a tour of Aquitaine, suddenly and unexpectedly entered into marriage. The bride was a young girl in her early teens, Isabel, the heiress of the important Aquitainian county of Angoulême.

John's motives in selecting his young wife seem to have arisen from both love and politics. Isabel was apparently a charming girl, and Angoulême was one of the more troublesome feudal principalities in turbulent Aquitaine. By establishing firm control over Angoulême, John could extend his authority in southern France quite considerably. But as it happened, Isabel of Angoulême's hand was already promised to the neighboring lord of another important Aquitainian principality: Hugh the Brown of Lusignan. In making Isabel his wife, John had forestalled a dangerous feudal alliance between Lusignan and Angoulême, but he had also gravely offended the Lusignan family. According to the custom of the day, he might have assuaged the Lusignan hostility by granting Hugh the Brown certain territorial compensations, but the headstrong king chose to scorn the Lusignans and thereby earned their fierce enmity. In the months that followed, John alienated a number of other Aquitainian barons by seizing their lands and accusing them of treason. He was creating a dangerous legacy of hatred in his continental dominions.

In the spring of 1202 King Philip Augustus made his move. Taking advantage of an appeal by the Lusignans to his feudal court, Philip summoned John to Paris to answer their complaints.

---

[4] The collapse of the Angevin Empire under John is treated masterfully and in great detail by Sir Maurice Powicke, *The Loss of Normandy* (2nd ed., 1961).

As king of England John was subject to no one; but as duke of
Aquitaine and Normandy, count of Anjou, and lord of numerous
other continental principalities, he was the vassal of the king
of France. As such he was bound by feudal custom to answer
the summons to his lord's court, and when he refused to do so
Philip formally deprived him of his French fiefs. Philip Augustus had managed to place himself in the position of the good
lord whose vassal had wronged and defied him, and he sent his
armies against Normandy with the full force of feudal law
behind him.

The campaign went well for John at first. In a bold military stroke he succeeded in capturing Hugh the Brown and
several of Hugh's Lusignan kinsmen together with Arthur of
Brittany. But John nullified his momentous victory by his subsequent foolishness. He released the Lusignans in return for
a ransom and promises of loyalty which they did not keep, and
he apparently murdered his nephew, Arthur, in a drunken rage.
Conclusive proof of the murder has never been forthcoming,
but rumors of it spread quickly, and John's reputation was
darkened still further. Meanwhile, the king was abusing his
barons, friend and foe alike, and increasing his unpopularity
among his continental vassals.

Ultimately John had to depend on the loyalty of these
vassals for the defense of his continental inheritance, and his
mistreatment of them was a fatal error. In the course of the
year 1203 one castle after another fell to Philip Augustus while
John moved aimlessly and lethargically around Normandy
watching his patrimony crumble. In December 1203, with
much of Normandy still under his control, he left for England
apparently in panic. By the middle of 1204 all Normandy was
in King Philip's hands. Meanwhile Maine, Anjou, and indeed
all of John's former continental territories north of Aquitaine
had fallen to the French monarchy. All that remained were
portions of distant Aquitaine whose turbulent barons preferred
a remote and ineffective lord like John to a powerful monarch
near at hand. The Angevin Empire was now defunct; John had
sustained a monstrous military and political disaster.

England's French territories were not severed from her
completely and would not be until the mid-sixteenth century.
But from 1204 onward England was far more autonomous than
before and her kings tended to devote the bulk of their attention
to the island kingdom itself. Modern Englishmen, looking at
events in retrospect, are inclined to regard this development as
a fortunate one. To John, however, it was a profound humilia-
tion that had to be avenged. For the next decade he devoted
his considerable political and diplomatic talents to the creation
of an alliance system designed to crush Philip Augustus and
permit the reconquest of Normandy and Anjou.

The Struggle with the Papacy

In the meantime, John became involved in a violent conflict with the papacy over the selection of a new archbishop of Canterbury to replace Hubert Walter (d. 1205). The archbishopric of Canterbury had been a storm center in the reigns of William Rufus, Henry I, and Henry II. Under John, as on these previous occasions, the basic issue was ecclesiastical independence *versus* royal sovereignty over the English Church. It was, as before, a trial of strength between the claims of the universal Church and the English state. But far more than before, the Church-state struggle in John's reign was a direct confrontation between the English monarchy and the Roman papacy.

The Investiture Controversy had been settled long before in compromise, but the question of lay control over the appointments of bishops and abbots remained unresolved. The kings of England normally subscribed overtly to the policy of free canonical election but in fact controlled appointments to important offices in the English Church through subtle – or sometimes not so subtle – maneuvering. So long as royal influence was applied quietly and without serious opposition all was well, but should the king act clumsily and create an issue, the papacy might be expected to intervene in behalf of proper canonical practices. This was particularly true in the opening years of the thirteenth century when the papacy was occupied by Innocent III, a man of outstanding intelligence, energy, and self-confidence. Innocent III was history's most powerful pope, and it was John's misfortune to come to grips with such a man.[5]

Hubert Walter had been a brilliant and devoted royal servant but a less than inspiring archbishop. The monks of Canterbury, who enjoyed the traditional canonical privilege of electing the archbishop, were anxious not to have another royal tool on the Canterbury throne. And John was just as anxious to place one of his own loyal subordinates in the exalted position. Working quickly to forestall the king, the Canterbury monks elected one of their own number and sent a delegation to Rome to have him confirmed. Infuriated at this display of independence, John forced the monks to retract their choice, to elect his own man, and to send another delegation to Rome to obtain confirmation of the new candidate. Thus the issue had been

---

[5] A number of recent historical studies on Innocent III, many of them with conflicting views, have been published together in J. M. Powell (ed.), *Innocent III: Vicar of Christ or Lord of the World?* (Heath: *Problems in European Civilization,* 1963).

raised, and Innocent III was in a position to adjudicate the dispute. He made good use of his opportunity by repudiating both nominees and persuading the Canterbury monks in Rome — now a goodly number — to elect a churchman of his own choice. The new archbishop was a distinguished English scholar, Stephen Langton, who had been out of the country for some years teaching on the Continent.

John refused to accept an "outsider" and rebelled furiously against Innocent III's interference. Every archbishop of Canterbury in memory — even troublesome ones like Anselm and Thomas Becket — had been royal nominees, and John refused to give up the privileges of his royal forebears and abandon control of the Canterbury succession to the papacy. Accordingly, Stephen Langton was barred from entering England. Innocent III, for his part, regarded Langton's election as strictly canonical and gave him full support. As a result of the impasse Innocent laid England under interdict, suspending all church services and all sacraments except baptism and confession for the dying.

The interdict lasted for seven years. John survived this awesome ecclesiastical penalty remarkably well and even turned it to his financial advantage by confiscating ecclesiastical revenues. But in the end he was obliged to submit. Innocent III was threatening to depose John and was encouraging Philip Augustus to undertake an invasion of England. And John himself, whose grand design for the reconquest of Normandy and Anjou was reaching its climax, needed all the support he could obtain. Hence he made peace with the papacy in 1213 and in the following year the interdict was lifted. Stephen Langton was admitted to England and installed in his archbishopric, and John agreed to restore at least a portion of the confiscated revenues.

Having surrendered, John determined to salvage as much as possible from the situation by winning the full support of the previously hostile pope. Of his own accord, so it seems, he made England a papal fief and undertook to become Innocent III's vassal. He took the further step of vowing to lead a crusade against the Holy Land. The projected crusade never materialized for John always claimed more urgent business at home, but by his submission to papal vassalage and his crusading vow he succeeded in capturing the friendship of Rome. Consequently, historians have credited John with snatching victory from defeat. This interpretation seems doubtful, since Innocent III's future support was of no great use to John and since Archbishop Stephen Langton turned out to be a man of independent spirit who tended to favor the barons in their forthcoming struggle with the crown. Nevertheless, in 1214 John still had hopes of transcending his previous disasters. With the papal struggle at an end, he was ready at last to move decisively against Philip Augustus.

During the years of the interdict John had been building a coalition of French and German princes against the French monarchy. In 1214 the chief parties in the coalition were (1) Otto of Brunswick, John's nephew and a serious contestant for the throne of the Holy Roman Empire, (2) the counts of Flanders and certain neighboring principalities, and (3) John himself. After several false starts John set forth for the district of Poitou in northern Aquitaine with as many English knights as he could persuade to accompany him. His expedition was intended as one part of a grand design: he was to attack Philip Augustus through Poitou while his German and Flemish allies were to invade France from the northeast. The strategy was well-conceived but it ended disastrously. John subdued Poitou and incorporated a large number of Poitevin knights into his army, but when these knights encountered an army led by Philip Augustus's son they refused to fight, claiming that they could not engage in armed conflict against their overlord. John was obliged to retire in rage and frustration.

Philip Augustus himself led an army against John's German and Flemish allies and won an overwhelming victory over them at Bouvines. This crucial engagement extinguished John's last hope of recovering the lost continental fiefs. It also marked an exceedingly significant advance in the authority of the French monarchy which thereafter replaced Germany as the great power on the Continent. Thus the disintegration of the Angevin Empire in 1204 was confirmed by the momentous French triumph at Bouvines in 1214. John's careful plans were ruined by a battle at which he was not even present.

Magna Carta

John's alliance system had been cemented with subsidies and bribes which in turn had obliged the king to tax England ruthlessly. In the wake of Bouvines the calamitous failure of John's foreign policy was manifest to all. His prestige had never been lower, and the tax-ridden English barons were ready for rebellion. Early in 1215 the insurrection began, and by early summer it was obvious that the king could not contain it. Accordingly, in June 1215, John came to terms with his vassals on the meadow of Runnymede and affixed his seal to Magna Carta.[6]

---

[6] On the Great Charter see W. S. McKechnie, *Magna Carta* (revised ed., 1914), and, more recently, J. C. Holt, *Magna Carta* (1965).

The Great Charter was a product of elaborate negotiations involving John, Archbishop Stephen Langton, and English barons of various degrees of hostility toward the king. Its sixty-three clauses embraced the full spectrum of baronial grievances. Despite the intensely specific and practical nature of many of the provisions, collectively they reflect — at least by implication — the rudiments of a coherent political philosophy.

Historians have not always agreed on the implications of Magna Carta. Until fairly recently it was widely regarded as the fountainhead of English liberty and the bulwark of constitutional monarchy. Subsequent historians, reacting to this rather naive view, described Magna Carta as a reactionary document — an assertion of feudal particularism at the expense of the enlightened Angevin monarchy. In reality, the Great Charter was both feudal and constitutional. It looked backward and also pointed forward. It marks a profoundly important step in the transition from the ancient Germanic notion of sacred custom and the feudal idea of mutual contractual rights and obligations to the modern concept of limited monarchy and government under the law. Earlier efforts to limit the arbitrary exercise of royal authority — the revolts of Stephen's reign, for example — had tended to be parochial in spirit, anarchic in consequence, and conceptually confused. In 1215, the barons were once again seeking to curb an autocratic king — perhaps, indeed, the entire autocratic tradition of the Angevin dynasty — but in doing so they were moving, haltingly and doubtless unconsciously, toward constitutional monarchy. At this moment, for the first time, the English barons were beginning to represent a national viewpoint. They incorporated into Magna Carta the concept that the king was limited by tradition and custom in his relations with free Englishmen of every class — burghers and peasants as well as knights and barons: "No free man may be arrested or imprisoned or deprived of his land or outlawed or exiled or in any way brought to ruin, nor shall we go against him nor send others in pursuit of him, except by the legal judgment of his peers or by the law of the land." The exact nature of "the law of the land" remained vague, but the barons felt it important to assert that there was such a law, to be discovered in custom and traditional usages, and that the king was bound by it. The concept was expressed more precisely a generation later by the great legist, Henry Bracton: "The king should be under God and the law." And political philosophers of the twelfth and thirteenth centuries were drawing sharp distinctions between the king who abided by the law and the tyrant who abused and ignored it. In Magna Carta these notions receive practical expression.

John had said, "The law is in my mouth." Such a doctrine

was not only offensive to the feudal spirit but subversive to baronial interests. The king whose will was law could charge reliefs, levy scutages, and confiscate property as he pleased. Magna Carta forbade such practices in specific clauses: "Scutage and aid shall be levied in our kingdom only by the common council of our kingdom...." "No widow shall be forced to marry so long as she wishes to live without a husband." "No one shall be distrained to render greater service from a knight's fee or from any other free holding than is thence owed." It was with practical building blocks such as these that the structure of the English limited monarchy was built. For implied in the numerous specific and highly practical provisions of Magna Carta, reissued numerous times in the generations to come, is the momentous concept of an overarching body of law which circumscribed the power of the king.

There remained the problem of creating some kind of machinery to force the king to honor his concessions. Henry I had promised many things to his subjects in his coronation charter, but he ignored these promises once the crisis of his accession was passed. Clearly, mere royal promises were not enough to restrain an unscrupulous king with the full power of the royal administration behind him. The search for some institutional means of limiting royal authority in fact as well as in theory was to occupy England for centuries to come. The later Middle Ages found a tentative solution in parliament. The barons of 1215 employed a far cruder sanction: a watchdog committee of twenty-five barons who were to act against the king, if he should violate the Charter, by summoning the English people "to distrain and distress him in every way possible." In effect, the barons had no better reply to a royal repudiation of Magna Carta than the desperate sanction of popular and baronial rebellion.

Unfortunately the sanction had to be applied almost immediately. For as far as John was concerned, Magna Carta was merely an expedient to escape a temporary difficulty. He had no intention of honoring his promises, and he quickly obtained from his sympathetic papal overlord absolution from his oath to the barons which was, he argued, obtained under duress. Consequently, John ended his reign in the midst of a full-scale civil war. The barons appealed for aid to Philip Augustus, and the wily French monarch sent an army to England led by his son, Prince Louis. John died in 1216 with the French in London and the country wracked by war.

In one sense the barons were fighting to reverse an age-long tradition of royal absolutism which had begun with the Norman kings and been carried still further by their Angevin successors. But in another sense they were fighting against a single man – a monarch who had earned their opprobrium by his duplicity and ruthlessness. This fact is dramatically demonstrated by the speed with which the baronial insurrection dissolved in the wake of John's passing. In the words of an earlier historian, "John's death virtually ended the war.... [The French] enterprise was doomed to fail when the kingdom ceased to be divided against itself; and the one insuperable obstacle to the healing of its divisions was removed in the person of John." *

---

* Kate Norgate, *John Lackland* (London, 1902), p. 286.

Chapter 6

The **Thirteenth Century:**
MONARCHY AND COMMUNITY

Henry III (1216–1272): The Minority

WHEN King John died in 1216 he left as heir his nine-year-old son, Henry III, who governed and misgoverned England for the next fifty-six years.[1] During the first decade of his long reign Henry was merely a nominal king, for the royal government was in the hands of regents. Fortunately for the realm, the young king's regents included men of singular ability and generous purpose. One was the legate Cardinal Guala who exercised the right of guardianship in behalf of England's papal overlord. Another was William Marshall, England's most illustrious and chivalrous baron, a doughty and aged warrior who had risen from the tournament circuit to become earl of Pembroke and who had remained faithful to King John through all his various moods and fortunes. A third was the talented

---

[1] The most thorough recent work on this period is Sir Maurice Powicke, *The Thirteenth Century* (Oxford History of England, Vol. IV, 2nd ed., 1962). It is detailed and formidable. Another magisterial work by the same author is *King Henry III and the Lord Edward* (2 vols., 1947). Bertie Wilkinson, *Constitutional*

justiciar, Hubert de Burgh, who had ascended from a minor knightly family to the highest post in the royal administration and had won for himself the earldom of Kent. These three men, together with several others, comprised a select group of leading barons and high ecclesiastics who ruled England in the name of the child king. Together they worked to heal England's old wounds and restore unity. Louis of France was forced to abandon his campaign, Magna Carta was reissued, and England was freed of strife and permitted to enjoy unimpeded the buoyant prosperity of the age.

As the years passed, the personnel of the governing group changed. Cardinal Guala left the country in 1218 and William Marshall died the following year. In the meantime Archbishop Stephen Langton, having returned from a visit to Rome, assumed an important position in the regency. In the early 1220s Langton and Hubert de Burgh were the chief instigators of royal policy, and although Hubert was the object of a certain amount of baronial jealousy the regency government continued, by and large, to prosper. At length, in 1227, the young king declared himself of age. At nineteen, he felt ready to assume the responsibilities of government, and in retrospect it can perhaps be said that he was as ready at nineteen as he would ever be. Stephen Langton died the following year, but the young king remained more or less under the influence of Hubert de Burgh until Hubert's fall from power in 1232.

One of the chief reasons for Hubert's downfall was his opposition to an ill-considered military campaign which Henry III was determined to undertake. Never one to permit good advice to temper his impulses, Henry was a man who longed for the unhampered exercise of the royal prerogative yet knew not how to use it wisely. For although possessed of many talents, he was an uninspiring leader and an ineffective king. He was intelligent, even learned, but not in matters of statecraft. He was pious, but his piety was narrow rather than profound. He was a man of discrimination, but only in judging art, not men. Generous with his friends, loyal to his papal overlord, he was suspicious of nearly everybody else, and his moody disposition, his mercurial temperament, and his sarcastic tongue lost him the respect of his barons. At times he could seem firm, but his firmness was actually mere obstinacy. He had the will to rule without the skill to rule, and his reign, although long, was inglorious.

History of England, 1216–1399 (3 vols., 1948–58), is lively and provocative. The constitutional history of the thirteenth century is skillfully treated in F. Thompson, *The First Century of Magna Carta* (1925).

The Civilization of the Thirteenth Century

Despite the petulant incapacity of its king, England in the reign of Henry III was participating fully in the vibrant climax of high medieval civilization. Although centered on France, the culture of the High Middle Ages made a profound impact on England as well. On both sides of the Channel the expansion of arable lands proceeded at a rapid pace. The towns continued to grow in size, in wealth, and in privileges. Commerce increased in scale and intensity, and the economy was kept lively by a process of gradual inflation. The great trade of English wool for Flemish cloth grew ever larger, while at the same time a flourishing cloth industry began to develop in England itself. With the rising productivity of English fields, more and more surplus grain was produced which served not only as a significant export commodity but also as a cushion against famine years. The peasantry itself seems to have profited only modestly from this prosperity, but the lesser knights (the later gentry) and the townsmen became increasingly affluent and important, and the greater barons now lived on a scale previously undreamed of. The grim, cramped castles of the eleventh century gave way to elaborate stone fortifications and ample and relatively well-furnished manor houses.

Throughout the twelfth and thirteenth centuries the birthrate of all the classes seems to have been rising while, as a result of increased food production and greater internal security, the death rate was diminishing. Consequently, the population of England appears to have at least doubled between the late eleventh century and the late thirteenth. The England of Domesday Book had a population of perhaps a million and a half, whereas later thirteenth-century England contained approximately three million inhabitants who were generally better-fed than their eleventh-century ancestors. These statistics, although exceedingly approximate, testify unmistakably to England's notable economic progress in the post-Conquest centuries.

The economic vigor of the thirteenth century was accompanied by a remarkably intense cultural creativity which saw the significant artistic and literary traditions of twelfth-century Europe develop into rich maturity. In the field of architecture, for example, the reign of Henry III, and that of his illustrious French contemporary, St. Louis IX, marked the apogee of the Gothic style. England experienced perhaps the supreme moment in her architectural history, and the moment was frozen and immortalized in austere and superbly proportioned cathedrals such as those at Salisbury and Lincoln, and in the graceful splendor of Westminster Abbey, reconstructed under the per-

High Gothic architecture: nave and choir, Salisbury Cathedral (1220–58).

sonal direction of Henry III himself. In structures such as these the soaring lines of the pointed arches, the brilliant colors of the stained-glass windows, and the somber realism of the sculpture combine to produce an integrated and deeply moving work of art.[2]

The literature of the age, although less significant than its architecture, is nevertheless impressive. The growing lay literacy of the twelfth century had by now reached the point where written records were being kept at many baronial courts and manors. Secular vernacular literature flourished in a variety of forms: the political song, the round (England's first known round, "Sumer is icumen in," dates from this period), and most notably, the romance. English was becoming gradually more important as a literary vehicle, but French retained its dominance in England and in the romance it found a congenial form of expression.

The romance is a synthesis of two earlier literary forms: the *chanson de geste* (song of great deeds) and the lyric poem. The former was immensely popular in northern France and England during the Anglo-Norman era. It was a rough and bellicose narrative poem that stressed the heroic virtues of loyalty and warlike prowess typical of the earlier feudal aristocracy. Its characteristics are splendidly exemplified in the Song of Roland, an exciting and rather bloodthirsty tale of a battle between a powerful Moslem army and a small knightly band led by one of Charlemagne's loyal vassals. The Song of Roland is said to have been a favorite of William the Conqueror himself.

The lyric poem, a product of the very different cultural milieu of southern France, was sometimes witty, often romantic, but seldom bellicose. In the course of the later twelfth century, the southern lyric, with its emphasis on idealized love and refined behavior, was transmitted by aristocratic southerners such as Eleanor of Aquitaine and her daughter Marie, Countess of Champagne, into the courts of northern Europe. There, it contributed to the softening and romanticizing of the knightly ideal and to a significant transformation in poetic expression from the rough and intensely masculine epic style of the *chanson de geste* to the thirteenth-century romance. This new literary style was narrative in form like the *chanson de geste*, but romantic in mood like the lyric poem. The thirteenth-century

---

[2] Two excellent works that relate Gothic architecture to the cultural background of the High Middle Ages are Erwin Panofsky, *Gothic Architecture and Scholasticism* (1951), and Emile Mâle, *The Gothic Image* (new ed., 1958). On a somewhat more popular level see the beautifully illustrated book by Jean Gimpel, *The Cathedral Builders* (new ed., 1961).

romances drew heavily for their subject matter on a series of
tales relating to the court of the half-legendary British monarch, King Arthur—tales which originated in England and were
beautifully and imaginatively developed by poets in France and
Germany. The sensitivity of the thirteenth-century romance,
contrasting sharply with the crude power of the *chanson de
geste*, attests to the growing sophistication of medieval European civilization.

Secular culture achieved much in the thirteenth century,
yet it remained deeply influenced by the ideals of Christianity.
The Church remained a powerful force not only in the daily
lives of its members but also in the arenas of regional and international politics. The papacy reached the height of its power,
and controlled the universal Church as never before through its
legates, its authority over bishops and abbots, and its superbly
developed central administrative machinery. But success and
affluence are always likely to present dangers to a spiritual institution, and there can be no question but that the thirteenth-
century Church had lost its lean and hungry look. Its prelates
were becoming increasingly absorbed in the fascinating problems of political power at the expense of their spiritual and
pastoral responsibilities, and pious reformers could point to
shocking instances of corruption. An archiepiscopal visitation
to a small thirteenth-century Norman nunnery yielded these
unedifying data:

> Johanna de Alto Villari kept going out alone with a man
> named Gayllard, and within a year she had a child by
> him. The subprioress is suspected with Thomas the
> carter, her sister Idonia, with Crispinatus, and the prior
> of Gisorcium is always coming to the convent for Idonia.
> Philippa of Rouen is suspected with a priest of Suentre,
> of the diocese of Chartres; Margurita, the treasuress,
> with Richard de Genville, a cleric; Agnes de Fontenei,
> with a priest of Guerreville, of the diocese of Chartres. . . .
> All wear their hair improperly and perfume their veils.
> Jacqueline came back pregnant from visiting a certain
> chaplain who was expelled from his house as a result of
> this. Agnes de Monsec was suspected with the same
> chaplain. Emengard and Johanna de Alto Villari beat
> each other. The prioress is drunk almost every night.

Instances such as these are far from typical, however.
Widespread ecclesiastical corruption was a product of subsequent centuries. The great weakness of the Church in the
thirteenth century was not vice but complacency. If there were

licentious nuns in Normandy there was also a stern and pious
archbishop to discipline them. The Church retained a powerful
impulse toward piety and reform which manifested itself in
the spiritual dedication of countless lay and clerical believers,
in the exemplary lives of many great prelates and, above all,
in the dynamic activities of the new mendicant orders.[3]

Arising in the early thirteenth century, these orders – the
Franciscan and the Dominican – brought new dynamism to the
spiritual life of Western Christendom. The Franciscan and
Dominican friars lived by a rule, as monks did, but unlike their
monastic predecessors they shunned the walls of the monastery
and traveled far and wide to preach among the people – especially the people of the rising towns who were exhibiting a
spiritual thirst which the traditional ecclesiastical organization
could not quench. The friars dedicated themselves to chastity,
obedience to their superior, and both individual and corporate
poverty. In the beginning the Franciscan and Dominican orders
had no property at all, and even though their immense success
and popularity soon forced them, in the interest of organizational
coherence, to accept jurisdiction over houses, churches, and
small parcels of land, they never remotely approached the vast
landed wealth of the earlier Benedictines or Cistercians. In
England, as on the Continent, the mendicant orders brought
vigorous new life to the Church by their fervent, compassionate
preaching, their unpretentious holiness, and their boundless
enthusiasm. To these virtues the Franciscans added still another: the gay and artless simplicity which they inherited from
their remarkable founder, St. Francis of Assisi (d. 1226).

Despite their original simplicity, however, the Franciscans
were quick to join the Dominicans in enriching the intellectual
life of the European universities which were now rising to great
prominence. Several important universities – most notably,
Paris, Bologna, and Oxford – had arisen in the vibrant intellectual environment of the twelfth century but became organized
and established educational institutions only in the thirteenth.
Bologna was Europe's greatest center for the study of civil and
canon law. Paris excelled in philosophy and theology, which
were regarded as the supreme intellectual disciplines of the day
and which the scholars of the thirteenth century developed and
elaborated in brilliant fashion. Franciscan and Dominican theologians of remarkable ability graced the Paris faculty which
included, at one time or another, the three most profound philo-

---

[3] On English monasticism in general, one should consult the works of Dom David
Knowles: *The Monastic Order in England, 943–1216* (1940), and *The Religious
Orders in England, I, 1216–c. 1340* (1948).

sophical minds of the age: the Dominicans St. Albertus Magnus and St. Thomas Aquinas, and the Franciscan minister-general, St. Bonaventure. In his severely analytical *Summa Theologica* and *Summa Contra Gentiles*, St. Thomas Aquinas created an exhaustive, compelling fusion of reason and Christian revelation which brought medieval theology to a point of mature synthesis and culmination. His intellectual system stimulated vigorous controversy in its own time and has done so ever since, but it has proven remarkably durable and retains, to this day, its power to win intellectual converts. It is an impressive illustration of the profundity of thirteenth-century culture and, indeed, one of the great achievements in the history of thought.

England shared in the intense intellectual life of the thirteenth century, particularly through its two universities – Oxford and Cambridge. Here, as at Paris and Bologna, distinguished faculties offered courses in law, medicine, theology, and the liberal arts.* Among the various subdivisions of philosophy was one known as "natural philosophy" which was roughly equivalent to what we know as science. And it was in science, above all else, that England made its distinctive contribution to medieval learning. Indeed, it has recently been argued that the real progenitor of modern European science was the great English scholar-churchman Robert Grosseteste (d. 1253), bishop of Lincoln and first chancellor of Oxford University.[4] A master of Greek, a theologian, an ecclesiastical statesman active in the political affairs of his day, and a keen student of both Platonic and Aristotelian philosophy, Grosseteste did his great pioneering work in the field of scientific methodology. His own attempts to explain such phenomena as comets, rainbows, and color seem crude by later standards, but in his emphasis on mathematics and, above all, his articulation of a coherent experimental method, he prepared the way for the impressive scientific advances of subsequent centuries. Grosseteste wrote extensively on methodology, outlining a procedure that contained most of the crucial ingredients of the modern scientific approach: careful observation, the framing of a hypothesis, and the checking of the hypothesis against the actual behavior of natural phenomena – a process akin to what we would now term experimental verification. Sound methodology is basic to science, and in Grosseteste's works it was set forth in detailed rational

---

* The "liberal arts" in medieval curricula were seven in number: arithmetic, geometry, astronomy, music, grammar, rhetoric, and dialectic (logical philosophy).
[4] A. C. Crombie, *Robert Grosseteste and the Origins of Experimental Science* (1953), presents the fascinating argument that Grosseteste was the key figure in the articulation of modern scientific methodology.

form for the first time. Grosseteste cannot be regarded as the father of science, for he drew heavily from his Greek and Islamic predecessors, but from the western European standpoint it is surely no exaggeration to regard him as its foster father.

Robert Grosseteste exerted a deep influence on his successors, particularly among English scholars of the Franciscan order. Although no Franciscan himself, he was instrumental in establishing the order at Oxford, and Franciscan friars were among his most devoted students. The scientific orientation of English Franciscanism, deriving from Grosseteste's inspiration and perhaps also from the deep love of nature exhibited by St. Francis himself, is particularly notable in the works of Roger Bacon. Roger was a Franciscan friar of the later thirteenth century whose extensive writings contain, alongside a good deal of superstitious fancy, a passion for experimentation and for the application of mathematics to scientific investigation: "Reasoning does not disclose these matters; on the contrary, experiments are required, performed on a large scale with instruments and by other necessary means." At times, Roger Bacon almost assumes the role of a scientific prophet: "Experimental science controls the conclusions of all other sciences. It discloses truths which reasoning from general principles [the favored method of the Paris theologians] would never have discovered. Finally, it sets us on the way to marvelous inventions which will change the face of the world." Is it mere coincidence that the land which produced Robert Grosseteste and Roger Bacon would one day produce Isaac Newton?

An age that achieved so much in the realms of art, literature, and thought might well be expected to demonstrate its creativity in politics as well. And such was the case. The thirteenth century witnessed a momentous growth in the power of the French monarchy, beginning with King Philip Augustus's conquest of much of the old Angevin Empire and his stunning victory at Bouvines, continuing with the distinguished reign of the saint-king, Louis IX, and concluding with the accession of the powerful, ruthless Philip IV (the Fair) whose royal administration achieved an unprecedented degree of efficiency and centralization. Drawing from the great heritage of Roman law, and drawing also from the precocious administrative institutions which the Angevin monarchs left behind them in Normandy, the Capetian kings of France made their kingdom the richest, mightiest, and most illustrious in Europe.

Yet France, with its vast extent and its legacy of local particularism, remained less centralized, less subordinated to its royal government, than England. For England, too, made impressive progress during the thirteenth century in law and administration. This progress will be discussed at length in the pages to come. For now, suffice it to say that the achievements of the twelfth century were continued and developed. The rising affluence of the lesser knights and the burghers was accompanied by a growing sense of political responsibility and an increasing participation in local administration. The shire courts, which were coming to play an ever greater role in the royal judicial system, were operated by members of the knightly gentry. The town governments and town courts fell more and more under the control of the burghers themselves—in particular, the wealthy merchants and master craftsmen. Accordingly, political responsibility was slowly filtering down from the great magnates to the prosperous middle group of shire gentry and well-to-do townsmen. The great majority of the population remained relatively impotent and inarticulate, but the political base was nevertheless broadening. Even the semifree serfs became slightly more involved in the affairs of the kingdom. For prior to the thirteenth century only freemen were allowed the privilege of bearing arms—indeed, the possession of arms had traditionally been a mark of free status—whereas in the thirteenth century arms were permitted to the serfs, who thereby assumed some small share of the responsibility for defending the land and maintaining internal order. It would be hazardous to make too much of this new privilege, which was also a new obligation, but it would be equally dangerous to ignore it.

Out of this diffusion of responsibility there arose a concept vital to the politics of the age and to the future development of English constitutional government: the notion of a "community of the realm." The concept of "community" by no means embraced all Englishmen. At first it was restricted to the king and his barons, but gradually it came to include the prosperous and increasingly responsible members of the lesser knightly class and the burghers. These groups contributed much to the operation and enrichment of the kingdom, and it was felt that they ought to have some voice in its governance. There was much disagreement as to precisely what their political role should be, but as the century progressed the notion became firmly rooted that a ruler who ignored the interests of the "community of the realm" was no king but a tyrant.

This notion was by no means subversive to the continued growth of a centralized government. The issue was not whether a strong royal administration should exist but how it should be controlled. In the course of the thirteenth century the struggle for control over the central administrative machinery was at times violent, but the machinery itself became steadily more elaborate and efficient. And the expansion of the royal bureaucracy was accompanied by a parallel growth in the scope and sophistication of royal law.

The reign of Henry III produced an impressive, systematic legal treatise—Henry de Bracton's *On the Laws and Customs of England*—a thoughtful and humane study which far transcended Glanville's work of the previous century and illustrated clearly that English law had come of age. Bracton, at once a widely experienced royal judge and a serious student of the principles of Roman law, devoted his treatise chiefly to an analysis of the vast accumulation of precedents on which the English common law was based, but he was able also to look beyond the precedents themselves to what he regarded as the fundamental principles that lay behind them. One such principle was the notion that the king, although subject to the law himself, was the ultimate source of justice in the realm. Henry I and Henry II had been moving toward this goal, and in Bracton's time it was coming ever closer to realization.

The thirteenth century saw the establishment of a coherent and comprehensive legal system, based on royal courts now staffed for the first time by what can be described as professional judges, and given a sturdy juridical and philosophical foundation by Bracton's great treatise. With the evolution of a strong royal bureaucracy, a structured and professional judiciary, and the vital concept of community, feudal monarchy was being left far behind. Yet it was the contractual assumptions of feudalism and cognate systems—the notion of subjects' rights before the lord king—that gave the English monarchy of the thirteenth century its tone and its direction.

Henry III: *The Limitation of the Royal Prerogative*

The age of Henry III was a crucial epoch in the history of English constitutional development. The historian G. O. Sayles has aptly described the reign as "a commentary upon the Great Charter." More than that, it was a commentary on one of the central problems inherent in Magna Carta and in medieval political theory as a whole: Given that the king's authority is bound by customary limitations—that "the king should be under God and the law," as Bracton put it—how might such a principle be translated into workable political institutions? The answer was gradually found in the concept that the king should govern in the interests and with the cooperation of the "community of the realm."

English government had always been, at least to some extent, the product of a dialogue between monarchy and community. The Anglo-Saxon kings acted on important occasions in consultation with their Witan; the Norman and Angevin kings usually summoned their Great Councils to advise them on cru-

cial decisions. And more and more, the monarchy was coming
to depend on the more responsible burghers and shire knights
who attended to the details of local government. But the Witan
and Great Council had neither a veto power nor a standardized
membership, and if a king chose to abuse his barons, ignore their
advice, and overtax his subjects, there was seldom any recourse
short of rebellion. The search for some such recourse underlay
the politics of Henry III's reign, and toward its end the barons
— many of them at least — were beginning to conclude that their
greatest hope lay in the frequent convening of Great Councils
known as parliaments.

If parliament can be said to have arisen in any one century, that century was undoubtedly the thirteenth. Yet even at
the century's end it was not generally understood that an institution existed known as parliament. Rather there was an institution known as the *curia regis* — the Great Council — which met
with increasing frequency, and the word "parliament" was used
to describe the meetings themselves. Accordingly, as Christopher Brooke has expressed it, the thirteenth-century "parliament" was not an *institution* but an *occasion*. Only later was
"parliament" used to describe the Great Council itself, meeting
with growing regularity, exercising increasingly specific powers,
governing jointly with the king. In the thirteenth century, all
this lay in the future.

Much effort has been devoted to the problem of what, precisely, constituted a parliament in the thirteenth century. What
were its functions? What classes were represented in it? Scholars have now learned that no specific answers can be supplied
to these questions — that, indeed, the questions themselves are
inappropriate. For in the thirteenth century, "parliament" was
an exceedingly amorphous concept. The Great Council, meeting in a parliament, might include only the leading magnates
and prelates; or the magnates and prelates together with
knightly representatives of the shires; or the magnates and
prelates together with representatives from the towns; or all
these groups at once. Its functions were equally varied: it
might advise the king on some important political problem,
render its support to the monarch in some crisis, judge important legal cases, grant the king an extraordinary tax, or do any
number of other things. We must beware, above all else, of
seeking to apply strict definitions to the parliament of the thirteenth century.

At first, the word "parliament" meant simply a meeting of
any kind at which views were exchanged — a parley. The term
is used in the eleventh-century Song of Roland to describe a
mere dialogue. By the twelfth century it seems to have acquired
the meaning of a larger deliberative meeting. It is used, for

example, in connection with Henry II's dispute with Becket at Northampton and John's confrontation with his barons on the occasion of Magna Carta. Meetings of the Great Council could likewise be called "parliaments" as, indeed, could meetings of the Small Council. It was only in the later thirteenth century that "parliament" came to apply specifically to an important meeting of the Great Council, and not until the fourteenth century did the term acquire any strict institutional significance.

The evolution of the concept of "parliament" in the thirteenth century was a product of political trends that were affecting all Europe, but in England the process was stimulated by Henry III's intransigence and the consequent alienation between the monarch and his barons. The magnates, for their part, were anxious to transform the implications of Magna Carta into living reality and to reverse the long trend toward royal absolutism that had been so evident under the Norman and Angevin kings. In Henry III they saw another despot, and an unheroic, incompetent one at that.

As the rift between King Henry and his magnates increased, he tended more and more to forgo their advice and exclude them from participation in the central government. And the more he did so, the more the rift widened. Particularly after about 1234 the king surrounded himself with his own professional administrators and with favorites whom the barons described contemptuously as "foreigners"—relatives of his wife, Eleanor of Provence, who were only too anxious to enrich themselves through royal favor in this rich island kingdom. The Great Council of magnates and prelates was all but ignored.

Of course Henry II was by no means the first king to rule without serious regard for the advice of his great magnates. The English political tradition was as yet sufficiently amorphous so that a king could rule arbitrarily as long as his policies were reasonably successful and palatable to the barons and as long as he did not squeeze them too hard. King John failed and squeezed, and Magna Carta was the result. Henry III's nonbaronial government engendered a vigorous reaction for two reasons: (1) His policies—which involved huge, chimerical foreign schemes and lavish spending—seemed ill-conceived and subversive to baronial interests; he was obliged to appeal frequently for baronial aids, and the barons granted them with increasing reluctance. (2) The barons were mindful of the recent example, during the regency, of a flourishing, successful government which had been based on baronial advice and council. This memory sharpened in the barons' minds the traditional notion that they were the king's "natural counselors."

The Crisis of 1258–1265

For nearly a generation, resentment and conflict grew between Henry III and his magnates, but the king managed to muddle through from crisis to crisis without major challenge from the baronage. At length, however, in 1258, a crisis arose that proved to be too much for King Henry, and as a consequence the royal government was forced to undergo a profound reorientation.

The crisis of 1258 came as a direct result of Henry III's grandiose ambitions in the field of foreign affairs. For a century the papacy had been engaged in a great power struggle with the Hohenstaufen dynasty of Holy Roman Emperors. Following the death of the brilliant and dangerous Hohenstaufen emperor Frederick II in 1250, the pope sought Henry III's cooperation in dividing the vast districts that the Hohenstaufens had ruled. In the 1190s this dynasty had added the rich Norman kingdom of Sicily and southern Italy to its extensive dominions which already included Germany and northern Italy. With the old Holy Roman Empire to its north and Sicily to its south the papacy was literally surrounded by the power of the hostile Hohenstaufens. To be sure, Germany was rent with princely particularism, and imperial authority in northern Italy was dissolving before the fierce independence of rising city-states. Still, the papacy was determined to sever Sicily and southern Italy from the remainder of the Holy Roman Empire and place it under a new dynasty. So it was that in 1254 the pope offered the Sicilian crown * to Edmund, the second son of King Henry III.

The offer was less generous than it might seem. The pope had been trying for several years to dispose of the Sicilian crown, and two important princes had already rejected it. They were probably wise to do so. Henry III accepted the crown for his son, but was obliged, in return, to assume the enormous debt which the papacy had incurred in connection with its campaigns against the Hohenstaufens in Sicily. It was a sum in excess of ninety thousand pounds, virtually as great as King Richard the Lion-Hearted's immense ransom. To make matters worse, the years following 1254 saw the actual control of the Sicilian kingdom fall into the hands of an able bastard Hohenstaufen named Manfred. Edmund's hopes of winning a kingdom to go with his new crown seemed dim indeed.

But once committed to paying the huge papal debt Henry III could not renege without great difficulty and embarrassment. He found himself committed to a ruinously expensive and fruit-

* The dominions of the king of Sicily included southern Italy as well.

less venture. When he fell behind in his payments the Vicar of Christ threatened to excommunicate him. Henry was obliged to turn to his barons for financial aid, and they agreed to help him only in return for radical political concessions. In 1258 he surrendered to the demands of his magnates and allowed them a significant degree of control over the royal administration.

Henry's Sicilian dream cost him dearly. It emptied his treasury and obliged him to sacrifice his royal independence which he prized so highly. Moreover, it forced him to come to terms at last with the French monarchy. In the Treaty of Paris (1259) he formally recognized the Capetian dominion over the former territories of the Angevin Empire in northern France and did homage to St. Louis for Gascony and other southern French lands that had remained more or less under English control after the catastrophes of John's reign. And in the end, Henry lost Sicily, too. For the papacy eventually found a more stalwart champion against Manfred in the person of Charles of Anjou, younger brother of King Louis IX. It was Charles rather than Edmund who finally won Sicily and southern Italy from the Hohenstaufens.

In 1258, however, the fate of Sicily was still uncertain, and Henry III was obliged to make terms with his magnates. His submission took the form of a letter in which he granted

> that by twelve faithful men of our council already elected, and by twelve other faithful men elected by the nobles, who are to convene at Oxford one month after the coming feast of Pentecost, the condition of our kingdom shall be ordered, rectified, and reformed in keeping with what they shall think it best to enact for the honor of God, for our faith, and for the good of our kingdom. . . . And whatever is ordained in this manner by the twenty-four elected by both sides and sworn to the undertaking — or by the majority of them — we will observe inviolably. . . . Moreover, the aforesaid earls and barons have promised that on the completion of the business stated above they will in good faith endeavor to arrange that a common aid is rendered us by the community of our realm.

The deliberations of the twenty-four men resulted in an agreement known as the Provisions of Oxford (1258) which sought at a blow to make the "community of the realm" a political reality. First of all, there were to be at least three formal meetings of the Great Council—three "parliaments"—each year, and they were to include in their membership not only the chosen counselors of the king but also twelve men "elected" by the "community"—i.e., selected by the magnates. It was further stipulated that "the community shall regard as binding whatever these twelve shall do." Moreover, a small permanent Council of Fifteen was established, largely baronial in membership, with the power of "advising the king in good faith regarding the government of the kingdom and all matters pertaining to the king or the kingdom, and of amending and reforming everything that they shall consider in need of amendment or reform." The Council of Fifteen was given a powerful voice in the royal administration through its power to appoint three of the great officers of state: the chancellor, the treasurer, and the justiciar. It had authority over the Exchequer and worked with the king to supervise the activities of sheriffs and other local officials.

The Provisions of Oxford also included a number of administrative reforms, designed particularly to correct abuses in property law, and additional reforms of a similar nature were established in a corollary document, the Provisions of Westminster (1259). In general, the magnates accepted the momentous advances in the central administration over the past several generations. By no means blinded by local particularism, they merely wished to share in the control of the administrative machinery until a new and more trustworthy king should accede to the throne. They sought what they conceived to be good government—government in the baronial interest—and they had despaired of enjoying such government so long as Henry III ruled unimpeded. Their methods of limiting royal authority—the frequent parliaments and the Council of Fifteen—represent a far more enlightened and mature approach than that of John's barons in 1215.

Still, their solution was exceedingly radical. The central administrative machinery remained as powerful as ever, but the king himself was reduced to a position of virtual parity with the greater magnates. Many barons, deeply troubled over the emasculation of kingship which the Provisions of Oxford implied, gradually became disenchanted with their more radical leaders. In time the experiment in limited monarchy became racked by baronial dissension, and by 1262 Henry III found himself in a position to abolish the Provisions altogether. Absolved of his oaths by the pope, he undertook once again to rule by his own authority.

Some of Henry's barons had evidently hoped that the king might learn from his misfortunes. They were badly disappointed, for Henry's renewed personal rule was just as willful, just as cavalier, as ever. Consequently, in 1263 baronial opposition asserted itself once again.

The leader of the insurgents in 1263 was Simon de Montfort, Earl of Leicester and brother-in-law of the king. Earl Simon was a remarkable character—brilliant, imaginative, and self-confident almost to the point of arrogance. He was a native of southern France who came to England earlier in Henry III's reign. Simon had once been a close friend of the king, but in time he, like so many other barons, was alienated by Henry's erratic personality. Simon was one of the powers behind the Provisions of Oxford, and had served on the Council of Fifteen. When Henry rescinded the Provisions in 1262 Simon had been forced into exile, but he returned in 1263 to lead the disaffected barons.

Toward the close of 1263 king and magnates agreed to submit their dispute to the arbitration of the saintly and universally respected Louis IX of France. St. Louis's impartiality was famous, but he had a profound respect for the prerogatives of royalty, and the baronial notions of cooperative government and "community of the realm" were entirely beyond his experience. His verdict, which was known as the "Mise of Amiens" (1264), constituted a ringing denunciation of the baronial cause:

> We suppress and annul all the aforesaid provisions, ordinances, statutes, and obligations, by whatever name, and all that has followed from them. . . . We also decree and ordain that the said king, of his own will, may freely appoint, dismiss, and remove the justiciar, chancellor, treasurer, counselors, lesser justices, sheriffs, and any other officers and ministers of his kingdom and household, as he was used and able to do prior to the time of the aforesaid provisions.

Left without a scrap of their hard-fought program, the baronial opposition felt that they had no recourse but to take up arms.

The rebellion of 1264–65 was not simply a struggle between king and baronage. For as has been suggested, the barons were by no means of one mind. Few of them approved of Henry III, but many had a keen respect for the royal office and distrusted the radical goals of the opposition leaders. Nobody, of course, wished to abolish the monarchy—the day of Oliver Cromwell was yet four centuries in the future—but insurgents such as Simon de Montfort would not hesitate to govern the realm in the name of a captive king.

Thus, there were barons on both sides, and not a few magnates switched teams in the midst of the struggle. The opposition was led by Simon de Montfort, the royalist force by Henry III's eldest son, the Lord Edward, now growing into stalwart manhood. There were many who looked longingly at this intelligent and chivalrous young warrior, wishing that he, not his father, were their monarch.

The first phase of the rebellion culminated in a pitched battle at Lewes in May 1264. The Lord Edward acquitted himself well, but the insurgents won the field. Henry III was obliged to submit to the rebellious magnates, and the Lord Edward was held hostage to insure the king's cooperation. For the next fifteen months Simon de Montfort was the *de facto* ruler of England, and although he ruled in Henry's name, the king had no voice whatever in the affairs of the realm.

Simon de Montfort attempted seriously to govern in the spirit of the Provisions of Oxford. He summoned parliaments frequently, and strove to broaden their representative structure. He shared his authority with two colleagues, the earl of Gloucester and the bishop of Chichester, and the three were assisted by a permanent council akin to the former Council of Fifteen but now reduced to nine members. Nobody could justly accuse Earl Simon of harboring dictatorial ambitions, but many remained deeply suspicious of his cavalier attitude toward the royal dignity. All in all, his government was far too radical a departure from the traditions of his age. As the months went by, he saw his party eroded by disaffection and his widespread support dissolve. His colleague, the earl of Gloucester, joined the royal cause, and in May 1265 the Lord Edward escaped from imprisonment and began to raise an army. At the battle of Evesham, in August 1265, Simon de Montfort's army was routed and Simon himself was slain. The experiment in baronial government was at an end, and Henry III resumed his authority.

King Henry was to live another seven years, but during this final phase of his troubled reign authority passed more and more into the hands of his able son and heir. The issues of the long crisis of 1258–65 were settled in the royal favor in the Dictum of Kenilworth (1266) and the Statute of Marlborough (1267), but the Lord Edward had the wisdom to be a gracious victor and to respect the interests and opinions of the "community." He rejected the severe limitations of royal power imposed by the Provisions of Oxford, but accepted the enlightened legal reforms which the barons at Oxford had urged. Hence, England was at peace with herself once again, and by the time Edward succeeded to the throne on his aged father's death in 1272 he had captured the hearts of his subjects.

The Evolution of Parliament

The struggles of Henry III's reign and the far-flung wars of Edward I's both contributed significantly to the evolution of

parliament.[5]   The institution arose, as we have seen, out of the
Great Council.   At the opening of the thirteenth century a convening of the Great Council was regarded merely as one of many
different kinds of "parliaments," but by the century's end the
term had come to be restricted almost exclusively to Great
Council meetings.   The parliaments of the thirteenth century
had many functions — consultative, judicial, political, and financial — but it would probably be safe to assume that the financial
motive was basic to the development of the parliamentary idea.
Ultimately, parliament's financial role was destined to be the
key to its power, but in the thirteenth century that role was
limited merely to the custom of approving extraordinary taxes.
"Scutage and aid shall be levied in our kingdom only by the
common council of our kingdom."   Such had been one of John's
promises to his barons in Magna Carta.   And as the thirteenth
century progressed, the concept of consent came to assume ever
increasing importance.   In 1297 the monarchy made the explicit concession that no extraordinary taxes would be levied by
the king without the assent of the whole "community of the
realm."   The "community" expressed its assent to uncustomary
taxes through meetings of the Great Council — through parliaments.   As the king's customary revenues became increasingly
inadequate to meet the rising costs of administration and war,
parliamentary grants became ever more essential.

It should not be concluded that the nonfiscal functions of
parliaments were merely a facade.   Far from it.   But under an
antibaronial monarch such as Henry III, parliaments tended to
be cherished chiefly for their financial support to the crown.
Their advice was not wanted.   This tendency is illustrated bla-
tantly in the parliament which Henry III summoned in 1237.
He put no business whatever before his barons on that occasion
but merely asked them to approve an aid.   It was the deep resentment engendered by this sort of royal treatment of the great
magnates — the "natural counselors" of the king — that underlay
the Provisions of Oxford and the crisis of 1258–65.

One of the most significant parliamentary developments
in the thirteenth century was the growing concept that parliaments need not be the exclusive business of king and magnates
alone.   As time went on, attendance at parliaments was occasionally extended to affluent members of what may be termed
the "upper middle class": the shire knights and the burghers.
Shire knights were summoned by John to a meeting of the Great
Council in 1213 and again by Henry III in 1254.   On both these

---

[5] A good recent survey of parliamentary origins in England is G. L. Haskins, *The
Growth of English Representative Government* (1948).

occasions their chief function seems to have been to speak for their shires in approving an aid to the king. In 1261 Henry III summoned them once again to give him moral and financial support in his struggle with his baronial opponents. The shire knights joined the barons in a parliament summoned by Simon de Montfort in 1264, and in 1265 Earl Simon summoned a famous parliament that included, in addition to the great magnates and prelates, two knights from every shire and two burghers from every town or city. Simon's chief purpose seems to have been to broaden the base of his revolution and to make manifest the notion of a "community of the realm" that embraced great landholders, townsmen, and shire gentry.

The burghers and shire knights again appear in some of the parliaments of Edward I. King Edward experimented constantly and creatively in the compositions of his parliaments. The two lesser orders were present at only four of the thirty parliaments held during the first quarter century of his reign, but during its final decade they were called regularly to serve alongside the great lords. Townsmen and shire knights were summoned to Edward's first parliament in 1275, "to discuss together with the magnates the affairs of our kingdom." A grant was made, but the new king was probably as anxious for their moral support as for their financial help.

Edward I's most famous parliament was the so-called Model Parliament of 1295, summoned at a crucial moment in his reign when a Scottish war, a Welsh rebellion, and a French invasion of Gascony combined to threaten the security of the realm. The three groups represented in the parliament of 1275 were summoned once again, and to them were added representatives of the lower clergy. Despite its name, the parliament of 1295 did not serve as a model for the future. The knights and barons met together in one group, the clergy met in a second group, and the townsmen in a third – on the pattern of the later French Estates General. In the fourteenth century the clergy resolved to exclude itself from parliaments altogether, preferring to meet separately and deal with the king in convocation. And the burghers and shire knights began to meet in a group that became the nucleus of the House of Commons. The magnates, left to themselves, evolved into the House of Lords.

The increasing participation of burghers and shire knights in the thirteenth-century parliaments was of notable constitutional importance, for it signified that the power of the English monarchy was to be limited not only by the magnates but by lesser classes as well. The "community of the realm" was significantly broadened and was becoming a potent political reality. Still, one must be careful when speaking of parliament and limited monarchy in thirteenth-century England. These concepts are apt to convey to the modern mind a degree of constitutionalism that was undreamed of in the High Middle Ages. As the century closed, the power of parliaments was still exceedingly vague. At best, it was the power to bargain modestly and discreetly for government favorable to the interests of the "community" in return for the granting of extraordinary fiscal support. And if any bargaining was done, either explicitly or implicitly, it was the magnates who took the lead. Lesser orders might sometimes be represented in parliaments, but they were as yet virtually inarticulate.

Why was it that these lesser orders came to be represented at all? The reason is not difficult to discover. In the thirteenth century they were growing in affluence and their political and social importance was increasing. They were forces to be reckoned with, and their allegiance and support were becoming more and more important to the central government, whether controlled by a Henry III, an Edward I, or a Simon de Montfort. Moreover, the shire knights and burghers in the thirteenth-century parliaments represented a considerable degree of wealth, and the monarchy needed the financial support of these orders to meet its soaring expenses. It is doubtless an over-simplification to say that the king summoned representatives of shire and town merely to get his hands on their money, but this was unquestionably one of his motives, and an important one. It is somehow reassuring to discover at the fountainhead of our most venerable representative institution the manifestation of a basic and profound human impulse: greed.

The political events of thirteenth-century England were not alone responsible for the evolution of parliament. For in the course of the High Middle Ages, parallel institutions were emerging throughout Western Christendom: the French Estates General, the Spanish Cortes, and similar representative bodies in Italy, Germany, and the Low Countries. Parliament, in short, was merely one of a considerable number of representative institutions that arose in thirteenth- and fourteenth-century Europe. Underlying them all was an old and widely shared tradition that the king was not absolute but was bound by custom and law. This view owed something, surely, to primitive Germanic custom, and something also to feudalism. It was reflected in the opinions of contemporary philosophers such as St. Thomas Aquinas who insisted that a king must rule in accordance with good law and in the interest of his people; otherwise he need not be obeyed. This was in no sense a democratic idea—St. Thomas was a dedicated monarchist—but it was, at least potentially, constitutional.

There is obviously nothing at all democratic about the thirteenth-century parliaments, nor can it really be said that they were instrumental in limiting royal power. The king's authority in thirteenth-century England was limited by the opinion of the "community" and the custom of the realm, and most of the parliaments of the age were summoned on *royal* initiative for the purpose of winning support for some policy or tax, and thereby overcoming these limitations. Simon de Montfort notwithstanding, the parliamentary idea developed in thirteenth-century England because the monarchy — particularly under Edward I — regarded parliaments as useful instruments of royal policy. On the other hand, we know that many centuries later parliament did become a deeply significant democratic institution, and in the broadest sense we can regard it as a bridge between medieval feudalism and modern democracy. But the kings and magnates of the thirteenth century, who would have despised democracy had they known about it, hadn't the slightest notion of engaging in institutional-bridge-building. They had problems enough of their own.

Edward I (1272–1307): Law and Administration

The reign of King Edward I, a crucially important epoch in the development of parliamentary custom, was notable and creative in other respects as well.[6] The new king had demonstrated his vigor and ability long before his father's death by his victory over Simon de Montfort at Evesham, and by his intelligent exercise of power during Henry III's final years. When Henry died in 1272 Edward was away on a crusade. As the illustrious and respected eldest son of the late king, he had no worries about his succession, and he therefore returned to England in a most leisurely fashion, settling affairs in Gascony on his way, and reaching home only in 1274.

Returning as a mature, self-confident man of thirty-five, he began at once to strengthen and systematize the powerful administrative and legal prerogatives which he inherited from his royal ancestors. Unlike his father, he was able to achieve many of his goals without incurring the hostility of his nobles. For Edward was a man whom the earls and barons could trust and admire. He was a courageous and skillful warrior, a man

---

[6] In addition to the works cited in note 1 of this chapter, see, on the reign of Edward I, George Holmes, *The Later Middle Ages, 1272–1485* (Nelson History of England, Volume III, 1962). Like the previous volumes in the Nelson series, this work is up-to-date and written in an engaging style. On Edward's legal achievements, see T. F. T. Plucknett, *The Legislation of Edward I* (1949).

of chivalrous instincts, a nobleman among noblemen. But he was also a king, and he never forgot it. He possessed a profound respect for law which characterized the best of an age that had produced a Bracton and a Thomas Aquinas. Like them, he had a passion for system and definition, which led him to bring to completion the great legal achievements of Henry II, Hubert Walter, and the administrators of Henry III. Edward I has been called "the English Justinian," and like the great emperor of sixth-century Byzantium he created a powerful and durable synthesis of the legal traditions of past centuries.

In the words of a seventeenth-century chief justice, "The very scheme, mould and model of the common law was set in order by the king [Edward I], and so, in a very great measure, has continued the same in all succeeding ages to this day." Edward I gave structure and system to the common law, but in doing so he rendered it far less flexible than before. No longer could monarchs extend their jurisdiction merely by deciding to create new writs — new forms of action; no longer could the law develop freely from precedent to precedent. For through the extensive series of statutes under Edward I, the latitude and individual interpretation previously exercised by royal judges were severely limited. By and large, judge-made law gave way to enacted law, and only by the issuing of new statutes could significant changes be introduced thereafter into the legal structure.

It was under Edward I that "statute" became a meaningful concept. The ancient notion that law was traditional and un-changing had long been inconsistent with the realities of legal development. As far back as Alfred the Great, the promulgation of law was coming to depend on the judgment of the king, and the "assizes" of the Angevin kings unquestionably bore the mark of original legislation. Nevertheless, according to con-temporary legal theory the Anglo-Saxon dooms merely "clari-fied" and "interpreted" existing law, and the Angevin assizes were regarded either as elucidations of ancient custom or as mere administrative regulations. By Edward I's time, however, it was gradually coming to be understood that the government might indeed change old laws and create new ones of its own volition. But original legislation, in view of the ancient tradi-tion, was regarded as an act of unusual significance and solem-nity. It could only be done in the form of a statute, and statutes could only be enacted by the king in parliaments. The necessary association between parliaments and statutory law was of enor-mous importance in future generations, for it led eventually to parliament's power to legislate. In Edward's time, however, the parliaments were relatively subservient and the king took the initiative in issuing statutes.

Bracton had insisted that the king was the fountainhead of all justice – that magnates and prelates who operated courts of their own did so only by royal leave. It was Edward I's goal to translate this theory into reality. The royal administration insisted that private franchises * would be recognized only if they could be shown to date from before the reign of Richard I (1189–99) or if they had been granted since that time by royal charter. As early as Henry III's reign, efforts were made to enforce this principle through writs of *quo warranto* ("by what warrant?") which initiated investigations of the legal foundations of private franchises. When Edward returned from his crusade in 1274 he began to initiate *quo warranto* proceedings on a large scale, with the result that illegal franchises were eliminated and legal ones were subjected to a greater degree of royal control. The Statute of Gloucester (1278) carried this royal policy considerably further:

> ... All those who claim rights of jurisdiction by charters of the king's predecessors as kings of England, or by any other title, shall come before the king or the itinerant justices on a certain day and at a certain place to show what sorts of franchises they claim to have, and by what warrant.... And if those who claim to have such franchises fail to come on the aforesaid day, those franchises shall be taken into the king's hand by the local sheriff. ..."

The Statute of Gloucester was followed by a period of complex disputes in which the monarchy asserted its jurisdictional rights firmly but with sufficient restraint to avoid widespread hostility. In 1290 Edward's policy culminated in the Statute of *Quo Warranto* which provided that rights of jurisdiction unsupported by explicit royal grant must be confirmed by the king's charter regardless of how long the rights had been exercised. Again, Edward was often willing to confirm previously unchartered franchises, but in the process of doing so, the principle of private justice only by royal delegation was firmly established. The absolute primacy of royal jurisdiction, toward which the monarchy had so long been moving, was achieved at last.

Edward's statutes also made significant contributions to property law, clarifying and simplifying some of the bewildering issues arising from the labyrinth of feudal tenures. Feudalism,

---

* i.e., areas in which the legal machinery was operated by some great private landholder.

as we have seen, was never a simple affair, and by the later thirteenth century, William the Conqueror's original land distributions had become hopelessly entangled by many generations of disputes over rights, inheritances, marriage settlements, "temporary" grants, forfeitures, and subinfeudations. Great chains of lord-vassal relationships, running down through many degrees of subordination, created considerable confusion regarding rights to land and often resulted in endless buck-passing when it came to performing feudal obligations. A certain Roger of St. German, for example, held an estate in Huntingdonshire in fief from Robert of Bedford, who held it of Richard of Ilchester, who held it of Alan of Chartres, who held it of William le Boteler, who held it of Gilbert Neville, who held it of Devorguil Balliol, who held it of the king of Scotland, who held it of King Edward I. Such a situation could hardly have commended itself to Edward's systematic mind.

Consequently, Edward strove to bring some degree of order to the chaotic and anachronistic feudalism of his day. The Statute of Westminster of 1285 undertook to specify the conditions under which a lord might confiscate the land of a tenant who failed to perform his required services and to establish clear rules governing conditional and temporary land grants. The Statute of Mortmain (1279) prohibited land grants to the Church without the license of the grantor's lord, for once an estate was granted to the Church—which never "died"—the land was permanently alienated from lay control. Most significant of all was the Statute of *Quia Emptores* (1290) which established an absolute prohibition against all further subinfeudation. Thereafter, if a tenant wished to sell a part of his land he could do so only by foregoing any claim of lordship over the buyer. The buyer would then hold the land of the seller's lord, and the seller himself would drop out of the feudal chain altogether. *Quia Emptores* by no means illegalized feudalism, but it did have the effect, as time went on, of diminishing the importance of lord-vassal relationships below the level of the king and his tenants-in-chief. It was an important though partial step from the feudal concept of dependent landholding to the modern concept of outright ownership of land.

The same passion for system which infused Edward's statutes prompted him to undertake creative reforms in the machinery of local and central administration. The assertion of royal legislative supremacy in the statutes of Gloucester and *Quo Warranto* was paralleled by the growth and systematization of the king's legal machinery. The highest tribunal in the land consisted of the king himself sitting in parliament or passing judgment with the advice of his council. But unless a legal case involved particularly important persons or raised some unusually difficult legal subtlety it was handled by one of the three royal courts sitting at Westminster or by itinerant judges working in the countryside. At Westminster were the courts of the King's Bench, Common Pleas, and the Exchequer. All three were staffed with professionals – trained lawyers in the case of the King's Bench and Common Pleas, and expert accountants at the Exchequer. The King's Bench handled cases of special royal concern, the Exchequer dealt with cases involving royal revenues, and the remaining cases went to Common Pleas.

The Exchequer was of course not only a court but also, and preeminently, the key institution in the royal fiscal system. Exchequer, Chancery, council, and household were the four chief organs of governmental administration under Edward I. The Exchequer, usually supervised by the treasurer, continued to serve as the central accounting office for royal revenues. By Edward's time it was responsible not only for the accounts of the sheriffs but also for those of numerous other local officials who collected money for the king. Chancery – which, like the Exchequer, continued to sit at Westminster – remained the royal secretarial office. Its supervisor, the chancellor, had custody of the Great Seal by which royal documents were authenticated, and its well-trained clerks prepared the numerous royal letters and charters and preserved copies of them for future reference.

Heretofore we have distinguished between Great Council and Small Council, but now, more and more, the Great Council was developing into the institution of parliament, and the term "council" therefore came to apply exclusively to the smaller group of royal advisers – judges, administrators, and magnates – which we have previously called the Small Council. This group remained flexible and ill-defined in membership and continued to accompany the king as he traveled through his lands. In 1258 the magnates had attempted to assert control over the council, and they would make further attempts in the course of the fourteenth century, but in Edward I's reign it was an effective and thoroughly controlled royal instrument.

The household, too, accompanied the royal person. It had evolved considerably since late-Saxon and Norman times, but it retained its essential character as a body of royal servants whose tasks ranged from menial duties to important administrative responsibilities. Since Chancery and Exchequer had become rooted at Westminster, it was necessary for the king to maintain smaller parallel institutions in his own household so that he could transact business quickly no matter where he was. The Great Seal was kept at Westminster, but the traveling household included its own staff of writing clerks and a keeper of the Privy Seal who could authenticate royal letters and avoid the delay involved in routing them through Chancery. Similarly, the clerks of the royal Wardrobe supervised receipts and disbursements in the king's household, sometimes assuming responsibility for paying the wages of troops and other military expenses when the king was engaged in foreign campaigns. Considerable tax revenues went directly into the Wardrobe without being received or recorded by the Exchequer, and at times when baronial supervision of the Exchequer was threatening the independence of the king, he might extricate himself by depending more fully on the Wardrobe which, being a part of the royal household, was subject to greater royal control.

In the twelfth century, the sheriffs and itinerant justices had been the chief connecting links between crown and countryside. Both these institutions continued to function in Edward I's reign, but in the meantime many new royal officials had emerged at the local level. Local justice was sometimes handled by royal judges on special commission to hear a particular case or series of cases. At other times a group of royal judges and important men of the district was empowered to hear, in the king's name, all the cases in a particular shire. As had always been the case, the efficient execution of royal justice at the local level resulted in a notable augmentation of royal revenues, and it was now becoming increasingly apparent that the king's judges were, in effect, draining money from the countryside. Hence, the general county eyre was coming to be regarded as unduly oppressive, and as the fourteenth century progressed, popular opposition forced the monarchy to limit somewhat the activities of its traveling justices.

Royal administration in the counties involved a delicate balance between central authority and local initiative. This balance was a matter of immense importance in the evolution of English government, for it meant that the royal administration could function effectively at the local level without suppressing the political vigor of the counties themselves. Rather than fighting blindly against the royal administration or being crushed by it, local notables could participate in it, protecting their own interests and gaining political experience in the bargain. Accordingly, magnates and gentry became involved not only in their own regional affairs but in the affairs of the realm, and their sense of community and local responsibility was significantly enhanced.

The remarkable nature of this phenomenon can best be appreciated by contrasting Edward I's England with contemporary France. In general, the French royal government ruled the countryside through officials sent from the royal household — men without local roots, who were transferred regularly from one jurisdiction to another. This fact undoubtedly contributed to the twin evils of royal autocracy and local particularism which afflicted France in the early modern centuries. In England, however, important local men participated vigorously in the royal administration of the countryside. They accompanied the royal judges on eyres of the counties. They often served as the king's sheriffs. And they occupied numerous local offices charged with maintaining peace and collecting royal revenues. The coroners, who investigated murders and other felonies, were normally drawn from the local gentry, as were the keepers of the peace, who saw to the maintenance of order and apprehended criminals. And local men were strongly represented among the host of assessors, customs officials, and tax collectors who served the king in shire and town.

A man who functioned as a royal official might hope thereby to rise, through royal favor, to a higher social and economic position. Royal service was by no means an unobstructed road to riches, but the patronage system pioneered by Henry I continued to flourish and expand, and more than one spectacular career was built on royal rewards for faithful service. By a skillful use of the vast patronage at his disposal, an able king such as Edward I could usually count on the devoted service of his acquisitive subordinates. At a time when the once-powerful feudal concepts of homage and fealty were dissolving, greed and ambition were rising to take their place as incentives for loyalty between a lord and his men.

Even in the early days of Anglo-Norman feudalism money had been used to buy loyalty and hire troops; now feudalism was becoming hopelessly anachronistic and money was more than ever a dominant force in society. Feudal personal ties continued, after a fashion, but their gradual decay was hastened by Edward I's prohibition of subinfeudation. The feudal aristocracy remained, by and large, in its former dominant position in society, and many feudal ideas persisted—even intensified— as magnates came to revel increasingly in elaborate tournaments, heavy armor, heraldic devices, and self-conscious chivalry. But the fundamental concept of service in return for land tenure was dead, and the armies of Edward I fought for wages.

Edward I's reign witnessed the development of the longbow and the progressive decline in the importance of knightly cavalry. Mounted knights now merely formed the small cores of armies that abounded in mounted archers and infantrymen. Edward's Statute of Winchester of 1285 defined the military responsibilities of the English population along the lines of Henry II's Assize of Arms (1181) which had already been amended and expanded more than once under Henry III. It now became customary for the king to grant "commissions of array" to local notables licensing them to raise forces in their

shires from among the local inhabitants whose military obligations were set forth in the Statute of Winchester. The knights
who were owed to the king by his tenants-in-chief might still
be summoned, but they now demanded wages for their services.
More important was the use of mercenaries under contract.
Edward I employed the policy—which was developed much
more fully in the fourteenth century—of entering into contracts
for life with important lords, binding the lords to supply mercenary contingents for the army in return for regular retaining
fees. This arrangement—known as the indenture system—was
extended to contracts between the lord and his own military
followers. Just as the lord undertook to supply troops to the
king in return for regular payments, so the lord's own men
undertook to follow him into battle in return for similar payments. Since the payments were normally contracted for life,
the relationships created by the indenture system tended to be
stable and permanent, and the subordination of man to lord
which the system entailed gradually took the place of the older
feudal relationships. The vastly expanded indenture system
of the fourteenth century has been called "bastard feudalism"; it was, in effect, a social hierarchy bound together by
money.

Under Edward I the indenture system was still in its in-
fancy, but it was already becoming a burden on the royal treasury. Indeed, the numerous wars of Edward I were immensely
expensive by the standards of the age. Edward was a vigorous
warrior king whose ambitions far outran the normal resources
of the monarchy, and he was obliged to exploit every conceivable
source of revenue. His desperate need for money was one very
important motive behind his summoning of numerous parliaments, and he frequently wrung from them the authority to
collect a substantial percentage of his subjects' chattels or
annual rents: a fifteenth in 1290, a tenth in 1294, a twelfth in
1296, a ninth in 1297, etc. He taxed the clergy with similar
severity, and thereby aroused vigorous opposition from the
archbishop of Canterbury and the pope. He collected heavy
customs dues, particularly from Italian merchants who were
virtually monopolizing the export of English wool, and he turned
to these same Italian merchants for large loans when his tax
revenues failed to meet his expenses. In return, he took the
Italian merchants under his special protection. Previous kings
had depended for loans on the English Jewry, but Edward expelled the Jews from England in order to confiscate their property. Yet for all his skillful and sometimes cruel ingenuity,
Edward failed to balance his books and his heirs were left with
a debt-ridden government.

The Wars of Edward I

The reign of Edward I falls into two distinct periods. Between his return from the crusade in 1274 and the beginning of his war with France in 1294 his foreign policy was remarkably successful and he pursued his domestic policies of administrative and legal centralization without significant opposition from his subjects. But from 1294 to his death in 1307 his wars were frustratingly inconclusive and his relations with his subjects were stormy.

Edward reigned in an age when the older concept of feudal monarchy was gradually giving way to a new concept of national sovereignty. We should not regard Edward I's England as a national state in anything like the modern sense, yet in England, France, and other European states of the time, the political authority of kings was steadily superseding that of feudal magnates. There was still a good deal of feudalism in Edward's soul, but it usually took the form of exploiting his rights of feudal lordship to the fullest in order to increase his own power and prestige at the expense of his vassals. This was particularly true in his relations with Wales and Scotland, over which English kings had long claimed a rather vague suzerainty. Edward's troubles with France arose from the fact that his great French contemporary, King Philip the Fair,* shared his policy of exploiting rights of lordship over vassal states. Edward, as duke of Aquitaine, was Philip's vassal for his lands in Gascony, and he resented Philip's behaving toward Gascony as he himself was behaving toward Wales and Scotland.

Edward's greatest triumph was his conquest of Wales. The Anglo-Welsh controversy had been going on ever since the Anglo-Saxon invasions, and the steady aggressions of the Anglo-Norman frontier lords had resulted in a significant westward extension of English authority at Welsh expense. Still, despite innumerable royal expeditions into Wales the independence of that mountainous Celtic land endured.

Edward's Welsh campaign began in 1277 as a result of hostility arising from Prince Llywelyn of Wales' refusal to do homage. Edward invaded Wales and succeeded in winning Prince Llywelyn's homage and restricting his authority, but in 1282 Llywelyn and other Welsh magnates rose in rebellion once again. Edward invaded for a second time, and in the course of the struggle Llywelyn was killed (December 1282). By the spring of 1283 all Wales was in Edward's hands, and its

---

* Philip IV (1285–1314).

independence was permanently lost. Thereafter, it was re-garded as an integral part of the English realm; the term "Prince of Wales" no longer referred to an independent Welsh ruler but became the customary title for the king of England's eldest son. Such it has remained ever since.

Considering the antiquity of the Anglo-Welsh conflict, Edward's conquest was remarkably rapid and easy. The Welsh rebelled in 1287 and again in 1294–95, but although the latter rebellion succeeded in embarrassing Edward and delay-ing a projected expedition against France, neither of the two uprisings threatened seriously to undo the conquest of 1282–83. Edward's achievement proved to be permanent.

The struggle with Scotland promised for a time to bring Edward an even more notable victory, but in the end Scotland eluded Edward's grasp. Again the issue turned on Edward's claims to overlordship. As overlord of Scotland, Edward was called upon by the Scottish nobility in 1290 to adjudicate a dis-puted royal succession. He began his task by demanding and receiving the allegiance of the Scottish magnates, and there-upon took temporary possession of Scotland while pondering the relative merits of the two royal claimants – Robert Bruce and John Balliol. At length, late in 1292, he decided in Balliol's favor. For the next three years he engaged in a heavy-handed assertion of his overlordship, violating custom by hearing judi-cial claims of Balliol's Scottish subjects at Westminster, and even going so far as to summon Balliol himself to answer a complaint of one of his own countrymen. Some Scottish mag-nates evidently preferred Edward to Balliol, but the English king's imperious behavior was creating a dangerous legacy of resentment. In 1295, at a time when Edward was deeply involved in French matters, Balliol and the Scots rebelled.

Abandoning for the moment his plans to invade France, Edward turned his attention northward and in 1296 led a bril-liantly successful expedition against the Scots. Balliol was forced to abdicate and Edward assumed direct control over Scotland. He dramatized his impressive achievement by bringing back to England as a souvenir of his campaign the Stone of Scone on which, by ancient custom, the Scottish kings were crowned. As it happened, the unification of England and Scotland under one monarch was quickly challenged by the fierce independence of the Scots. In 1297 a new rebellion broke out, led by a member of the lesser nobility named William Wallace. The rebellion alternately flared and simmered as repeated English invasions failed to reestablish Edward's power in its former fullness. At length, in 1304, most of the Scottish nobles submitted to Edward and the uprising was brought to an end with the capture of Wallace himself in 1305.

In the following year still another insurrection broke out, led this time by Robert Bruce, grandson of the former claimant to the Scottish throne. Bruce, as it turned out, was the real hero of this Scottish war of independence. Crowned king of Scotland by his rebellious followers in 1306, he was defeated in battle by Edward but retained his poise and carried on the struggle. Edward I died in 1307 on the road to Scotland, still seeking the tantalizing prize that had often seemed within his grasp yet always escaped him. His son, Edward II, proved no match for Robert Bruce, and consequently Scotland was able to consolidate her independence. Not until the seventeenth century were the two crowns joined at last in a single person, and even then it was a Scottish king who became king of England.

Scottish independence was won by the fierce tenacity of the Scots themselves, but their cause was aided immeasurably by the fact that at crucial moments in the conflict Edward I was preoccupied with his struggle against Philip the Fair of France. The Anglo-French controversy had begun long before, with the Norman Conquest, when the English monarchy first became involved in the preservation and extension of vast French territories. The rivalry persisted, off and on, into the nineteenth century. Over this vast span of time relations between the two kingdoms were characterized by repeated wars separated by peaceful intermissions, sometimes of considerable duration. When Edward I ascended the throne, England and France had not engaged in serious hostilities for more than half a century, and the outstanding issues between the two monarchies had been resolved by the Peace of Paris of 1259. This agreement, as we have seen, provided that the English king should hold Gascony as a vassal of the king of France.

In the course of the thirteenth century England and Gascony had developed a considerable degree of economic interdependence. Gascon wine was exchanged for English cloth, grain, and other products, and the trade between the two lands gradually assumed such importance that the prosperity of Gascony came to depend heavily upon its English connection. Edward himself valued Gascony highly; he spent a number of months establishing order there on his return journey to England from the crusade in 1273–74, and in the later 1280s he spent the better part of three years there strengthening his authority. Edward was highly sensitive about his rights in Gascony, and could not be expected to relinquish them without a vigorous struggle.

There were several reasons for the renewal of the Anglo-French conflict, but the most basic of them was Philip the Fair's insistence on exercising to the fullest possible degree his rights of overlordship over Gascony. For the first two decades of Edward's reign England and France were at peace, and Edward was able to concentrate without serious interruption on his highly successful efforts to subdue Wales and Scotland and systematize the English administration. In 1293, however, Philip the Fair, on the pretext of a dispute between English and Gascon pirates, summoned Edward to his court. Like John nearly a century before, Edward refused the summons, and Philip replied in 1294 by undertaking to conquer Gascony.

It has been said that only after 1294 did Edward I's ambitions become too great for his resources. This is not altogether true. Broadly speaking, his three fundamental goals, the conquest of Wales, the establishment of hegemony over Scotland, and the retention of Gascony, had all been vigorously asserted long before 1294. Edward was by no means master of events in the 1290s; his difficulties arose largely from the aggressive new policy of Philip the Fair, and so far as the Gascon situation was concerned, Edward was on the defensive.

The hostile actions of Philip the Fair prompted Edward to take vigorous and expensive countermeasures. He wove a network of alliances against France, much as John had earlier done, and prepared for a large-scale invasion. But in committing himself to the enormously difficult task of reasserting his authority in distant Gascony in the teeth of the powerful French monarchy, he presented a tempting opportunity to his previous victims. A dangerous Welsh rebellion in 1294–95 caused him to delay his French expedition, and the Scottish uprising of 1295–96 necessitated still another postponement. By 1297, when the French expedition was ready at last, the alliance system had broken down and Edward's prestige was badly damaged. English opposition to royal centralization, which had remained dormant during the years of Edward's great military triumphs, now asserted itself at last. Royal taxation had intensified between 1294 and 1297 in order to provide the revenues necessary for the coming French war and the new Welsh and Scottish campaigns, and by 1297 Edward's subjects were sullen and rebellious.

The French expedition was launched in the summer of 1297 in an atmosphere of unrest and disaffection, and returned in early fall after an inconclusive campaign. After several years of complex negotiations, peace was finally established between England and France in 1303 on the basis of the *status quo ante bellum*. Nothing was gained and, from the territorial standpoint, nothing was lost. The pact was sealed by marriages between Edward I and Philip the Fair's sister, and between King Edward's son (the future Edward II) and King Philip's daughter Isabella. The latter marriage was destined to provide future English kings with a claim to the French throne, thereby contributing to the outbreak of the Hundred Years War in the fourteenth century.

Edward I succeeded in retaining Gascony, but the struggle with France proved costly indeed with respect to the king's relations with his English subjects. 1294 marked the end of a long honeymoon, and thereafter Edward's reign was marked by protracted conflict in England itself. Only once, however, did the conflict reach the threshold of open rebellion, and even then the insurrection was averted by timely royal concessions.

The great domestic crisis of Edward I's reign occurred in 1297. It arose from the confluence of a number of separate but related problems: (1) Edward's foreign policy was straining English resources almost to the breaking point, and the Gascon expedition together with the concurrent uprising of Robert Bruce in Scotland constituted a military and diplomatic crisis of major proportions. (2) The savagely taxed nobles, gentry, and burghers resisted additional exactions for a foreign policy of questionable outcome; the gentry violently opposed Edward's effort to make everyone with an annual landed income of twenty pounds or more take up the burdensome responsibilities of knighthood; and some of the magnates refused to serve in distant Gascony. (3) The Church, led by the firm and dedicated Archbishop Winchelsey, refused to pay additional taxes without express papal approval. In taking this stand, English churchmen were following the policy of the pope himself. In 1296, Pope Boniface VIII – the last of the great medieval popes and perhaps the most overbearing of them – issued the bull *Clericis Laicos* which specified that every single occasion of royal taxation of the clergy required specific papal permission. Whatever the canonical grounds for this bull, it was contrary to the custom of recent years and aroused violent royal opposition in both England and France. The struggle between Philip the Fair and Boniface VIII over royal taxation of the clergy is a dramatic and well-known episode in European history, but it is necessary to understand that the controversy raged in England as well.

Edward managed to weather the crisis of 1297. Never again was he able to assert full control over Scotland, although he continued to try; never again were his relations with his subjects as untroubled as they had formerly been, although after the French settlement of 1303 he was in full control of the domestic situation. The conflict with the Church subsided toward the end of 1297 when Pope Boniface modified his bull. The laity was assuaged by a royal confirmation of Magna Carta in 1297, accompanied by new concessions which granted, among other things, that extraordinary taxes should thereafter be levied only by consent of the "community of the realm." *

Despite these and other concessions, Edward was as jealous of his prerogatives in England as in Wales, Scotland, and Gascony, and in his final years he began once again to tighten his hold on the English realm. On the election of a docile pope in 1305 he secured papal backing for the repudiation of some of his earlier concessions and succeeded in arranging the suspension of his old antagonist, Archbishop Winchelsey, who was thereupon forced into exile. Edward was a determined man, and events seemed once again to be going in his favor. It is possible, indeed, that he might have won Scotland, too, for at his death in 1307 he was on his way northward with a powerful military expedition. But in his closing years he was obliged to belabor England with a stick rather than entice her with a carrot, and it was abundantly clear that his realm had been severely overstrained by his remorseless insistence on his self-styled "rights" at home and abroad.

Despite Edward's severity, and despite the inconclusive outcome of his Scottish wars, his reign remains one of the most impressive in the annals of England. It was a period of immense accomplishment and of crucial constitutional development—an age in which the common law reached maturity and parliaments became a normal part of the machinery of government. As medieval England's greatest lawgiver, Edward fully merits the laudatory title, "The English Justinian," which later historians gave him. But his similarity to Justinian was not limited to the field of law. As Professor Helen Cam has pointed out, it extended also to war and finance: "Like Justinian, Edward had overtaxed the resources of his realm, and his successors, like Justinian's, had to pay the penalty."†

---

* See above, p. 173.
† H. M. Cam, *England Before Elizabeth* (Harper, New York, 1960), p. 113.

Chapter 7

The Early ***Fourteenth Century:***
War and Social Change

The Change in Mood

THE ADJECTIVE "transitional" can be applied with some justice to any historical epoch, but it is particularly appropriate to the fourteenth century.[1] In this era many of the crucial institutions of the Middle Ages were in decay yet their modern counterparts had not yet appeared in recognizable form. The fourteenth century was not an age of feudalism but of bastard feudalism. Devotion to the medieval Church was beginning to give way to rebellious anticlericalism but patriotic devotion to the state lay in the future. The medieval intellectual synthesis was breaking up but nothing comparable was yet arising to take its place. The century closed in a mood of deep dissatisfaction with the traditional political, social, economic, and religious structures, but there was little consensus as to what new forms should replace the old. Hence, although certain trends

---

[1] The standard work on fourteenth-century England is May McKisack, *The Fourteenth Century* (Oxford History of England, 1959). The appropriate volume in the Pelican History is A. R. Myers, *England in the Late Middle Ages* (1952). Another excellent survey, covering the period from 1307 to 1485, is V. H. H. Green, *The Later Plantagenets* (1955).

in the fourteenth century can perhaps be described as "progressive" or "modern," the general atmosphere of the age smelled of decay. The equilibrium of the High Middle Ages was giving way to turbulence and social struggle as England groped toward an uncertain future.

On the Continent no less than in England the prosperity and the cohesion of high medieval civilization were giving way to a new mood of violence and unrest. In the eleventh, twelfth, and thirteenth centuries the population had been rising rapidly on the wings of a vigorous and prosperous economy, and the frontiers of Catholic Christendom had undergone a significant expansion. Within Europe vast quantities of new farmland had been created out of forests and swamps, and in Spain, Sicily, Syria, and the Baltic, Western Civilization had been pushed far outward beyond its earlier boundaries. But as the fourteenth century opened, these external and internal frontiers ceased to expand and after a time began to recede. The population underwent a long period of decline. The clearing of forests and marshes ceased, and marginal lands that had been brought into cultivation during the High Middle Ages were abandoned. The Christian reconquest of Spain came to a halt; Granada — the one remaining Moslem foothold in the Iberian Peninsula — continued under Islamic control until 1492. The Teutonic Knights, who had pushed German-Christian power far eastward and northward along the Baltic shore, were gradually being driven back. In 1291, Acre, the last important bridgehead of the Crusaders in the Holy Land, was lost, and by the mid-fourteenth century a dangerous new Moslem power, the Ottoman Turks, was beginning to move into the Balkans.

The new age was disheartened by a protracted economic recession which manifested itself in falling land revenues and a reduction in agrarian productivity owing to the decline in the labor force and the consequent abandonment of fields and villages. This unhappy situation was in part a product of the devastating famines and plagues of the age, particularly the Bubonic Plague or "Black Death" which struck Europe with tremendous severity midway through the century.

These catastrophes caused unimaginable suffering among the peasantry. But by decimating the peasant population they created a labor shortage which worked ultimately to the peasant's advantage and tended to subvert the economic position of the great lord. Unchallenged in the social structure of the High Middle Ages, the nobility now suffered not only from reduced land revenues but also from a progressive decline in their military importance as a knightly cavalry force. Common infantry, which had always played an important role in English warfare, became more significant than ever with the advent of the longbow under Edward I, and in the battles of the fourteenth century a body of trained archers was often the key to victory. With the coming of gunpowder and the development of artillery later in the century, the armored knight was becoming an anachronism. The decline of the nobility relative to other classes in society is illustrated by the notable increase in the power of townsmen and gentry in fourteenth-century parliaments. Still, the decline must not be exaggerated. At the end of the century, and for many generations to come, the landed nobility remained powerful. It had to share its power more and more with other classes, it was forced to undergo a severe economic squeeze, but despite all, it managed to retain its position at the top of the social order.

While land income was dropping, the commercial structure of England was experiencing major changes. During the first half of the century, Italian merchants continued by and large to serve as the chief royal bankers and to take a vigorous part in the English wool trade. But more and more, English merchants themselves were striving to control this trade and to enjoy its considerable profits. Under Edward I, foreign merchants — Italians, Flemings, and Germans from the cities of the Hanseatic League — controlled about two thirds of the wool trade, but already the English merchants were undertaking a serious struggle to get more of the trade into their own hands. They sought to concentrate the selling of English wool in one particular foreign trading center under English control — in a single town which would be given a royal monopoly on wool exportation. Such a center was called a "staple."

The first staples were created at Dordrecht and Antwerp in the Low Countries by Edward I in the 1290s. Anxious to build up his war chest, Edward I found it advantageous to concentrate the wool trade in spots where it might be easily supervised and efficiently taxed. Edward II established the first compulsory staple at St. Omer in 1314, and Edward III, responding to the financial pressures of the Hundred Years War, established staples at one time or another at Antwerp and Bruges. Foreign merchants still played an important role in the trade, but now, unless specially privileged, they were obliged to buy their wool at the staple from English traders.

After mid-century the collapse of two Italian merchant firms on which Edward III had particularly depended for loans — the Bardi and the Peruzzi — prompted the monarchy to favor English merchants more wholeheartedly than before. In 1363 the king established a staple at Calais — in northeastern France but under English occupation — and gave control of it to a group of English merchants known as the "Company of the Staple." This company was granted an absolute monopoly of the wool trade with the one exception that wool could still be shipped by sea to Italy. The wool monopoly was lucrative indeed to the Company of the Staple, enabling it to dominate the trade for many years thereafter. But during these years the wool trade as a whole was declining as a result of the steady rise of the English cloth industry. English wool was being consumed more and more in the manufacture of English cloth, and the amount remaining for export decreased steadily. English cloth makers were exempt from the high royal duties on wool and, being relative newcomers on the economic scene, were less bound by anachronistic guild regulations. They were therefore able to undersell their continental rivals and, in time, to win large markets not only in England but across the length and breadth of Europe. As the fourteenth century closed, English merchants themselves were beginning to penetrate deep into the Continent, competing successfully in areas that had long been dominated by the merchants of Flanders and the Hanseatic League. No longer merely a source of raw materials, exploited by foreign traders, England was now a great textile producer and her merchants were beginning to demonstrate the sort of initiative that would, in later centuries, make her the commercial nexus of the world.

English towns also underwent fundamental changes in the fourteenth century. The economic forces of the age brought about the decline of many towns – Oxford and Lincoln, for example – which were centers of agriculture or of the faltering wool trade, but the concurrent rise of cloth manufacturing transformed other towns such as Norwich, York, and Coventry into thriving textile centers. The intensification of the cloth trade made the great city of London more prosperous than ever, and the port of Bristol, on England's opposite shore, was becoming London's chief rival. In general, the labor shortage brought about by the population decline had the effect of presenting tempting new opportunities to the lesser urban classes – the journeymen and minor craftsmen – whose services were much in demand. But these opportunities, opened momentarily by social and economic change, were closed by political force. The wealthy and privileged merchant guilds, and the more important craft guilds such as those connected with cloth manufacturing, guarded jealously their traditional control of urban economic life and town government. Ruling as narrow oligarchies over the English towns, they clung to their valuable monopolies, repressed the rising organizations of journeymen and the guilds of the lesser crafts, and did everything in their power to keep wages down. Consequently, the later fourteenth century witnessed a series of severe class struggles in the English towns. The ruling merchants were dangerously threatened from time to time, but in the end they succeeded in maintaining their power. Even though the lesser classes had the economic trends of the age on their side they advanced only very slowly. And the towns themselves, although winning ever wider privileges and increasingly generous charters from the king, remained under royal control. Independent city-states of the sort that abounded in contemporary Italy and northern Germany were quite unknown in England.

In both town and countryside the labor shortage worked to the advantage of the lower classes of employees, and the dominant groups reacted by bending every effort to the forceable preservation of the economic status quo, suppressing dangerous lower-class organizations and passing statutes in parliament which aimed to fix wages at artificially low levels. The rebellious unrest that arose from these repressive policies culminated in the savage Peasants' Revolt of 1381, which will be discussed in the next chapter. Similar revolts were occurring throughout the fourteenth century on the Continent—a particularly ferocious one broke out in France in the later 1350s. Fourteenth-century Europe suffered from an upsurge of violence, rebellion, and murder, a sharpening of class conflict, and increased factionalism among the nobility. Added to this were the twin horrors of plague and war. England did not suffer much directly from the warfare of the fourteenth century, but France was devastated by contending armies and rampaging companies of ill-disciplined mercenary soldiers. An age of transition is seldom comfortable, and the transition which Europe underwent in the fourteenth century was painful indeed.

The passing of high medieval civilization is equally evident in the realms of art and the intellect. The soaring and dignified Gothic style of the later twelfth and thirteenth centuries gradually evolved in the fourteenth into a highly decorative architectural style known as "perpendicular" which was sharply different in mood. The awesome nobility of the earlier Gothic interior gave way to an interior space brightly illuminated by large windows high in the walls and crowned by a heavily-ornamented roof. The result was a sense of spaciousness and openness, but at the expense of the relative restraint and mysterious heavenward thrust of high medieval Gothic. It would be fruitless to argue that one of these styles is "greater" than the other, but they are unquestionably expressions of two distinctly different spirits.

The breakdown of the high medieval intellectual synthesis consisted chiefly of a series of powerful attacks against the fusion of reason and revelation which had been achieved by the thirteenth-century scholastic philosophers, St. Thomas Aquinas in particular. The work of demolition was begun by

Early Perpendicular Gothic architecture:
choir, Gloucester Cathedral (after 1330).

the English Franciscan, John Duns Scotus (d. 1308), and was carried to its climax by another English Franciscan, William of Ockham (d. 1349). Duns Scotus was far from a mere destroyer; he constructed an elaborate philosophical system of his own, so complex indeed as to discourage and even repel many later scholars. But his system of thought tended to place rather narrow limits on man's ability to approach God and religious truth through reason. Following somewhat in the tradition of the Franciscan scientists, he taught that the most appropriate object of human reason was the natural world rather than the supernatural, and although his Christian belief was as strong as that of St. Thomas, he maintained that a number of Christian dogmas which Aquinas had regarded as rationally verifiable could be accepted only on faith.

William of Ockham went much farther, insisting on a radical distinction between rational facts and Christian doctrines. He believed in both, but concluded that the dogmas of the Catholic religion transcend reason. The existence of God should be taken on faith. It could not be proven, and all efforts to create a rational theology were doomed to failure. The supreme intellectual achievement of the thirteenth century was the welding of logic and faith into a single coherent system, and the fourteenth-century philosophers worked tirelessly to destroy that system. In so doing, they were accomplishing on an intellectual level what was being achieved concurrently on the social, economic, and cultural levels: the destruction of an old ethos and a tentative, uncertain approach toward a new one.

The Reign of Edward II (1307–1327)

Three kings ruled England in the fourteenth century: Edward II (1307–27), Edward III (1327–77), and Richard II (1377–99), and of these three, two had their reigns cut short by rebellion and deposition. Edward II was the weakest and least successful of them, and his inadequacies stand out in sharp relief against the iron strength of his father, Edward I, and the popularity of his son, Edward III.[2] He inherited from his father an overly ambitious foreign policy, a debt-ridden treasury, and a restive nobility, but Edward I failed to pass on

---

[2] On Edward II's reign see T. F. Tout, *The Place of the Reign of Edward II in English History* (2nd ed., 1936), and J. C. Davies, *The Baronial Opposition to Edward II* (1919). An interesting contemporary history of the reign is N. Denholm-Young (tr.), *Vita Edwardi Secundi* (1957).

to him the intelligence and fortitude necessary to cope with these problems. Even as a youthful Prince of Wales, Edward II had demonstrated his willfulness and incapacity, and before accepting him as their king the barons forced him to take a coronation oath of unusual scope. The oath took the form of a series of questions posed to the prospective king by Archbishop Winchelsey of Canterbury (who had returned from exile on Edward I's death):

> "Sire, will you grant and keep and confirm to the people of England by your oath the laws and customs given them by the previous just and God-fearing kings, your ancestors, and particularly the laws, customs, and liberties granted the clergy and people by the glorious king, the sainted Edward, your predecessor?" "I grant and promise them."

> "Sire, will you in all your judgments, to the best of your ability, preserve to God and the Holy Church and to the clergy and people full peace and concord before God?" "I will preserve them."

> "Sire, will you, to the best of your ability, have justice rendered rightly, fairly, and wisely, in compassion and truth?" "I will so do."

> "Sire, do you grant to be held and kept the laws and just customs which the community of your realm shall choose, and, to the best of your ability, defend and enforce them to the honor of God?" "I grant and promise them."

The last of these four promises was the most novel and doubtless the most important, embodying as it did the concept of "community" which had been the source of such fierce struggles in the thirteenth century. By now it was coming to be understood that parliament was the instrument through which the community expressed its will, and of necessity Edward II summoned parliaments frequently. The new king was as willing to make promises as most of his predecessors had been, and just as ready to break them. The coronation oath is useful in disclosing to us in very general terms what the community expected of its king, but more than an oath would be required to tame the obstinate Edward II.

Edward was a mercurial, unchivalrous weakling whose many-faceted personality is admirably described by Bishop Stubbs: "He was a trifler, an amateur farmer, a breeder of horses, a patron of playwrights, a contriver of masques, a

The Fourteenth-Century Kings

HENRY III = ELEANOR *of Provence*
1216–1272

EDWARD I = ELEANOR *of Castile*
1272–1307

EDMUND, *Earl of Lancaster*

THOMAS, *Earl of Lancaster*

EDWARD II = ISABELLA *of France*
1307–1327

EDWARD III = PHILIPPA *of Hainault*
1327–1377

EDWARD, *the* = JOAN
Black Prince   *of Kent*
d. 1376

LIONEL, *Duke of Clarence d. 1368*

JOHN OF GAUNT, *Duke of Lancaster d. 1399*

EDMUND, *Earl of Cambridge, Duke of York d. 1402*

THOMAS *of Woodstock, Earl of Buckingham, Duke of Gloucester d. 1397*

RICHARD II
1377–1399

HENRY IV
1399–1413

HENRY V
1413–1422

HENRY VI
1422–1461

smatterer in mechanical arts; he was, it may be, an adept in
rowing and a practiced whip; he could dig a pit or thatch a
barn; somewhat varied and inconsistent accomplishments,
but all testifying to the skillful hand rather than the thoughtful head. . . ." In short, Edward was an absurd eccentric who
lacked the confidence of his sober and conservative magnates.
Since he was lacking in all the chivalric and military virtues
of the knight, he was consequently incapable of winning the
respect of his barons who were still sufficiently medieval to
prefer their kings to be warriors and heroes, not dilettantes
or businessmen. To make matters worse, Edward was probably
a homosexual. His coronation ushered in a generation of
bitter civil strife.

Throughout his career Edward II demonstrated a dangerous and self-defeating tendency to form powerful emotional
relationships with ambitious young men and to fall hopelessly
under their influence. The first such man, and one of the most
important, was Piers Gaveston—a Gascon knight of modest
birth whose courage and ability were overshadowed by his
arrogance and ruthless ambition. Gaveston had been exiled
prior to Edward I's death because of his influence on the Prince
of Wales, but when the prince acceded to the throne he brought
Gaveston back to England and made him earl of Cornwall.

The friendship with Gaveston caused Edward II endless
difficulties. As one contemporary expressed it:

> [baronial antagonism] mounted day by day, for Piers
> was very proud and haughty in bearing. All those whom
> the custom of the realm made equal to him, he regarded
> as lowly and abject, nor could anyone, he thought, equal
> him in valor. On the other hand the earls and barons
> of England looked down upon Piers because, as a for-
> eigner and formerly a mere man-at-arms raised to such
> distinction and eminence, he was unmindful of his
> former rank. Thus he was an object of mockery to
> almost everyone in the kingdom. But the king had an
> unswerving affection for him. . . ." *

It must have seemed to the barons that the bad old days
of Henry III had returned, for Edward II ignored the will of
the community, scorned the advice of his nobles—his "natural
counselors"—and listened only to the vainglorious upstart
Gaveston. The magnates, for their part, were driven to form a

---

* *Vita Edwardi Secundi*, p. 3.

coalition against the king which shortly fell under the leadership of Earl Thomas of Lancaster, Edward II's first cousin and one of the wealthiest and most powerful magnates that England had ever known. At his height Earl Thomas held five earldoms concurrently—Lancaster, Leicester, Derby, Salisbury, and Lincoln—together with vast estates in northern and central England, and he defended his lands and his interests with a large private army. His impact on English history would have been still greater were it not for the fact that his policies were shortsighted, capricious, and limited, by and large, to the satisfaction of his own personal ambition. Recent attempts to present his career in a more favorable light fail to dispel the impression that he was a witless blunderer.

Nevertheless, Earl Thomas's royal opponent was at least as witless as he. And Edward II's fruitless attempts to carry on his father's aggressive Scottish policies put the monarchy in desperate need of money. Edward and Gaveston exploited every possible source of tax revenue and borrowed heavily from Italian bankers, particularly the Frescobaldi of Florence. Ultimately, however, the king was obliged to seek extraordinary financial support from parliaments.

Edward's financial dependence enabled the magnates to establish a degree of control over the unwilling king. In 1310 they forced him to accept a committee of notables who were empowered to draw up a series of ordinances for the proper governing of the realm. The product of their work, the Ordinances of 1311, were somewhat similar to the Provisions of Oxford half a century earlier but were much more elaborate and thorough-going. They provided that both Gaveston and Edward's chief banker, Amerigo dei Frescobaldi, should be exiled from England. Parliaments were to be summoned at least twice a year and were given the power of consent to the appointment of great administrative officers such as the chancellor and treasurer. More than that, the parliaments were given a veto over the appointment of important officials in the king's household itself—the master of the Wardrobe and the keeper of the Privy Seal. As a further check on the financial independence of the household, the Wardrobe was forbidden to receive tax revenues directly but could draw funds only through the Exchequer. Finally, and perhaps most humiliating of all, the king could declare war only with parliamentary approval.

In 1311, as in 1215 and 1258, the magnates forced the monarchy to accept a comprehensive series of limitations on royal power. And now, as before, the royal submission was merely temporary and was followed by a period of civil turbulence. The irrepressible Gaveston returned to England from exile late in 1311 and by Christmas was again at Edward's side.

The furious magnates responded by taking up arms, seizing the royal favorite, and having him hanged. With Gaveston's execution Edward II's reign entered a new phase, unhappier than the last.

The murder of Gaveston cost the insurgents some support, for several magnates, restive under Thomas of Lancaster's inept leadership, felt that opposition to the king had become too extreme. The land was on the verge of civil war when, in 1313, a reconciliation was arranged between king and magnates. For the moment the Ordinances of 1311 were forgotten. Open war was avoided but the condition of the kingdom remained far from peaceful. For now the many complex and bitter rivalries among the nobility, which had troubled Edward II's reign from the beginning, reached their climax. The second and third decades of the fourteenth century are marked not only by a continual struggle between monarchy and nobility but also by savage conflicts between magnate and magnate which sometimes reached the point of private war. In 1317 the personal armies of the earls of Lancaster and Surrey clashed openly. And throughout this period the English spirit was darkened by military disasters in the conflict with Scotland.

Edward II had great difficulty with the Scots from the beginning, and in 1314 the entire northern policy of the first two Edwards was shattered by an overwhelming Scottish victory over a large English army at Bannockburn. The Scottish triumph was so complete as to doom all further efforts to subdue the northern kingdom. In the years that followed, the Scots took the offensive against England, often with the support of dissident English earls, until Edward II arranged a peace with them in 1323. Scotland had won her independence and Robert Bruce ruled his kingdom unchallenged. And Edward II's prestige, none too high to begin with, was tarnished still further by his humiliating military failure.

Meanwhile the king continued to have trouble with his magnates and his parliaments. Earl Thomas of Lancaster, who had held aloof from the disastrous Scottish campaign of 1314, was now more powerful than ever, and in a parliament held in the autumn of 1314 he succeeded in reestablishing the Ordinances. In 1316 and 1317 he was the king's chief counselor and the supreme figure in the royal administration. He never succeeded, however, in winning Edward's confidence, nor indeed did he even try. Not only Edward II but many of his magnates were becoming alarmed at Lancaster's immense authority, and in 1318 a more moderate group of barons rose to power in the court. Lancaster remained a potent force in the English government, but he was no longer supreme. The new men were suspicious of Lancaster and less interested than he in forcing royal government under the rigid control of the Ordinances. It is ironic that this generally moderate group included a youthful nobleman of ruthless ambition — Robert Despenser the younger — who rose quickly to a position of inordinate power by managing to win from Edward II the affection which the susceptible king had once lavished on Gaveston.

Despenser was the son and namesake of a royal official who had rendered good service to both Edward I and Edward II. Hence the younger Despenser could not be denounced as an upstart foreigner like Gaveston. But Despenser was even more dangerous than Gaveston had been. The finer virtues which Gaveston had displayed on occasion were utterly suppressed in Despenser by a naked will to power. And by 1321 Despenser had risen, through the affection of the king, to a position of almost total authority in the royal court. It was Despenser rather than Edward II or his nobles who now ran the government of England.

Once again the magnates formed a coalition against the king and his favorite, led by great notables such as Thomas of Lancaster and the Mortimers — a family of Marcher lords who deeply resented Despenser's brazen policy of collecting lordships for himself in the Welsh Marches. Now, at last, the struggle between king and insurgents broke into open warfare, and at the crucial battle of Boroughbridge in 1322 Lancaster was routed by a royal army. The earl was executed shortly thereafter, and the king — or rather Despenser — won unchallenged dominion over the kingdom.

During the four years following the battle of Boroughbridge, Despenser ruled imperiously over king and kingdom, amassing estates and enemies. But his immense political power made him overconfident, and he carelessly allowed a new coalition to develop which would ultimately prove fatal to his grandiose ambitions. Lord Roger Mortimer, imprisoned after the battle of Boroughbridge, escaped from the Tower of London in 1323 and took refuge in France. Two years later Queen Isabella, whose place in the royal affections had been usurped by Despenser, was sent across the Channel to negotiate with her brother, King Charles IV of France, on the long-standing Anglo-French dispute over Gascony. Once in France Isabella broke with her husband and became the mistress of Roger Mortimer, and in 1326 Mortimer and Isabella returned to England with an army. With them was the young Prince Edward, son of Edward II and Isabella, and heir to the throne.

Mortimer and Isabella at once became the center of a general uprising of English magnates against the despised Despenser and his crowned puppet. The royalist force collapsed with remarkable speed; late in 1326 the king was captured and imprisoned, and Despenser was executed. And in January 1327, a parliament formally deposed King Edward II in favor of his fourteen-year-old heir, Edward III. The act was sealed by Edward II's enforced abdication and by his murder later in the same year. Edward III inherited the kingdom, but he was still too young to rule. Actual power passed to Mortimer and Isabella, who dominated the regency government.

The deposition of a king, unprecedented in English history, was an awesome occurrence. Parliament was the immediate instrument of the deposition, but the events of 1327 by no means illustrate a significant degree of parliamentary power over the monarchy. The real agents of Edward II's downfall were Mortimer and Isabella, aided by the pent-up hostilities of the English magnates. Edward II was defeated and imprisoned by means of armed rebellion; the parliament of 1327 was under the control of the insurgents and merely ratified their wishes. Nevertheless, the very fact that the formalities of royal deposition should be carried on in a parliament is significant in itself. It was through parliaments that the "community of the realm" spoke, and in 1327 the "community" gave legal sanction to what otherwise would have been an act of treason.

In Edward II's time the royal element in English government reached its nadir. The monarchy was still the fulcrum of English politics, and for this very reason the reign of an incompetent and feeble king such as Edward II robbed the kingdom of its political balance and brought on a state of general turbulence. Despite the ever-growing importance of English political and administrative institutions, the strength and wisdom of the monarch was the fundamental factor in the well-being of the community. Edward III was a far abler king than his father, and when he came to power the whole political orientation of England changed dramatically. For after a generation of violence and semianarchy a strong monarch once again occupied the English throne.

The immediate effect of the revolution of 1327, however, was a renewal of the bitterness and disaffection from which England had so long been suffering. Mortimer proceeded to enrich himself from the lands of Edward II's defeated supporters, and the baronial faction that supported the revolution soon turned to internal bickering and even armed conflict. Moreover, the relationship between Mortimer and Isabella was becoming a national scandal. The two were well on their way to making as many enemies as Despenser when in 1330 they were unexpectedly brought to ruin. Seemingly secure in their control of England, they fell victim to a court conspiracy led by the young king himself. Mortimer was seized in his room in Nottingham Castle by followers of Edward III, tried by a parliament, and hanged. Isabella was permitted her freedom and a generous allowance but was deprived of power. And young King Edward, having proclaimed his coming of age in this exuberant fashion, proceeded to the essential work of healing England's divisions by restoring vigorous royal leadership to his troubled kingdom.

Edward III (1327–1377): The Hundred Years War

Like Richard the Lion-Hearted, Edward III was a warrior king.[3] Chivalrous, magnanimous, a bit lax on matters of royal prerogative, he was immensely popular except during a brief constitutional crisis in 1341 and in his final years of voluptuous senility. Historians have accused him of being a grandiose fool, addicted to empty pageantry and spectacular but ultimately fruitless military campaigning. Yet he succeeded to a remarkable degree in maintaining the loyalty of his magnates and his six sons. Earlier kings of England—William the Conqueror and Henry II in particular—had been tormented by the rebellious infidelity of their offspring, but the sons of Edward III respected and supported him. The key to his success was his ostentatious chivalry which historians have so often and so wrongly condemned. Chivalric pageantry and campaigning were the very things that the magnates loved, and Edward III's seemingly theatrical behavior won for him a tangible and exceedingly valuable prize: the admiring loyalty of his barons and the obedience of his subjects. Edward III was an honored king, and consequently England was at peace with herself during most of his reign.

Peace at home and war abroad characterized the age of Edward III. Between 1333 and 1336 he led a series of successful if inconclusive expeditions into Scotland, and later on, in 1346, the English won a notable victory over the Scots at the battle of Neville's Cross, taking King David II of Scotland into captivity. Edward III's chief military efforts, however, were directed against France, and it was there that he won his greatest glory.

Edward's French campaigns mark the opening phase of

---

[3] There is no adequate modern biography of Edward III. On political institutions in the early part of his reign, see J. F. Willard and W. A. Morris (ed.), *The English Government at Work, 1326–37* (3 vols., 1940–50). An excellent survey of the Hundred Years War is E. Perroy, *The Hundred Years War* (W. B. Wells, tr., 1951). On the early phase of the war see the sound and sophisticated account of A. H. Burne, *The Crécy War* (1955).

The Hundred Years War

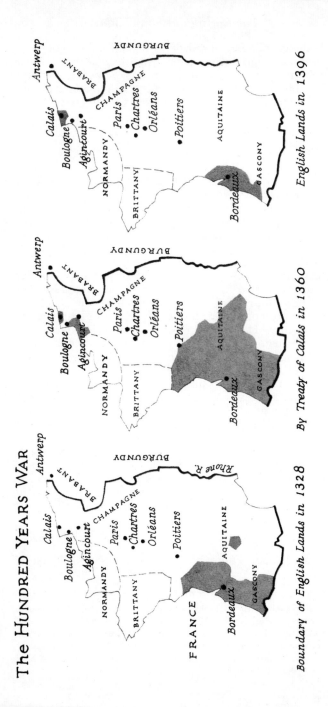

Boundary of English Lands in 1328

By Treaty of Calais in 1360

English Lands in 1396

a protracted military struggle known as the Hundred Years War. The name is inappropriate for several reasons. For one thing, the "war" lasted not for 100 years but for 115 years – from 1338 to 1453. For another, the campaigns of this period were separated by prolonged truces, often lasting a great many years. One might reasonably regard the "Hundred Years War" as consisting in fact of a series of much shorter wars. And it should be obvious by now that the conflict between the medieval kingdoms of England and France began not in 1338 but in 1066. Almost every king since the Norman Conquest had campaigned against the French at one time or another, and the "Hundred Years War" was in many respects merely a continuation of these earlier struggles. Nevertheless, the term has been hallowed by custom and will be used here for the sake of convenience.

One theme which links the various campaigns of the Hundred Years War and separates them from previous Anglo-French conflicts is the English monarchy's claim to the French throne. When the last of the Capetian kings died childless in 1328, Edward III became a serious contender for the French royal succession through his mother Isabella, daughter of King Philip the Fair. But the French, not wishing to be ruled by an English monarch, denied that the royal succession could pass down through the female line, and gave the crown to Philip VI (1328–50), the first monarch of the Valois dynasty. Edward did not at first dispute this decision, but later on, when other matters prompted him to take up arms against the French, he revived his claim and used it to justify his invasions. Subsequent kings of England were also to claim the throne of France, and the Valois succession was not finally recognized in England until after the war's end in 1453.

In the middle and later 1330s Anglo-French relations were severely strained by a number of further disputes. The two lands were at odds over Flanders, which France had long been endeavoring to control but which was extremely important to England as a market for her wool. Moreover, the French had been supporting the Scots in their warfare with England. The old dispute over the remaining English fiefs in southern France remained very much alive and reached a crisis in 1337 when Philip VI ordered the confiscation of Gascony. And underlying these issues was the fact that the young King Edward and the chivalrous young noblemen whom he had gathered around him were hungry for adventure and for the pursuit of military glory on the fields of France. In short, a warrior king and a warrior nobility needed a war.

So it was that in 1338, after elaborate preparations, Edward III led a glittering and hopeful army southward across the English Channel. His plan was to invade France through the Low Countries—to attack on a huge scale not only with his own soldiers but with those of his continental allies as well. For Edward III, like John and Edward I before him, had created an elaborate system of alliances with important princes in the Netherlands and Germany. Such an alliance system required staggeringly heavy expenditures for subsidies and bribes, and imposed a considerable strain on English resources. Edward attempted to finance his soldiers and diplomats by means of heavy taxes on wool and by various complex but ineffective schemes to create artificial wool shortages and thereby raise prices and customs revenues. But Edward found that his allies' thirst for bribes was unquenchable and that when the time for action came they demanded more money than he was able to give them. Accordingly, the campaigning between 1338 and 1340 accomplished very little except to drive the English monarchy far into debt. Edward salvaged one victory from the early phase of the war when his fleet annihilated a large French armada in 1340 at the battle of Sluys off the Flemish coast. Sluys was an impressive triumph which enabled the English to control the Channel for the next several years. But Edward's initial land campaigns were both frustrating and expensive.

During the 1340s and thereafter Edward altered his military strategy significantly. Finding that an alliance system was costly and inefficient, he undertook to send English armies directly into France, lightly supplied but prepared to forage off the land. The new policy proved its worth in 1342 when a series of English raids against Brittany resulted in the establishment of English control over that strategic province. Again in 1345 Edward sent armies into France—one to Brittany, another to Gascony—and in 1346 the king crossed the Channel himself with an army of some 10,000 men, immense by the standards of the age. Campaigning in Normandy, he plundered the important town of Caen and from there led his force first southeastward toward Paris, then northward into Ponthieu. At Crécy, a few miles from the Channel, he encountered the French army, and the two forces clashed in the first great land battle of the Hundred Years War.

The battle of Crécy, fought on August 26, 1346, resulted in an overwhelming victory for Edward III. It was, indeed, the most stunning military triumph of his career. Edward's longbowmen decimated the mounted French nobles to such a degree that their military capability was crippled for some years to come. In August 1346 the English occupied the key Channel port of Calais, which was destined to remain in English hands until the mid-sixteenth century. The campaign of 1346 gave Edward the success and prestige to which he had aspired only in his wildest dreams, and brought the hegemony of medieval France to a decisive close.

A decade after Crécy the English, depending heavily once again on their longbowmen, won another major victory over the French cavalry at Poitiers. Edward III was not present at the battle; the English army was led by his eldest son, a talented young warrior known as the Black Prince. Although badly outnumbered, the English put the French to rout, captured the incompetent French king, John the Good, and returned triumphantly to England with their royal prisoner.

Crécy and Poitiers were separated by the cataclysmic arrival of the Black Death in Europe. Shattered by two momentous military disasters, the fearful plague, the loss of its king, and the harrying of mercenary companies, France in the later 1350s was virtually prostrate. In 1358 a large-scale rebellion of French peasants was put down only after a savage struggle, and in 1359 the Black Prince was able to lead his army across France from the Channel to Burgundy virtually unopposed. At length, in 1360, the two kingdoms concluded a truce on terms exceedingly favorable to Edward III. King Edward temporarily dropped his claim to the French throne but was given vast territories in France, comparable even to those of the twelfth-century Angevin Empire. And King John of France was ransomed for the staggering sum of half a million pounds, five times the ransom of Richard the Lion-Hearted in the twelfth century.

The impressive gains which the English had won by their brilliant French campaigns of the 1340s and 1350s were lost in the course of the next two decades. This reversal in military fortunes resulted from a notable revival of French royal authority and the dogged, unrelenting pressure of French armies against the overextended English positions. England prospered during the greater part of the 1360s; Edward III basked in the prestige of his earlier victories, and the royal treasury was richly nourished by French ransom payments. But as the 1360s drew to a close, the relative quality of French and English leadership was undergoing a fateful transformation. Edward III was slipping into an early dotage, and passed his later years as a mere tool of unscrupulous courtiers and his even more unscrupulous mistress, Alice Perrers. His eldest son, the Black Prince, fell victim to a lingering illness. On the French side, the inept King John died in 1364 and was succeeded by his intelligent and energetic son, Charles V (1364–80). King Charles had the good fortune of being served by an able military commander, Bertrand Duguesclin, who was reputed to be the ugliest man in France and the best general in Europe. Charles and Duguesclin adopted a military policy of remorseless harassment. They avoided major battles but won a great many minor ones. This policy, as it turned out, was the best possible one for France. From about 1369 onward England's French possessions dissolved steadily until, by the time of Edward III's death in 1377, the English held only Calais, Cherbourg, a little territory around Bordeaux, and a few Breton harbors. A generation was to pass before England, under the vibrant leadership of King Henry V, made any serious attempt to recover her losses and resume her quest for the throne of France.

Parliament in the Fourteenth Century

Against the background of foreign military campaigning that characterized much of the fourteenth century, parliament underwent a significant development.[4] Huge military expenditures forced the monarchy to depend increasingly on extraordinary taxation, and the revenues which the kings so desperately needed could be obtained only by parliamentary consent. Hence, the parliaments of the fourteenth century were in a powerful bargaining position. But the magnates of Edward III were generally enthusiastic about the French war and were not inclined to be parsimonious in giving the king their financial support. Edward III's policies and his chivalric personality placed him in close rapport with his nobles. Fourteenth-century parliaments included other classes than the nobility, however, and Edward III's aggressive and expensive policies seemed far less captivating to the townsmen and gentry. It was they who objected most strongly to the repeated subsidies necessary to finance his grandiose campaigns, and consequently it was they who profited the most from his dependence on parliamentary grants.

As the fourteenth century opened, parliament had come into being but was as yet ill-defined in membership and function. By the end of the century much of its potential had already been realized and it was coming to assume something of its modern form. It had split into Lords and Commons, and the Commons in parliament had acquired a crucial role in taxation and legislation. By 1399 the parliamentary tradition had become sufficiently etched into the English political system to survive the anarchy of the fifteenth century, the discreet absolutism of the Tudors, and the divine-right monarchy of the Stuarts, to become the fundamental institution in modern English government.

---

[4] On parliamentary developments see the splendid essays of G. T. Lapsley, *Crown, Community and Parliament in the Later Middle Ages* (1951). A brilliant, monumental work on the English administrative structure is T.F. Tout, *Chapters in Medieval Administrative History* (6 vols., 1923–35).

The fourteenth century, therefore, was a crucial epoch in the rise of parliament and, more specifically, in the rise of the Commons. By the time of Edward I's death the summoning of representatives of townsmen and gentry was becoming customary, and although they were present at only three of the first seven parliaments of Edward II, they attended all but two of the parliaments between 1310 and 1327. They became a normal element in the parliaments of Edward III and were invariably present from the mid-fourteenth century onward.

At the very time when representatives of town and shire were becoming an integral part of parliament, the two groups were in the process of coalescing into a single political force. Gradually they came to realize that they had strong common interests. The shire knights remained more powerful and more articulate than the burghers in fourteenth-century parliaments, but the economic resources of the burghers were expanding throughout this period relative to those of other classes, and both gentry and townsmen discovered that they could accomplish far more by working in close cooperation than by endeavoring to defend their interests alone. Their community of interests was cemented by frequent intermarriages between members of the two classes. And before the fourteenth century was half over they had fused politically into a single parliamentary group: the House of Commons.

This process of fusion began under Edward II and reached its completion under Edward III. Representatives of town and shire probably met together in 1332, and they unquestionably did so in 1339 to deliberate jointly over a royal grant. They were described in the Rolls of Parliament at that time as "men of the Commons." Thereafter, joint meetings became normal, and the Commons took its place as a vital element in the government of England.

The development of Commons as a separate parliamentary group meant that the members of parliament who were not included in the Commons became, in effect, a separate group themselves. These men—the great magnates and prelates of the realm, who had long been the core of parliament—became a distinct body known as the House of Lords. The term "House of Lords" does not actually appear in our documents until the sixteenth century, but the institution itself was in existence from the mid-fourteenth century onward.

In the thirteenth century many great notables had regarded attendance in parliaments as a burden, but as the fourteenth century progressed they came increasingly to consider it a valuable privilege. Eligibility for attendance in parliaments was now much more rigorously defined than before, and under Edward III there emerged a definite group of barons who alone and invariably received parliamentary summonses. This select group came to be known as the "peerage." And although the term "peer" literally means "social equal," actually the peers, to paraphrase George Orwell, were more "equal" than anyone else in the realm. Fourteenth-century barons who were eligible for a parliamentary summons fell into two groups: (1) the greatest magnates and prelates, who received individual summonses to Parliament, and (2) lesser lords whose tenures were regarded by custom as "baronial" rather than merely "knightly" and who answered a general parliamentary summons. The right of a lord to attend parliament became hereditary and was passed down, like a great baronial estate, from father to eldest son. Thus, the peerage became a permanent and clearly defined group at the apex of the social order.

The process of selecting particular individuals to represent their shires or towns in the House of Commons was far more fluid and complex, and many of the details of the selection process are hidden from us. Normally the shire representative was chosen at a meeting of the shire court, which was usually attended only by the more substantial men of the district. The sheriff was the chief figure at these meetings and was often able to manipulate the elections in his own favor or in behalf of the monarchy. Indeed, the electoral procedures were frequently so ill-defined that the sheriff could simply name his own slate of representatives. Similarly, a powerful local magnate might overawe the court with his private army of retainers and secure the election of his own henchmen. In the later fourteenth century, John of Gaunt exerted virtually absolute control over the selection of shire knights from his vast palatinate of Lancaster, and the great magnates of Yorkshire appear to have dominated the elections of Commons representatives from their county. Such manipulation was still more common in the fifteenth century when the military power and local autonomy of the great lords was at its height. Prior to 1399, manipulation of county elections by sheriffs or magnates, although widespread, was far from universal. Left to themselves, the county courts were apt to elect knights or squires of unusual wealth and substance, and the same was true of the towns where electoral arrangements were so varied as to defy generalization. Whatever the details, the Commons representatives were generally pillars of their community (unless they were paid royal or baronial agents), and one will look in vain in the fourteenth-century Commons for lower-class protest or revolutionary ferment.

Nevertheless, the emergence of Commons and the progressive extension of its power is a matter of immense significance in the development of English constitutionalism. The fourteenth-century Commons rose to power by means of its implied power to approve or disapprove extraordinary royal taxes on the classes which it represented. And at every opportunity it sought to tighten its control of taxation – to make its power over the royal purse strings increasingly explicit.

In the crisis of 1297 the royal government of Edward I had conceded that all uncustomary taxes must be approved by the "community of the realm." It was generally assumed at that time, although not specifically stated, that the "community" was embodied in parliaments. Under Edward III this power to approve taxes, now inherent in parliament, passed gradually into the hands of Commons. It was to be the key to all of Commons' future power, and the members of Commons seem to have understood this important fact. For when they approved a particular grant, they would often demand and receive greater control over grants in general. Commons was in a strong position, for the increasingly affluent classes which it represented were supplying the monarchy with the bulk of its tax revenues. Accordingly, by the end of the fourteenth century the Commons was coming to exercise the exclusive right to originate parliamentary taxation. In 1395 a parliamentary grant was made "by the Commons with the advise and assent of the Lords." This was the first time these exact words were used, but they became the normal formula in years thereafter.

Thus, by 1399 parliament – and more specifically Commons – had a controlling voice in royal taxation. Parliamentary approval was required for all taxes, direct or indirect – even tolls and customs from merchants. Parliament was even supervising and auditing tax revenues and was beginning to specify the uses to which particular taxes could be put. Profiting from the military dangers and general unrest of Richard II's reign (1377–99), parliament used its fiscal power to establish an ever greater control over government policies. In 1377 it insisted on overseeing the use to which its grant was put and succeeded in securing the appointment of two London merchants as treasurers of war. And in 1382 the parliamentary representatives imposed their own foreign policy on the royal government by insisting on a military campaign in Flanders. The right to grant or refuse taxes, they were discovering, was an effective avenue to political power.

The relationship between taxation and power is nowhere better illustrated than in the gradual acceptance of Commons' right to legislate. This function, undreamed-of at the close of the thirteenth century, was well established a hundred years later. Edward III's first parliament, meeting in 1327, introduced for the first time a Commons Petition – a list of grievances which the parliament expected the monarchy to consider seriously in return for the granting of taxes. Parliaments had long been accustomed to receiving and passing on to the king petitions from individuals or groups. The Commons Petition differed from these earlier individual petitions in that it dealt with matters of general interest to the "community of the realm." The Commons Petition of 1327 was concerned with such matters as the maintenance of Magna Carta, the soundness of English currency, and the size of cloths sold in English markets. Coming at a time of grave political crisis it received the sympathetic attention of the royal government and gave rise to two statutes and several ordinances and decrees. More important, it set a fateful precedent; similar petitions were introduced in the parliaments of 1333 and 1337, and they appeared regularly from 1343 onward. Fourteenth-century parliaments used the Commons Petition repeatedly as a device to put pressure on the king to grant their wishes, and as time went on it became increasingly customary for a Commons Petition to give rise to royal statutes. Thus, the Commons Petition was a significant step in the direction of parliamentary legislation. In later years the Commons Petition evolved into the Commons Bill, and the will of the House of Commons became the law of England. Indeed, after the mid-fourteenth century most statutes resulted directly from Commons Petitions or Commons Bills. The mechanism for Commons legislation was thereby established, and it remained only to refine it.

Originally, the normal procedure was for Commons to make a Petition and vote a grant. The king would then approve the Petition and it would be translated into statute. But if some item in the Petition was offensive to the king he might ignore it or alter its meaning. In order to prevent this sort of royal tampering and to achieve complete identity between Petition and statute, the Commons developed the principle of "redress before supply." Only if and when the king satisfied their Petition both in matter and spirit would Commons make the requested grant. This principle was an effective weapon indeed against a monarch such as Edward III who needed money desperately in order to fight his wars and was not inclined to quibble so long as he received his grant. "Redress before supply," which had become a normal procedure by the early fifteenth century, was a key factor in the transformation of parliament's privilege to petition into parliament's right to make law.

In the course of the fourteenth century, therefore, parliament—and Commons in particular—acquired two momentous privileges: consent to taxation, and control of legislation. By the century's end parliament had established itself firmly and permanently in the English political fabric. A hundred years of war, plague, and social turbulence had seen England move far along the road toward constitutional monarchy.

Law and Administration

The evolution of other branches of the English government in the fourteenth century was much less spectacular than that of parliament. The royal council became steadily more elaborate and differentiated and the bureaucracy was gradually becoming a force in itself, but in essence the council retained the structure that it had assumed in the thirteenth century. Baronial attempts to control council and household, which began in 1258–65 under Henry III, were revived, as we have seen, under Edward II but without lasting success. Under Richard II, in the final quarter of the century, magnates and parliament succeeded far more completely than before in establishing a grip on the council and influencing the household, with the result that much of Richard II's reign was dominated by what may be termed a "conciliar government."

The English judicial structure evolved slowly along the general lines established by Edward I. There were no "English Justinians" in the fourteenth century, and the common law remained in general what it had been at Edward I's death. At the local level, townsmen and gentry came to exercise ever greater responsibility in the operation of the government. As the century progressed, the important role in local administration formerly exercised by the sheriffs was falling increasingly into the hands of a new group of officials – usually drawn from the gentry – known as justices of the peace.

The fourteenth-century justice of the peace was to remain a dominant figure in the administrative and judicial organization of the counties for centuries to come. The office evolved out of Edward I's keepers of the peace who exercised police functions under the authority of the sheriff. A statute of 1330 gave the keepers of the peace the responsibility to indict criminals as well as apprehend them, and this new judicial function was greatly broadened by a statute of 1360 empowering the keepers to try felons and trespassers. The statute of 1360, in effect, transformed the keepers of the peace into justices of the peace. Their judicial functions were further elaborated in 1362 when they were directed to hold courts four times a year. These "quarter sessions" – as the four yearly courts were called – gave the justices of the peace preeminence in legal affairs over all other county officials, including sheriffs. By the century's close their jurisdictional supremacy had ripened into a general supervision of the county administration, and the quarter sessions had virtually superseded the older shire courts and county eyres. The justices themselves had by then assumed the obligation of supervising the recruitment of shire levies and had become, withal, the chief royal officers in the counties and the essential links between crown and shire. No mere bureaucrats or royal agents, they were largely local men with local interests who were nevertheless exceptionally useful to the king and council in the governance of the realm.

Chapter 8

THE STRANGE DEATH OF 𝕸𝖊𝖉𝖎𝖊𝖛𝖆𝖑 ENGLAND

Upheaval in the Later Fourteenth Century

DURING the second half of the fourteenth century England's foreign struggles and constitutional transformation occurred against a background of plague, cultural disintegration, and growing social upheaval. The Black Death destroyed what remained of the confidence and optimism of the High Middle Ages. It served as the somber backdrop to a deepening economic crisis, a bitter popular insurrection known as the Peasants' Revolt, and growing social tensions and religious restlessness. These themes recognize no arbitrary dating such as is so often imposed on them by historians. They are problems which tormented English society well after 1399, the terminal point of this present book, and many of them will be discussed more fully in the next volume of this series. Together, they constitute a dark and turbulent epilogue to England's medieval experience.

The Crisis of the Later Fourteenth Century:
The Black Death

The culture of the High Middle Ages, and the general prosperity that accompanied it, were beginning to fade in the opening decades of the fourteenth century. Very likely the population began its downward trend with the terrible floods and famines that struck England between 1315 and 1317. But with the political and military successes of Edward III's reign the kingdom seemed to be recovering its coherence and self-assurance. Then, in 1348–49, the Black Death struck, carrying away at a single blow perhaps a quarter to a third of the English population. Already the Black Death – or bubonic plague – had wrought its devastation on the Continent, and all Europe was stunned by the catastrophe. The plague was carried by fleas which infested black rats. Having spread with fearful speed across mid-fourteenth-century Europe, it returned periodically for the next three centuries, keeping people in a general state of anxiety for their lives and the lives of their families. The population of England and the Continent dropped drastically in the wake of the plague, and continued to decline for the next century or so. It began to rise again after about the mid-fifteenth century, but only very slowly. The population of mid-fifteenth-century England has been estimated at about two and one half million – a million or so less than at the beginning of the fourteenth century.

The Black Death brought incalculable suffering and terror to the English. Those who endured the first onslaught were saddened by the loss of beloved friends or members of their families. Although they survived the catastrophe without social collapse it broke their confidence and darkened their spirits. The personal grief brought by the plague is immeasurable, but it is possible to comprehend its toll in more tangible ways – in the deserted villages, the decline of the European wool market, and the severe shortage of labor. The Black Death cannot be said to have changed the course of history, but it did have the effect of vastly accelerating the already evident breakdown of high medieval civilization. Among other things it hastened the demise of the old manorial regime. With the rising wages brought about by the labor shortage, and the declining grain market which resulted from the population drop, land profits and land values fell. Demesne farming became increasingly profitless and gradually disappeared almost entirely. Landlords now tended to abandon the practice of direct farming, preferring to divide their old demesne lands into individual peasant plots and to live entirely off the rents of their tenants.

The Crisis of the Later Fourteenth Century: Political and Social Conflict

Social turbulence had been intensifying early in the century during Edward II's reign, and in the later years of Edward III it increased still more. The Black Death had much to do with this, as did the failing leadership of the king. Most important of all was the unhealthy trend toward bastard feudalism that had been gaining momentum ever since Edward I's reign. By the later fourteenth century the custom of assembling permanent private armies of retainers – supported by their lords' wages and clad in their lords' liveries – was reaching its height. This practice of "livery and maintenance" was, in effect, the old feudal household system gone wild. The contract, or "indenture," between king and lord and between lord and military retainer had become fully developed in the course of Edward III's French campaigns, and, in the decades following, it contributed much to the general social chaos. Private military retinues often terrorized the countryside, bringing about a breakdown of local government and an epidemic of local warfare. The justices of the peace did their best to keep order in their districts, but frequently they were unable to cope with the private armies of powerful local lords. The English countryside had been relatively peaceful in the High Middle Ages; in the fourteenth and fifteenth centuries it was afflicted by an accelerating trend toward violence.

The social crisis reached its peak in Edward III's final years and in the reign of his successor. When Edward passed from his long dotage at last in 1377, he was succeeded by a ten-year-old child, Richard II (1377–99), son of the Black Prince. For the next decade England was ruled by a regency government dominated by contending baronial factions. Plague, social disorder, and weak royal government all contributed to the general gloom of the period, as did the series of military humiliations which England was then suffering at the hands of the French. The years between 1377 and 1380 were darkened by fear of a French invasion of England – a fear which ceased only with the death of the able French monarch Charles V. But France had been suffering, too, and the succession of a young child to the French throne in 1380 - the fitfully insane Charles VI – brought on a long era of civil strife centering on the rivalry of two royal uncles: the dukes of Burgundy and Orleans. France, which had been tormented so long, was now obliged to endure still more. But England gained no immediate advantage from France's plight; the duke of Burgundy was sufficiently strong to maintain the military pressure against the English, and Richard II was anything but a warrior king.

The Crisis of the Later Fourteenth Century: Religious Ferment

The turmoil and pessimism of the later fourteenth century were accompanied by a powerful upsurge of protest against the structure and substance of the medieval Church. Outcries against the wealth and spiritual hollowness of the clergy had been known for centuries, but they were more strident now than ever before. Plague and social upheaval had created a mood of violence and radicalism at the very time when the Church was becoming particularly deserving of pious condemnation. Early in the century the papacy had abandoned Rome for Avignon. There it remained for seven decades, under the shadow of the French monarchy, devoting itself more and more to administrative matters, and collecting its revenues with ever greater efficiency. To many, the papacy seemed to have forfeited its international character, and its grasping fiscal policies were therefore all the more resented. For the English, who were at war with France during much of the fourteenth century, allegiance to a French pope was difficult indeed. Hostility to the papacy is aptly illustrated in the contemporary observation that the pope was supposed to lead Christ's flock, not to fleece it. The scandal of papal misgovernment was heightened after 1378 when the Church was split into two fragments, one led by a pope at Avignon, the other by a pope at Rome. This tragicomic schism persisted to the end of the fourteenth century and beyond.

Opposition to the papacy and the Church proceeded along several lines. The great English Franciscan philosopher, William of Ockham, contended not only against the faith-reason synthesis of St. Thomas but also against the complacency, greed, and corruption of the contemporary Church. An avowed enemy of papal absolutism, he insisted that the Church should be governed and reformed through ecclesiastical councils, the selection of which was to begin at the parish level. On the Continent similar and even more radical views were finding expression. The clergy, it was suggested, should renounce its wealth or be deprived of it, and the pope should withdraw from politics and devote his attention to purely spiritual matters.

The later fourteenth century witnessed an upsurge of mysticism in such works as *The Revelations of Divine Love* by the anchoress Juliana of Norwich. The medieval Church had always found room for mystics but had never been entirely comfortable with them. For mysticism involves a direct relationship between the believer and God which, without necessarily questioning the sacraments and the priesthood, has the effect of transcending them and diminishing their importance. The Church, as mediator between God and man was, strictly speaking, unnecessary to the mystic who needed no intermediary in his quest for the beatific vision.

The alienation of the ecclesiastical hierarchy from the individual believer is illustrated in quite different ways in the writings of two great literary figures of the late fourteenth century, William Langland and Geoffrey Chaucer.[1] The works of these two men mark the reassertion of the English language as a dominent literary vehicle after centuries of French linguistic supremacy. And both men disclose – each in his own manner – the growing popular hostility toward the ecclesiastical establishment. Langland, like the contemporary mystics, had no great interest in the sacramental functions of the priesthood. But unlike the mystics he was a moralist rather than a contemplative. He loved the Church as it should be but despised the Church as it was. Perhaps one might more properly say that his love for the essential Church – the Body of Christ – prompted him to condemn the corrupt behavior of contemporary churchmen all the more severely. Langland was neither a revolutionary nor a heretic. He revered the Church as the agent of man's salvation and the vehicle of divine love, but he denounced the friars for their greed, the theologians for their needless complexity, and the papacy for its malign influence on simple Christian believers. More than anything else, Langland condemned the avarice and arrogance of the wealthy and the selfish cruelty of those in power, whether churchmen or laymen. Wealth, to Langland, hardened men and made then uncharitable, and the Church should therefore return to a condition of apostolic poverty. In his masterpiece, *Piers Plowman*, he writes:

Ah, well it may be with poverty, for he may pass untroubled,
And in peace among the pillagers if patience follow him.
Our prince, Jesus, and his apostles chose poverty together,
And the longer they lived the less wealth they mastered. . . .
If possession is poison and makes imperfect orders,
It would be well to dislodge them for the Church's profit,
And purge them of that poison before the peril is greater.

Not only the Church, but all society has been corrupted by wealth:

---

[1] See B. Ford (ed.), *The Age of Chaucer* (Penguin Guide to English Literature, I, 1954). A recent study of the great religious reformer of the later fourteenth century is J. A. Robson, *Wyclif and the Oxford Schools* (1961).

As weeds run wild on ooze or on the dunghill,
So riches spread upon riches give rise to all vices.
The best wheat is bent before it ripens,
On land overlaid with marl or the dungheap.
And so are surely all such people.
Overplenty feeds the pride which poverty conquers.

William Langland was bitterly critical of his society, yet like a Hebrew prophet he softened his protests with a strain of hope—hope for a purified humanity moved by love rather than greed. His intense moral sensitivity contrasts sharply with the mood of his genial and worldly-wise contemporary, Geoffrey Chaucer (c. 1343–1400). Chaucer's marvelous literary genius derived in part from his ability to portray with remarkable insight the personalities and motivations of his characters. He entered into them, displayed them for all to see, yet was able to remain personally aloof. He was not a conscious reformer, not a prophet crying out against the sins of his age, but an acute observer of human character. In this role he was able to illuminate vividly the vices and virtues of contemporary churchmen. The pilgrims depicted in his *Canterbury Tales* include the Poor Parson, a compassionate and well-intentioned village priest, and the Oxford Clerk, absorbed in his disinterested devotion to scholarship. They also include less attractive ecclesiastical types: the superficial, mannered Prioress, the Pardoner who was essentially a salesman of indulgences, the lecherous Summoner, the Monk who was addicted to the pleasures of the hunt, and the corrupt Friar:

Highly beloved and intimate was he
With country folk wherever he might be,
And worthy city women with possessions;
For he was qualified to hear confessions,
Or so he said, with more than priestly scope;
He had a special license from the pope.
Sweetly he heard his penitents at shrift
With pleasant absolution, for a gift.*

Criticism and resentment of the contemporary Church found expression also at the political level. During the later thirteenth and early fourteenth centuries the papacy considerably expanded its right of "provision"—of exercising direct

---

* Tr. Nevill Coghill, in Geoffrey Chaucer, *The Canterbury Tales* (Penguin Books, Baltimore, 1952).

Four Canterbury Pilgrims:
the Prioress, the Miller, the Squire, and the Clerk of Oxford;
from the Ellesmere manuscript (*ca.* 1390) of Chaucer's *Canterbury Tales*.

control over the appointment of English churchmen at all levels from parish and canonry to archdiocese. The right of papal provision – which was in keeping with the growing tendency at the time toward ecclesiastical centralization – gave the papacy the power to appoint a large number of churchmen in four-teenth-century England. Resentful of such extensive outside control of the English Church, Parliament gave its support in 1351 to the Statute of Provisors which succeeded in limiting papal provisions at least slightly. A second Statute of Provisors in 1390 was more effective, but the popes retained considerable influence on English ecclesiastical appointments for some time to come. And in doing so they insured that resentment would continue.

The old issue of appeals to the pope from the Church courts of England remained acute throughout the fourteenth century. Papal appeals, like papal provisions, were attacked by statutes. The first Statute of Praemunire (1353) sought to limit such appeals but actually had little effect on them. It was not until the third Statute of Praemunire in 1393 that the practice was seriously curtailed. Finally, Anglo-papal relations during the fourteenth century were clouded by an accelerating conflict over the pope's right to tax the English clergy. There were serious protests against papal taxation in 1375 and 1376, and on two occasions Richard II refused it altogether. These strug-gles, although inconclusive, had the effect of diminishing the papal hold on the English Church. They constitute a political expression of the rising anticlericalism that affected society at all levels.

Fourteenth-century anticlericalism reached its crescendo in the career of the great Oxford philosopher and ecclesiastical revolutionary, John Wycliffe (d. 1384). Wycliffe's thought was built on the strong tradition of anti-ecclesiastical protest which had already manifested itself in many ways – in popular oppo-sition to clerical wealth and corruption, in hostility between the English government and the papacy, in scholarly attacks on medieval theology and the Church hierarchy by men such as Ockham. The mystical doctrine of direct communion with God, short-circuiting the priestly sacramental system, also made a deep impact on Wycliffe. And by the later fourteenth century the Church itself was noticeably weaker than it had been in the High Middle Ages. Its moral authority was declining, it no longer inspired such awe as it once had, its monopoly on literacy and learning had long been broken, and laymen now occupied the high positions in the royal administration and judiciary which had once been the exclusive preserve of clerics. With the decline in land income brought about by the plague, the Church's revenues fell, and it found itself in bitter competition with the equally hard-pressed barons and monarchy for the taxes of the English laity. Many Englishmen were prepared to listen respectfully to Wycliffe's radical reform proposals, and some were even ready to follow him.

Wycliffe first attained repute as a highly gifted but fundamentally orthodox Oxford theologian. In the mid-1370s he passed under the protection of the most powerful magnate of the age, John of Gaunt, Duke of Lancaster, and fourth son of Edward III. Shielded by John of Gaunt's favor, he became active in politics for a time and began his fateful journey along the road of heresy. After 1378 his radical doctrinal views made it impossible for him to continue his political career, and he devoted his final years to writing. In these years his opposition to the Church and to traditional Catholic doctrine became sharper and more fundamental than ever before. He condemned ecclesiastical property and suggested that the king had the right to confiscate it. He attacked the traditional medieval doctrine of the eucharist. Inspired by the mystical doctrines that were then in the air, he rejected the entire priestly-sacramental system. To him, the organized Church was not a mediator between God and man, but merely an agency to aid man in his spiritual quest. Indeed, the *true* Church was not the ecclesiastical hierarchy at all, but the community of believers. Not merely the mystic but every man must confront God directly, without priestly intercession, guided only by his own conscience and Holy Scripture.

Such, in brief, were the religious doctrines of John Wycliffe. Most Englishmen, disenchanted though they were with traditional Catholic Christianity, were not yet ready for them. Langland's longing for a purification of the old order was far more congenial to the contemporary English mood than Wycliffe's call to revolution. Yet Wycliffe's scholarly prestige was great, hostility to the Church was growing, and there were some who adopted his extreme views. These men, known as Lollards, included a handful of Oxford scholars; most of them, however, were from among the poor and outcast. To them, Wycliffe's religious revolt carried strong overtones of social revolution. Within a few years the heresy had spread to the Continent and served as a powerful influence on the career of the Bohemian reformer, John Hus. In 1415 Hus was burned at the stake by the fathers of the Council of Constance, but the doctrines endured to influence and inspire the Protestant reformers of the sixteenth century.

Wycliffe appears to have caught English churchmen off guard. In time, however, they reacted to his teachings and had little difficulty in enlisting the support of the lay establishment. Wycliffe himself seems to have enjoyed John of Gaunt's protection to the end and was allowed to die peacefully and naturally in 1384. But Wycliffe's doctrines had already been officially condemned before he died, and during the later part of Richard II's reign it became royal policy to hunt down and execute Lollards. This policy of repression was strengthened by a statute of 1401 bearing the ingenuous title, the Statute on the Burning of Heretics. By the early fifteenth century the immediate crisis was over, but the seeds had been planted and continued to germinate.

The Crisis of the Later Fourteenth Century: The Peasants' Revolt

Ecclesiastical wealth evoked a powerful protest in the later fourteenth century, but as the poetry of Langland demonstrates, popular opposition was directed not only against wealthy churchmen but against wealthy laymen as well:

The poor may plead and pray in doorways,
They may quake for cold and thirst and hunger.
None receives them rightfully and relieves their suffering;
They are hooted at like hounds and ordered away.

These words illustrate a profound sense of grievance that translated itself into an increasing degree of class antagonism and, in 1381, into a savage uprising known as the Peasants' Revolt.[2] This tragic rebellion fed on the general gloom and unrest of the age. More specifically, it was a product of the growing conflict between landlord and tenant which arose from the Black Death, the falling population, and the shortage of labor. As the labor supply diminished, wages tended to rise sharply. The landlords, facing an economic squeeze between rising wages and contracting markets, sought through legislation to keep wages down. These landlords were not great magnates for the most part but members of the gentry. Their fears were manifested in a series of Statutes of Laborers, issued from 1351 onward in response to strong pressure from the House of Commons. The Statutes of

---

[2] The nature of peasant life in the period is illuminated in H. S. Bennett, *Life on the English Manor, 1150–1400* (1937). For a good earlier account of the Revolt see Charles Oman, *The Great Revolt of 1381* (1906). The affair is given a Marxist twist in R. H. Hilton and H. Fagan, *The English Rising of 1381* (1950). Important contemporary documents are collected in G. M. Trevelyan and E. Powell (ed.), *The Peasants' Rising and the Lollards* (1899).

Laborers, which aimed at freezing wages by legislative fiat, were successful in keeping them within bounds but not in halting their rise altogether. For landlords often found themselves in competition with one another for peasants' services, and a "black market" on labor seems to have developed. Nevertheless, the peasant felt wronged by this legislation and tended toward the opinion, not altogether unfounded, that the ruling orders were conspiring against him.

This conviction was powerfully reinforced by a series of "poll taxes" which were levied between 1377 and 1381. Traditionally, parliamentary grants had been borne chiefly by the wealthier part of the population, but the poll taxes were assessed on rich and poor alike by head. The Commons, hard-pressed by declining land revenues and convinced that the peasants were having things far too much their own way, were captivated by the idea of reducing their own tax burden at peasant expense. The most severe of the poll taxes, that of 1381, was the immediate cause of the Peasants' Revolt.

The Revolt lasted scarcely a month, from late May, 1381, to the end of June, by which time the rebels were suppressed and the old social order was everywhere restored. It was a hopeless, wretchedly led endeavor, but for a brief moment it shook society to its foundations. A violent protest against the miserable conditions resulting from political suppression, war, depression, and plague, it illustrates the deep insecurity that afflicted English society in the later Middle Ages.

The Peasants' Revolt was, on the whole, a confused affair. It began in Kent and neighboring Essex. Among its many leaders the most notable were the Kentishman Wat Tyler and the priest John Ball, whose famous couplet symbolizes the radical, Christian-based egalitarianism of the rebels:

> When Adam delved and Eve span
> Who was then a gentleman?

Having terrorized the lords and gentry of their respective shires, the two bands merged on London in mid-June and ran wild in the city for two days. The court took refuge in the Tower, and the archbishop of Canterbury was captured and killed. Although deeply hostile to the lords, the rebels remained respectful of the monarchy, and the frightened court had no recourse but to send out the fourteen-year-old king, Richard II, to negotiate with them. There were two parleys, on two successive days, between the young monarch and the rebel leaders, and from contemporary accounts of these meetings we are able to form an impression of the rebel goals. They demanded above all the abolition of villainage — that is, the freeing of all peasants from the traditional work service on their lords' demesnes. They further demanded a ceiling on rents — not to exceed fourpence per acre. Beyond these specific concessions they sought a series of reforms that would have had no less effect than to overturn society: equality of all men before the law, abolition of all lordship except the king's, confiscation and redistribution of all ecclesiastical property which was not essential to the direct sustenance of churchmen, and the elimination of all English bishoprics save one. Such goals might well find wide support in later centuries. In 1381 they were wildly unrealistic and, if adopted, would have led to social chaos.

Richard II, having no real choice, submitted for the moment to the peasants' demands. At the second of the two parleys, after the king had made his concessions, the lord mayor of London seized the rebel leader Wat Tyler and pulled him from his horse. Wat Tyler was immediately slain, and his followers, surprisingly, refrained from any violent reaction. At the king's request, they simply dispersed. Perhaps they were under the illusion that their cause had triumphed. In fact, however, once the rebels withdrew from London the revolt was doomed. Terror continued to stalk the countryside for the next week or two — abbeys were attacked, manors burned, and towns plundered — but the rebellion quickly lost its initial enthusiasm. By the end of June the rebel bands had been hunted down and the old social order returned. The concessions were of course forgotten.

The Peasants' Revolt had no real chance to overturn society, yet some of its leaders' goals were realized in the next few decades through the operation of basic economic forces. The old demesne economy was no longer paying its way, and English villainage was therefore rapidly disappearing of its own accord. A villain was essentially one who was bound to perform work services for his lord, and as demesne lands were divided more and more into tenants' plots, the necessity of work service disappeared. By the early fifteenth century the old manorial regime was all but dead and villainage was dying with it.

As the fourteenth century closed, the age of crisis was drawing to an end. The following century, although socially divided and deeply troubled, witnessed no repetition of the Peasants' Revolt and produced no heretic of Wycliffe's stature. Aristocratic warfare reached a new level of intensity, but there were no serious challenges to basic social or ecclesiastical institutions. The epoch of transition from medieval to modern England was far from over, but the first great social and cultural upheaval had passed.

The Reign of Richard II (1377–1399)

The young Richard II, who negotiated with Wat Tyler so courageously and insincerely, grew up to become one of England's less successful kings.[3] He was a moody man, lonely, despotic, alternately ambitious and lethargic. By inclination he was an artist rather than a warrior. His political objectives were projections of his own personality: autocratic government at home and withdrawal from continental warfare. These goals were essentially those of the later Tudor kings, and Richard II has therefore been described as the sort of man that might have reigned successfully in the sixteenth century. Unfortunately, his policies were several generations ahead of their time and were extremely unpopular among his own contemporaries.

Richard's reign falls naturally into three periods: (1) between 1377 and 1389 he was dominated more or less by baronial factions; (2) between 1389 and 1397 he ruled in his own right but was obliged to restrain his absolutist impulses in order to maintain baronial cooperation, (3) between 1397 and 1399 he defied his barons, crushed them momentarily, achieved the absolute power that he had long sought and was suddenly brought to ruin by a baronial reaction.

The long period of tutelage under a baron-dominated council made the young king restive and resentful. It would be a gross error to regard the barons of this period as a monolithic force. On the contrary they were perhaps more faction-ridden than ever before, and they were engaged in conflicts not only with one another but with the gentry and townsmen who now exercised considerable power through the House of Commons. Still another strong political force in this age was the royal court itself, dominated by the young king's close relatives and intimates and, as time passed, by the king himself. The conflicts of this period were complex and unedifying; ultimately they resolved themselves into a struggle between court and parliament. England's greatest landholder, John of Gaunt, Duke of Lancaster, was a powerful figure during Richard's early minority. As uncle of the king he had a foothold in the court, and as master of the vast Lancastrian inheritance he was a political figure of great note. But his very power made him enemies, and his support of Wycliffe earned him the hostility of

---

[3] The best biography is A. Steel, *Richard II* (1941). The reign can also be approached through R. Bird, *The Turbulent London of Richard II* (1948). The career of a great contemporary magnate is surveyed in S. Armitage Smith, *John of Gaunt* (1904).

several leading churchmen. He was able to influence English politics but not to dominate them.

As in earlier periods of weak royal rule, England in Richard's minority suffered from the absence of central leadership. The turbulent political activity of the age lacked focus and direction. But gradually, as the king grew older, he himself sought to fill the vacuum with his own personality. He began to surround himself with loyal friends, thereby creating a "court party" faithful and subservient to himself. He favored these friends with earldoms, duchies, and high offices at court, and with their advice and support he embarked on a high-handed policy of royal authoritarianism. Intimate with his court favorites and defiant toward the barons and gentry, he ignored the exhortations of his nobles for a more vigorous prosecution of the Hundred Years War and sought to diminish their role in royal government. These policies were sharply challenged by the parliament of 1386, known as the "Wonderful Parliament." Hinting at the fate which an earlier royal tyrant had suffered in 1327, the Wonderful Parliament deposed Richard's chancellor, Michael de la Pole, who had been one of the king's most powerful favorites, and impeached him for peculation and other misconduct while in office. It installed in his place a man more sympathetic to the magnates' interests. A council of magnates and prelates was now created to "advise" the self-willed young monarch and keep him under control.

Once the Wonderful Parliament adjourned, Richard began to assert himself again. He restored Michael de la Pole to favor, ignored the baronial council, and threatened to take legal action against those baronial leaders who had compromised his royal prerogative in Parliament. The king and his baronial opponents now faced one another as open enemies; Richard, lacking sufficient military power to enforce his claims, was obliged to submit to the baronial leaders and accept their "appeals" against his favorites. The so-called "Merciless Parliament" met in 1388 to hear the appeals of the baronial leaders—who became known as the "Lords Appellant." Dominated by the Lords Appellant themselves, the Merciless Parliament convicted a number of the king's counselors of treason and had some of them executed. In doing so they destroyed Richard's court circle and left him no choice but to cooperate with his barons and his parliaments. A new, baronially imposed governing council was created whose members swore to support the acts of parliament. For the time being, the king was checked.

The Merciless Parliament was the central political event of Richard's reign. It marks the zenith of parliamentary power and the nadir of the royal prerogative in fourteenth-century England. The Lords Appellant themselves may have justified their actions on constitutional grounds, but their motives betray an element of cruelty and vindictiveness. Like so many victorious barons before them, they went too far, and the very magnitude of their triumph evoked a reaction of internal factionalism and widespread dissent. In 1389 Richard declared himself of age at last (he was now 22), and owing to the selfish and incompetent administration and unpopular policies of the Lords Appellant he was able to recover a measure of support.

Richard mended his fences for the next eight years (1389–97) and cooperated with barons and parliaments in the governance of his realm. He did not become a convert to constitutional monarchy, but he did become a wiser autocrat who could grit his teeth, cooperate with his enemies, and bide his time. He arranged a truce with France, and sealed it by marrying the daughter of the half demented French king, Charles VI. And slowly he succeeded in building around him a new circle of trustworthy supporters in the royal administration. He was courteous and respectful toward the Lords Appellant, but in his heart he never forgave them.

By 1397 Richard had consolidated his position and lulled his opponents sufficiently to make one last bid for the absolute power to which he believed the royal prerogative entitled him. Working through his sheriffs and other local administrators who could sway the elections of parliamentary representatives, he packed the parliament of 1397 with his own supporters and overawed it with his military retainers. This royalist parliament wreaked artistic vengeance on all the king's old enemies – depriving them of their lands or their liberty, in some instances executing them or forcing them into exile. The three leading Lords Appellant were now obliged to suffer the ironic fate of being themselves "appealed" in parliament for treason. One of the three was murdered, a second executed, and a third banished. Lands were confiscated on an immense scale and redistributed among a new group of magnates, some of whom were close friends of the king. In a parliament of 1398 all the acts of the Merciless Parliament were revoked, and Richard II, anxious to secure greater financial independence from annual parliamentary grants, demanded and received a lifetime privilege of collecting customs revenues on wool.

Intoxicated by his total victory, Richard began to drift toward megalomania. He forced huge loans from the burghers and undertook to fine the shires for not supporting him in his struggle with the Lords Appellant in 1387. In the autumn of 1398 he banished the two remaining Lords Appellant, one of whom was Henry of Bolingbroke, eldest son of the wealthy and aged duke of Lancaster, John of Gaunt. When John of Gaunt

died early in 1399, the king, refusing to consider the claims of
the banished heir, seized the vast Lancastrian lands himself.

Richard's confiscation of the Lancastrian estates was a
grievous blunder. Ever since the Norman Conquest the inheritance of land had been of vital concern to the nobility. The issue
of normal inheritance underlay the civil strife of Stephen's
reign in the early twelfth century and now, 250 years later, England had a king who flaunted the rights of noble heirs. Richard's throne had never seemed so secure as it was in early 1399;
yet, in fact, the king could count on little support outside his immediate circle. He had sown hostility among all the articulate
classes in the land. Supremely confident, he led an expedition
into Ireland in the summer of 1399, and while he was away
Henry of Bolingbroke returned to England to claim his Lancastrian inheritance by force.

As a son of John of Gaunt and a grandson of King Edward
III, Henry of Bolingbroke was a man of royal blood, and when he
landed in Yorkshire and moved southward one great magnate
after another rallied to him. The aim of the rebels was not
merely to install Bolingbroke in his Lancastrian estates but to
make him king of England in Richard's stead. Richard returned
from Ireland to find his cause abandoned, and in August 1399 he
surrendered to the insurrectionists. Parliament received his
abdication in September, declared him deposed, and recognized
Henry of Bolingbroke as King Henry IV of England. The un-
fortunate Richard died in captivity early in 1400, and the new
Lancastrian dynasty was established on the English throne.

As in 1327, so in 1399 parliament was the instrument of a
royal deposition. In neither instance was parliament acting on
its own. Rather it was conferring a stamp of legality on an accomplished revolution. Parliament deposed Richard II in the
presence of Bolingbroke's army, and really had little choice in
the matter. In 1399 parliament was strong but far from supreme, and in the centuries immediately following, its power
was destined to decline rather than rise. In certain respects the
autocratic Richard II was an advance agent of a new age, dominated first by violence among barons and then by a growing
trend toward royal absolutism which culminated in the Tudors
and Stuarts.

Conclusion

The deposition of Richard II marks an appropriate end to a
century of violence and turmoil. It was, in every respect, a
fundamental revolution in English politics. A king had been

deposed in 1327, but was succeeded by his legitimate and un-questioned heir. With Richard II's deposition in 1399 the very concept of hereditary succession to the throne was subverted. For Richard was the last of the Plantagenet kings, and thence-forth England was ridden with the curse of a disputed crown. Legitimate succession was absolutely basic to the politics of the Middle Ages, and the shattering of that principle in 1399 shook the political order to its foundations. For the next century rival families contended fiercely for the throne, and ordinary English-men, ill-ruled and plagued by civil war, suffered terribly. Not until the coming of the Tudors in 1485 was the destructive work of 1399 undone.

The transition from the medieval to the modern ethos was far from complete in 1399. The spirits of Englishmen remained troubled by recurring plague, social unrest, and cultural groping. In emphasizing a change in dynasty one must not be misled into ignoring the far more subtle changes that were still in process and would remain so for generations to come. As our period closes, England's population was still falling, her struggle with France remained fundamentally unresolved, her economy was spotty, her faith was slowly dissolving, her countryside was turbulent. Yet, for all that, England in 1399 was not a society in decline but a society in process of transformation. There was anxiety and suffering, but there was also momentous creativity. Men such as Chaucer, Langland, and Wycliffe display original-ity of a degree that would ornament any age. More than that, all three demonstrate a heightened sense of national identity. Chaucer and Langland were crucial figures in the revival of English as an important literary vehicle, and Wycliffe dreamed of an English translation of the Bible and accorded the king a central position in the governance of the English Church. Richard II's reign was also a great creative age in the develop-ment of the perpendicular style in architecture—witness the naves of Canterbury and Winchester and the choir of York. Again, the new architectural style was not only impressive in itself but also less cosmopolitan, more distinctly English, than the earlier Gothic had been. At this very time English mer-chants, who had once allowed their foreign rivals to dominate English trade, were creating lucrative new markets for them-selves across northern Europe.

As the fourteenth century closed, all Europe was slipping gradually from medieval universalism toward modern national-ism. England was still a kingdom, not yet a nation, but it was becoming increasingly English as time went on and was thereby moving perceptibly toward the England of the Tudors and Stuarts. In many respects the transition from medieval to modern England involved a rejection of things medieval—

feudalism, scholasticism, Christian universalism. In other respects, however, modern England was built on sturdy medieval foundations — king, council, household, parliament, the university, the tradition of scientific scholarship, the silent conquest of fields from forest and marsh, the common law. More basic still was the growing awareness of Englishmen that they were a single people — a conviction that had begun long before with Bede and Theodore of Tarsus, and grew steadily as the Middle Ages progressed. In the broad view, many of the most fundamental ingredients of modern English society and culture are clearly in evidence by 1399. They illustrate unmistakably the essential medieval contribution to the making of England.

Index

Acre, fall of, 190
Adelard of Bath, 122
Agricola, 6
Agriculture, 5, 8, 10, 23, 73–74, 123–24, 156, 190–92, 224–26
Aiden, St., 37
Aids, 96–97, 152, 166, 172
Alan of Chartres, 178
Alban, St., 14, 144
Albertus Magnus, St., 161
Alcuin of York, 44, 49, 50
Alfred the Great, King, 45, 47, 52–59, 60, 61, 62, 69, 71, 74, 76, 85, 176
Ambrose, St., 13, 33
Angevin Empire. *See* Empire, Angevin
Angles, 21, 33
Anglo-Saxon Chronicle, 16, 45, 50, 56–58, 60, 75, 79, 102–3, 104, 105, 106, 112, 116
Angoulême, 146
Anjou, 81, 87, 95, 110, 115–38, 147, 149
Anselm, St., 106–7, 110–11, 131, 133, 149
Antonine Wall, 6–7
Antwerp, 191
Aquinas, St. Thomas, 107, 161, 174, 176, 193, 195
Aquitaine, 82, 108, 118, 139, 146, 147, 150, 183
Architecture, 89, 131, 156, 158, 193, 231; Gothic, 89, 131, 156, 158, 193, 231; Romanesque, 131
Arthur, King, 22, 159
Arthur of Brittany, 146–47
Artillery, 191
Asser, 52, 53, 55
Assize of Arms (1181), 124–26, 136, 181
Assize of Clarendon (1166), 127–28, 129
Assize of Northampton (1176), 127
Assize of Novel Disseisin, 129
Assizes, possessory, 128–29
Athelney, Isle of, 53
Athelstan, King of Wessex, 60, 62
Augustine of Canterbury, St., 30, 34
Augustine of Hippo, St., 13, 14, 33, 34, 106, 133

Bacon, Roger, 162
Ball, John, 225
Balliol, John, 184
Baltic Sea, 190
Bannockburn, battle of, 200
Bardi, 191
Bec, monastery of, 90
Becket, St. Thomas, 122, 132–35, 149, 166
Bede, 16, 21, 22, 24, 25, 27, 33, 36–37, 38, 40, 42–46, 55, 56, 79, 122, 232
Bedfordshire, 62
Benedict Biscop, St., 40, 42
Benedictine monasticism. *See* Monasticism
Benedict of Nursia, St., 32–33
Beowulf, 16, 40
Bernicia, kingdom of, 27, 35, 37, 45
Bertha, Queen of Kent, 34
Black Death, 190, 193, 207, 215, 216–17, 218, 222, 224
Black Prince, 207, 217
Blois, 95
Blood feud, 19
Boethius, 56
Bologna, University of, 160, 161
Bonaventure, St., 107
Boniface VIII, Pope, 187
Boniface, St., 43–44
Boroughbridge, battle of, 201
Borough courts. *See* Courts of law
Boudicca, 6–7
Bouvines, battle of, 150, 162
Bracton, Henry de, 151, 164, 176, 177
Bretwaldaship, 24, 25, 34, 35, 36, 45, 46, 47
Bristol, 123, 192
Brittany, 23, 83, 138, 206
Brooke, Christopher, 165
Bruce, Robert, 184–85, 187, 200
Bruges, 191
Burghal Hidage, Wessex, 52, 64
Burghers, 123, 163, 172–74, 187, 208–9, 213, 229
Burghs, 52, 59, 71, 88
Burning of Heretics, Statute on, 224
Byrhtnoth, ealdorman of Essex, 66, 67, 75, 98

Byzantine Empire. *See* Empire, Byzantine

Caen, 206
Caesar, Julius, 1–2
Calais, 191, 206
Cam, Helen M., 188*n*.
Cambridge, University of, 161
Cambridgeshire, 62
Canterbury, 34, 39–40, 110, 122, 135; archbishopric of, 39, 48
Canterbury Tales, 220
Canute, King, 58, 61, 65, 76–77, 78, 80
Carolingian Empire. *See* Empire, Carolingian
Cartae Baronum, 124–25, 136
Castles, 81, 83, 88, 89, 96, 98, 100, 124, 156
Cavalry, 81, 84, 89, 93, 98, 109, 181–82, 190, 207
Celtic Church, 28–31, 34, 37–40, 43
Celtic culture, 27, 37, 40
Ceorls, 72–73
Chamberlain, 68–69
Champagne, 95
Chancellor, 68–69, 145, 169, 179
Chancery, 179
Chanson de geste, 158–59
Charlemagne, 44, 47, 49, 50, 55, 61, 94
Charles IV, King of France, 201
Charles V, King of France, 207, 217
Charles VI, King of France, 217, 229
Charles of Anjou, 168
Chaucer, Geoffrey, 219–20, 231
Chichester, Bishop of, 171
Christianity: conversion to, 14, 20–21, 27–40, 43–44; in Roman Empire, 13–14, 20–21, 28. *See also* Church, English
Church, English: under Angevin dynasty, 111, 131–35, 148–50, 160–62, 178, 182, 187, 188, 218–20, 222–24; and Anglo-Saxons, 27–40, 42–44, 48, 60–61, 76–77, 78–79; and Investiture Controversy, 91, 107, 110–11, 131, 148; under Norman kings, 80, 88, 90–92, 105–7, 109, 110–11, 133; sacraments of, 131–32. *See also* Christianity; Monasticism; Papacy
Cicero, 3
Cistercian order, 123

Cities. *See* Towns
Civitas, 7, 11, 15
Clans, 19
Class struggles, 14th-century, 192–93
Claudius, Emperor, 2–6, 10
Clericis Laicos, 187
Cluny, monastery of, 61
Colchester, 7
Colonia, 7, 11
Columba, St., 30, 38
Comitatus, 18, 19, 20, 62, 64–66, 74, 93, 98
Commendation, 98
Commerce, 5, 7–8, 70–71, 77, 79, 89, 101, 122–24, 156, 191–92, 216, 231
Commissions of array, 181–82
Common Law, 68, 127–31, 176, 181, 188, 213, 232
Common Pleas, court of, 179
Commons, House of, 173, 208–13, 224–25, 227
Commons Bills, 212
Commons Petitions, 211–12
Community of the realm, 163, 164, 168–69, 173–75, 188, 196, 202, 212
Consolation of Philosophy. See Boethius
Constable, 68–69
Constance, Council of, 223
Constantine, Emperor, 13, 14, 28, 31
Constantinople, 13, 28
Constitutions of Clarendon, 133–35
Cornwall, 5, 23, 29
Corpus Juris Civilis, 130
Cortes, 174
Council of Fifteen, 169–71
Courts of law: borough, 71, 123, 163; ecclesiastical, 90, 132–35, 222; and Edward I, 178–80; feudal, 93, 96, 97, 98, 128–30, 132, 158; in 14th century, 213–14; and Henry II, 127–29; and Henry III, 163–64; hundred, 64–65, 67, 72, 77, 90, 97, 98, 128; under Norman kings, 101; shire, 62, 64, 67, 77, 90, 97, 98, 113, 128, 180, 181, 210, 213–14
Coventry, 192
Crécy, battle of, 206–7
Crusades, 90–97, 108, 109, 140–42, 149, 175, 177, 183, 185, 190
Curia regis. See Great Council
Currency, 47, 70, 72, 93, 101–2, 112

2 3 4 5 6 7 8 9 0